BAD KARMA

Confessions of a Reckless Traveller in Southeast Asia

Tamara Sheward

Academy Chicago Publishers

Published in 2007 by
Academy Chicago Publishers
363 W. Erie Street
Chicago, Illinois 60610

Published in 2005 by Summersdale Publishers Ltd.
Copyright © Tamara Sheward 2003

Printed in the USA.

Library of Congress Cataloging-in-Publication Data

Sheward, Tamara.
  Bad karma : confessions of a reckless traveller in Southeast Asia / Tamara
Sheward.
    p. cm.
  "First published in Great Britain by Summersdale Publishers in 2003"—T.p.
verso.
  ISBN 978-0-89733-565-2 (pbk.)
  1. Southeast Asia--Description and travel—Humor. 2. Sheward, Tamara—
Travel—Southeast Asia. I. Title.

  DS522.6.S53 2007
  915.904'54092—dc22
  [B]
                          2007027778

Contents

Pre(r)amble. 1

Smells Like Leprosy. 10

Please Wash These Filthy Curtains. 18

Udon Thani: Byword for Hell (Part I). 30

The Annoyance of Being Earnest. 44

Haight-Ashbury on the Mekong. 56

Animosity Bridge. 59

Begging to Differ. 74

Pills, Thrills and Green Around the Gills 83

Get Off the Monument. 94

The Kip Kid and the Queen of Whatever 107

If One Intestinally Ulcerates. 124

Boogie à la Rama 135

Hello to What Unfortunately Is 145

Savannakhet: Byword for Hell (Part II) 158

The Disco Bus 176

The Wannabe Bootlegger Blues 185

Hue Crazy: A Night at the Apocalypse 205

Don't be Lazy. 218

Jinxing the Hosts and Other Dinnertime Faux Pas. 228

Please Don't Do Anything Weird 242

Subterranean Hoedown. 258

Dumb Luck and Other Staples of Survival 275

The Most Godforsaken Place on Earth. 289

Slum Runners 297

Epilogue 303

Pre(r)amble

I'd never really had any interest in going to Southeast Asia.

When I was at school, I thought the Khmer Rouge was an oddly named cosmetic, Pol Pot simply the chorus in a Dead Kennedys song and Laos an annoying bug I got sent home for having in my hair.

As I got older, and none too wiser, my interest in going to a region where landmines were strewn around like old beer bottles and everyone was shorter than me peaked at nil. Singapore Airport was about as far as I was willing to venture, and then only because it was an unavoidable stopover on my way to assemble with the rest of the Ugly Australians Abroad in the swilling fields of London. Getting pissed on warm bottles of White Lightning, working in factories and dossing down in rat-infested sharehouses was, for me—as it was for many of my Antipodean peers desperately avoiding the real world—both a rite of passage and an introduction to the world of travel. But despite the obvious health hazards associated with finding rodents nesting in your sleeping bag, operating heavy machinery and going within a ten-kilometre radius of White Lightning, travel in the UK was safe. And easy. Why, I figured at the time, would I want to risk my life venturing into unfamiliar territory surrounded by people with names like Ng who would most likely make me drink snake semen? If I wanted to harm, debase or otherwise maim myself, I could do that quite easily at The Church in London's King Cross on a Sunday afternoon. And at least I could pronounce "Bruce."

But as age finally imparted a small shred of wisdom, it dawned on me that getting head-meltingly pissed and face-slappingly obnoxious surrounded by my equally rapscallion countryfolk in Old Blighty was a ridiculous and expensive hobby. Besides, I was starting to see less and less humour in bellowing "Waltzing Matilda" in far-from-tuneful slurs on midnight tube rides home, and was cringing every time I heard a phlegmy "G'day" coming from yet another Melburnian laid up in East Putney after too many nights of ecstasy and no jumper. Adventure called.

Summoning all my courage, most of it Dutch, I bade farewell to England and sought out new horizons. An extended rail junket across the USA. Coughing up a lung trying to communicate with the natives in Germany and Denmark. Coughing up the other lung in the hash bars of Amsterdam. A blurry year in the rough and tumble bars of Belfast. And while I enjoyed every minute of my rovings, one irritating theme remained constant throughout. Other bloody backpackers.

Whether I was sinking a stout with hooligans in a bullet-proof Falls Road pub or failing dismally at rollerblading with Puerto Ricans in downtown Miami, they always found me. While life on the road offered no real stability, I always knew I could count on some whining Australian to sidle up to me with a nasal "Owyagoin, maaate?" just as I was settling into an obscure bar or out-of-the-way pension. There seemed to be no escape from my countryfolk.

Don't get me wrong. It wasn't as if I only had something against those who thought that wearing an autographed Broncos jumper meant they were dressed to the nines, or that export VB was a life-giving elixir. No, I had enough intolerance to go around: I was sick to death of all backpackers. Pseudo-spiritual Americans, vocabulary-mauling Kiwis, Canadians and their bloody flags. And of course, the French. All of these people were free to do whatever the hell they wanted, just not within the city limits of wherever I happened to be.

Despondent and disillusioned, I returned home to Cairns, ironically one of the most popular backpacker meccas in the southern hemisphere. While spending the rest of my life in Far North Queensland was out of the question, I had some serious thinking to do. I wanted to stagger off the backpacker trail and to never hear another chorus of "Aussie Aussie Aussie, Oi Oi Oi!" coming from a foreign bar again.

I wanted adventure. I wanted action. I wanted danger. Well, maybe not too much danger—just enough to scare away any other potential backpackers. Different people, strange food, funny hats. India fitted the bill, but there were way too many backpackers there seeking ersatz-enlightenment from laced lassis and oily hash.

Russia, too cold. South America, too expensive and I was afraid of llamas. Israel, ditto India but throw in the horror of milking kibbutz cows at 3 a.m. And Koh Samui just sounded like a warmer London: more Australians scratching at their new goatees, loading up on chemicals and then whinging about everything on the comedown. Was there nowhere left on earth for an anti-social, gormless, slightly chickenshit twentysomething struck with travel fever?

＊

When the answer finally came to me, I was ill-prepared for it. Or maybe just ill.

After being off the travel trail for nearly a year, I'd managed to snare a job writing lies for the local rag and had stashed all my earnings in anticipation of my Next Big Trip, wherever the hell it might take me. While dreaming of my escape to a mythical place free of irksome backpackers, I'd forgone any so-called life in Cairns, preferring to spend my weekends staring mournfully at maps and travel guides, all of which just served to confuse me further. But on the eve of the anniversary of my return to Australia, I chucked the atlas to the shithouse and strode triumphantly to the door. Enough was enough. Ideal destination or not, it was time I made my grand re-entry into the big bad world. Or at least the corner pub. Five double Black Russians and two B52s later, I had what I like to think of as "a moment of clarity." I'd noticed him earlier, when I still had the ability to focus, and had thought nothing of it. Another old guy, a bit wiry and tough-looking but nothing to write home, or on the bathroom walls, about. With his pack of Winnie Reds, tattoos muddied by time and sun and the hard-faced peroxide blonde on his arm, he looked like the token Bloke found in every Far North Queensland pub. But it was when I—by that stage better equipped for hearing than seeing—copped an earful of his conversation to the token Shazza, that everything changed.

"You have no idea how bloody good it is to be surrounded by your own countryfolk," he rasped, waving around a stubbie of Fourex. "When you don't see an Aussie for months on end, you forget what a good mob we are." Shaz, who most likely hadn't been further than the annual Townsville Hog Rally, nodded warily, evidently doubting that there was anywhere on earth you could go without seeing another skip. Remembering the time I'd wandered into a ramshackle bar in the Texan wilderness only to be served by a twanging hick from Oodnadatta, I was just as doubtful. Unless this guy had been hiding down a mine shaft in the deepest Congo, there was no way he'd have been able to hide from the Aussie Invasion. Even then, there was no guarantee.

"And y'know, it's not just 'Stralians that I miss," he continued in a gravelly voice. "It's having anyone around that speaks English.

4

I mean," he bent to light a cigarette, "those folks have learnt a bit of the lingo, but it's not the bloody same."

While Shaz was content to nod again, secure in a Bundy-induced haze of vague disbelief and apparent disinterest, I was not. Buckling legs and slurred speech or no, I had to get to the bottom of this. By the way this guy was talking, it sounded like he'd stumbled across a piece of paradise.

I introduced myself with something that sounded like "Hey youse" and lurched my way to their table. While Shaz, who said her name was Glendene, seemed less than impressed with the intrusion of anyone not bearing rum, the old guy was thrilled. If nothing else, it gave him another Australian to surround himself with.

"Warren," he said. This being Far North Queensland, I knew what that meant. Wazza. He outstretched a callused hand. "Owareya?"

While how I was—drunk as a skunk—was fairly obvious, I appreciated Waz's efforts to ignore it. Buoyed by his lack of revulsion or attempts to call a bouncer, I launched straight into my spiel. I told him everything, from a rundown of my last trips abroad to my desire to explore a place bypassed by the backpacker trail. I told him of my exasperation in "discovering" hidden villages or beaches, only to run smack into a herd of American frat boys high-fiving it all over the place, and I told him of my near-desperate need to get out of Australia. "Okay, I get it. Y'wanna know where to go, hey? Place with hardly any foreigners, exciting, beautiful place, right?" I nodded, in awe of his powers of summation. It had taken me nearly forty-five minutes to get that same point across. "Well, missy, I can tell you right now." He paused to light his millionth cigarette of the night, and I held my breath, certain that despite his earlier ravings to Shaz/Glendene he was going to tell me I was out of luck.

He exhaled. "Southeast Asia."

✳

By the time the bouncers were hovering around our table, booming "Time" in ever more threatening tones, I was mentally booking myself a flight. Waz, as it turned out, had been living in Southeast Asia for the past sixteen years, most recently in Cambodia where he owned a resort. "Well, it's kinda a resort," he said mournfully. "More like a bunch of old huts on the beach. But nobody ever comes. I think people are still too afraid."

But his woes were my joy. While the region wasn't completely devoid of foreigners, backpackers, package-tour geeks and the like, it was still less affected than, say, Nepal or Tooting. And apparently, Cambodia wasn't the only place that seemed to have frightened off otherwise intrepid travellers. Laos, he said, was cautiously opening its doors for the first time, while Vietnam, which he assured me was "flippin' gorgeous," was only just beginning to take off as a destination, thirty years after the war. Though Thailand was already legendary for the hordes of Westerners intent on turning the entire country into a refuge for acid casualties, Wazza touted it as a good launching pad for the rest of the trip and promised there were still some places which retained a folksy innocence. "And the whole bloody place is as cheap as chips," he said. "It's a fuckin' paradise." *Lonely Planet* couldn't have put it better.

I left the pub, courtesy of the strong grip of an impatient bouncer, with Waz's phone number in my pocket and a billion dreams in my head. During my sober months of earning and yearning, I'd tried everything in my search for the ideal exotic, bizarre and Birkenstock-free destination. I'd sought out the experts: travel agents, the net, my globetrotting parents. But all I'd gotten out of that was misery. The selectively deaf woman at Flight Centre recommended a singles package tour of the Greek

Isles. When I typed "solo journeys" into the web search engine, all I'd found were vibrator ads. And my parents, who were thrilled by the fact that I'd managed to hold down a job that didn't involve the wearing of steel-capped boots, had nervously peppered their conversations with air-crash statistics and malaria horror stories. I should've known in the first place to look where answers are normally found. In the bottom of a beer glass.

$*$

I'd known Elissa since the day she arrived at school halfway through Year 11, and we'd hit it off straightaway. She was pretty in an unusual way, with long red hair and huge almond-shaped eyes, and her quirky humour and straight talking singled her out. We were both interested in reading, unlike many of our semi-illiterate peers, and she still liked doing tomboy things such as climbing trees or exploring the long drains that gurgled through most of the backyards in Cairns. We made up code names for ourselves and invented a language. For a few months, she honestly believed she was a vampire and I went along for the ride, writing gothic poems and taking secret oaths in moonlit parks. We were besties.

At university our dorky vampire fantasies gave way to fantasies about dorky English Lit boys, but we remained as close and ridiculous as ever. Between boyfriend debacles, graduations (hers) and dramatic dropouts (mine), we hung out in appropriately seedy student bars and went on little trips together. But most of all, we dreamed together. Okay, maybe most of all we bitched and gossiped and got pissed together. But we did dream. By the time we hit our early twenties, I'd already been to Europe a few times while she'd ventured off to places like Japan and New Caledonia, and we made vague, excited plans for the day we'd go globetrotting together. Getting carjacked in New York. Screaming at anacondas down the Amazon. Sharing a fag at the top of Macchu Picchu. It didn't really matter where we went. Wherever it was, though, it was gonna rock.

Unlike our scheme to infest the school captains with nits midway through Year 12, our plans were never realised. I took off for stranger pastures and El went back to Japan to teach English. It seemed that whenever she had holidays, I was either incommunicado or too broke to set up a halfway meeting point. And when I was free and cashed up, she was stuck in some obscure prefecture trying to explain to a bunch of kids named Akira the difference between "they're" and "their." It looked like it was never going to happen.

But Fate's a funny thing. One minute its Fickle Finger is flipping you the bird and the next it's pointing you towards a brighter destiny. And on the morning I rang El with half-hearted hopes of dragging her over to Southeast Asia with me, I swear it dialled the phone for me.

It hadn't taken very long to talk her into coming. Granted, she couldn't, as I'd initially suggested, walk out on a three-year teaching contract without better cause than "I just feel like it," but she did have holidays coming up. And while she only had three weeks or so, it was better than nothing. Besides, I was unfamiliar with Asia, Asians and anything even slightly oriental apart from the five-dollar Shandy Special, but El, with her years in Japan, would be able to make at least some sense of our surrounds. Or so I hoped.

"So whaddya reckon?" I asked after a brief rundown of the virtues of our would-be destinations. Brief, indeed, was the operative word. Apart from what Wazza had told me, and what little of that I could actually remember, I knew diddly about Southeast Asia. But I've always believed less in plans and facts than spontaneity and mood swings when it came to travel. If you didn't plan for something, you could never be disappointed when it didn't work out. Far better to bumble with no expectations. "You comin'?"

I listened to the static for a moment as she pondered the question. Either that or she was shovelling sushi into her mouth. El really knew how to adapt to her surroundings.

"So," I pestered after half a minute of having her chew in my ear. "Huh? Huh?"

She belched triumphantly. "What the hell," she yelled. "Let's do it!"

It was on.

Chapter One

Smells Like Leprosy

Flustered, sunburnt and instilled with a paranoia born of people chattering away in foreign tones while laughing at my flustered and sunburnt face, I paced nervously around the information booth at Bangkok's Don Muang Airport. Well, I would have paced, had my backpack not been so laden down with crap. Instead, I lurched. Nervously.

My hometown travel agent had forced me to take four days in Bali ("It's a free stopover!") before meeting up with El in Thailand and my introduction to Asia had proved to be an inauspicious adage-buster. In the future, if I wanted the best things in life, I would go out of my way to pay for them. Instead of arriving in Thailand prepped with cultural awareness and a confident grip on the Asian way of doing things, I'd landed with nothing more than a head full of plaits that made me look like a honky Snoop Doggy Dogg.

"Hey!"

Joy of all joys, it was El. If it had been humanly possible for me to jump for joy, I would've done it. But, as I was busily morphing into Quasimodo beneath the weight of my impedimenta, it was all I could do to raise a feeble cheer.

She hooted as she ran to greet me, before screeching to a halt. "Are you alright?" Crouched over with my nose nearly to my knees in an attempt to balance my shifting pack, and with a tomato-flushed face, I certainly didn't look alright. I looked like a menopausal packhorse. But I'd never felt better. After four scatty days spent in a frenzy of lonesome confusion, I was insanely relieved to be with my best friend.

"I'm bloody fantastic," I said without a shred of sarcasm. "Really."

"Right," she said, looking at me with concern. "We should get out of here before your spine curls under that pack. Do you have any idea where on earth we go from here?"

I shrugged, and winced as my shoulders groaned beneath forty kilos of clothes, boots, books and an illegal excess of duty-free cigarettes. "Anywhere," I moaned. "Just get me somewhere to lie down. For God's sake, somewhere normal."

"Normal, meaning?"

"Plain old normal. I have a feeling it may be the last shot we get at it for a while."

∗

Perhaps to the most debauched and nasally-challenged, Khaosan Road actually was normal. Billed as "the budget travellers' mecca," Bangkok's answer to the Sunset Strip was indeed cheap. And nasty.

Lined with crumbling and malodorous guesthouses that hid an inherent decrepitness behind cutesy monikers ("Hello," "Peachy") and those that were stark with seediness ("Porn"), Khaosan Road was the temporary home to cheapskates, freaks and weirdos from all corners of the globe. A sprawl of a street, Khaosan gasped and heaved in an eternal humidity, panting in time to the interminable bipping of drunken tuk tuk drivers, the solicitations of harlots and transvestites (cutely called "katooeys," I later discovered), and the raunchy yelps and belches of backpackers slouched over joints and sweaty beers. Beneath a smothering quilt of heat, garbage and diesel, sparking neon lights threatened electrocution under the guise of "Change Money Here," "Cheap Beer," "Buddha Tours" and all sorts of weird squiggly things that I soon guessed made up the Thai alphabet, while the stallholders who couldn't afford a shopfront vied for business by accosting passers-by: "You, beautiful! See my gems!", "Handsome man, you want buy watch?", "Hey, blondie! Special price for you!"

Bumping and blundering past touts, out-of-it Germans and people of indistinguishable gender, El and I slouched up Khaosan Road looking for somewhere to lay both our bags and some vague plans.

"Look El, what about here?" Ankle-deep in a mound of slippery filth that defied definition, I pointed at the closest guesthouse. "It looks great to me, hey?" When tendrils of what you hope is only slimy vegetation are creeping into your sandals, even an ooze-free cardboard box in a back alley looks like the Hilton.

"It looks a bit flash," El said, and she was right. Flash for Khaosan Road anyway, considering the place had walls and didn't smell like leprosy.

"Everything's supposed to be so cheap, though. Let's have a look."

Five minutes later we were back ploughing through the sludge and fever. "No rooms, my arse," I said.

"Yeah," El smirked. "Only because you wouldn't shag the receptionist."

I shuddered at the thought of the obese woman staffing the night desk. While El had gone off to use the hotel toilet, the clerk had started stroking my arm and staring at my non-existent chest. "I have special room only for you, miss," she'd cooed shyly. "You look like Xena, Warrior Princess. I like Xena." Vowing to grow out my thick fringe and rid myself of any other lesbian superhero traits, I'd leapt away from her. "No Xena?" she'd mourned. "Then no room."

"Shut up," I grunted, smacking a still-giggling El in the arm. "I think I need therapy after that."

"C'mon Xena," she tittered. "Let's just find us any old dive."

Khaosan Road was littered with Old Dives, New Dives, Dying Dives and the one Semi Dive that we were turned away from on account of me not jumping the bones of the chubby receptionist. But we hadn't figured on the Dive With Attitude.

"No. Go somewhere else."

"What do you mean, no?" El leaned over and pointed at the guest register, empty but for a few scrawls. "I don't see people queuing at the door."

The woman leaned back in her chair, gave us the slow once-over usually reserved for street gangs about to jump you or models sizing up the latest anorexic, lit a cigarette and smirked. "No." She dismissed us with a light wave of her hand. "Get lost."

In our cargo shorts and backpacks, we looked like every other dropkick kid on the block. The only difference between us and them was that, while they sat wide-eyed in their Red Bull singlets discussing Goa and Ko Phangan and Ibiza and any other exotic locale populated solely by itchy-scalped Westerners, we would be busy planning our escape from anywhere named in a commemorative techno CD. Did we have "jaded" painted on our foreheads? Were we not cool enough to stay in a loused-up flophouse simply because somehow this woman could tell that we wouldn't be ordering banana pancakes with the rest of the hippie herds? Or was it perhaps because I was spluttering a Tourette's syndrome litany of barks and curses from beneath my now unbearable backpack?

"Bloody hell . . . get this mongrel thing off me . . . Jesus wept."

"Out!"

We slunk dejectedly back on to the pavement, making "waaah" noises and glaring at everyone who wasn't buckling beneath an overstuffed bag. I felt like the guy who lugged his swag of sins across the earth in *Pilgrim's Progress*. Even worse, I felt the same way I did when I was forced to read *Pilgrim's Progress* at school. Bored and miserable.

"Right, that's it," El said, stomping the pavement. "Next place we find, we're staying."

The marketing geniuses behind the success of the Chart Guesthouse must have realised that smell is the most powerful sense, for they advertised their presence with an unmissable signature scent of body odour, socks and overflowing toilets. You could go past a billboard, but dry retching somehow manages to keep you in one spot for a while.

Man, these people were good. As we doubled over in a duet of spasms and heavings, rooted to the spot by revulsion and nausea, a smiling tout bounced out of the Chart and led us inside without a word. It's hard to object with a mouth full of bile.

*

The room was like every other along the Khaosan Road: tiny, windowless and seemingly decorated with three-week-old oatmeal. But the Chart, never an establishment to skimp on perks, also offered the added bonus of stench. No ordinary stench, mind you, but the whopper of reeks, sultan of stink, the macdaddy of putrid. Unlike in Australia, the Land of She'll Be Right, nobody in Asia seemed to do things by halves. People were rich or poor, shy or brash. The food was either gorgeous or repulsive—a point proven by the street café next to our guesthouse that offered only two main courses: green coconut curry or skinned pig's head on a stick. And if something had to have an odour about it, it was either jasmine and hibiscus or piss and toxic waste. I would have preferred a touch of the garden to my sleeping quarters, but the Chart management seemed to have other ideas. Excretion and emissions it was.

At least it gave us somewhere to peel off our bags, nurse our strap welts and eventually pass out. I'm not an aromatherapist, but I get the feeling that if you're subjected to the smell of urinal lollies and crusty backpackers' boots for long enough, your body will eventually flee the olfactory trauma by slipping into a scentless sleep. Or a coma.

After stomping the narrow beds for bugs, we stretched out to smoke, blather and attempt to decide where we wanted to go. We had no idea, and a quick glance through my guidebook hadn't done much to inspire a game plan. Aimless travel in the Western world is quite simple: if I see a town named "Truth and Consequence" or "Monster Beach," I know I must drop everything and head there at once, but a map clogged with placenames like "Chachoengsao" or "Phitsanulok" somehow fails to spark my imagination. Picking a destination on the vagabond travelling trail is a word association game. New York equals pretzels and freaks on the subway. Tasmania means inbreds and apples. Mexico City is gasmasks and swine in the streets. But what can you get with Khanu Woralaksaburi except a twisted tongue?

"I don't really care about staying in Bangkok," I said, stating the obvious. I'd been tearing along on my Tourette's theme ever since getting kicked out of the Dive With Attitude, with every string of curses now ending in the word "Bangkok."

"Jesus, no. Let's get the hell out of here tomorrow," El said.

"I would like to see more stuff here," I admitted. "The Golden Buddha, some of those temples, floating markets, chicks who shoot ping-pong balls out of their . . ."

"Yeah, you should," El interrupted. "I should too, actually, but I want outta here." El was of a similar mind to me when it came to travel. If it's got more than two hostels, we didn't want to know about it. "I'm already sick of looking at these dropkicks."

"Join the club." I inhaled deeply with the intention of sighing, but wound up dry retching instead. "I just want to get away from this ponging, hideous reek."

"And all the hectic crowds."

"And pig's heads on a stick."

"And . . ."

Something slammed into our door, shaking the hinges and rattling the knob. "Open up, youse cunts!" What a welcome wagon. Chernobyl wafting down the hallway and a slurring Liverpudlian. "I hear you, Aussies, open up and give us a spliff!"

Minus spliffs and any inclination to deal with deluded Brits on a bad comedown, we shouted from behind the locked door. "Fuck off!" (El and I are a women's chorus of charm.)

"Aussie sluts!" He throttled our doorknob a final time before clomping heavily down the hall and yelling at someone else.

El turned to me on the bed. "God, I love backpackers. The class, the eloquence, that communal feeling . . ."

"The extra chromosomes. That's it. Bangkok can bite my arse." Tourette's gripped me once again and I lay there swearing and ripping at my plaits until we both passed out.

✳

Over a breakfast of watery coffee and cigarettes, El had discovered the town of Nong Khai. The guidebooks said it was a small town, promised only a handful of backpackers and said it was easy to get to by train. Best of all, it was bang on the Thai-Lao border.

"So we could be in Laos in a couple of days?" I asked incredulously.

"Easy," El said, studying the book. "Look, it's right here." She pointed to a small dot, way north of Bangkok and overlapping the black band that signified the border with Laos. "We could stop on the way in a town called Udon Thani, which also sounds alright. See a bit of Thailand before racing off into the nether regions of Laos, hey?"

"Shit!" Somehow, despite all our chat and adventurous dreams, I'd never really believed that we would actually end up rambling around Laos, Cambodia or any smudge of a country that didn't really exist for me outside of disastrous news reports of war or cattle disease. But we were actually going to do it. I swelled with excitement.

"Let's hoon it!"

The train didn't leave until that night, so we decided to spend the day getting gypped by rogue tuk tuk drivers, looking for but never finding the ornate Grand Palace and schnarfing down some authentic Thai food. Determined buggers that we are, we managed to achieve two out of three of our objectives. Ridiculously lost, without a palace in sight and down hundreds of baht thanks to some swindling letch on a motorised rickshaw, we spent hours picking through sweaty, jabbering markets in an attempt to slurp down some fish soup or lemongrass anything. But to no avail. Everyone was either contentedly gnawing away at the by-now ubiquitous pig's head on a stick or walloping down a Whopper. Thailand may be the only Southeast Asian nation to have avoided colonisation by a foreign power, but someone forgot to fill in the American fast-food barons. Pizza Hut, McDonalds and Subway wrappers drifted across the Bangkok streets, flipping under the wheels of the neverending traffic beside banana peels and lost thongs. It was a pigsicle or Donut King.

"Phom yak ja dai kha-nom khek" is the way to order a jam doughnut in Thailand.

Chapter Two

Please Wash These Filthy Curtains

The Nong Khai Express made its rickety way out of Hualamphong Station at 8.30 p.m., and we waved goodbye to Bangkok, a crude Christmas of neon in the swampy darkness, with our middle fingers.

"See you later, you tuk tukking hoodwinkers!" I yelled.

"Bite me, backpackers!" El hollered.

"Be quiet!" barked the ticket inspector. "Give me your tickets."

After much thought, El and I had decided against posing as locals in the third-class wooden bench sleeping compartment ("and for warmth, you may enjoy the tepid drool of the peasant asleep on your shoulder") and opted to shell out a couple of hundred baht for a small but comfortable bunk bed in first class. Yeah, yeah, it's against the Code of the Hardcore Backpacker to engage in anything as decadent as a good night's sleep, but this is also the credo that would have us dining out on swine on a stick. Besides, who would we be fooling? What with me beanstalking it over even the tallest man on board, and El with her red hair and green eyes, there was no way we'd ever pass as humble Siamese.

And now, handing over our tickets to the sssh-ing ticket guy, we were even more positive we'd made the right choice. Instead of getting bitch-slapped with all the other plebs by the inspector, as we doubtless would have been in third class, this guy was only snarling at us. And instead of bedding down to a night of saliva and splinters, we'd scored our own little cubby house of blankets and real pillows where we could hunker down and gobble our stash of food in peace.

"Would madam care to partake in some feastage?"

"Indeed!"

Living like lords we were, high on the hog. Or maybe just hogs. Our first-class ticket stubs might have marked us as a couple of grand old dames, but when it came to cuisine, we were definitely nouveau-riche clueless. Instead of buying sensible food like, say, another doughnut, we'd stocked up on soggy bread, tins of random poultry pieces in curry sauce, a vat of jam and a pack of crackers that went under the alarming name of "Chicken Shake." I don't care what they have to do to get the chooks into the biscuit and I certainly don't think they should be bragging about it. But at least they'd shown some restraint. They could have called it "Chicken Mangle."

Nevertheless, curry, bird bits, jam and Chicken Shake all squashed together between two moulding flops of bread tasted a treat, although I'm certain that roasted dog's nose on a bed of cow dung would have stuck to my ribs just as nicely. I've heard people wax lyrical about the amazing effect eating outdoors has on the appetite, and after downing my fair share of yeasty potato salad à la fly colony, I can't say I disagree. But all that hale and hearty fresh air has nothing on the hunger generated by a sense of impending adventure. Outside, Thailand was clacking by, a dark wonderland of eight-syllable villages and chattering people and rogue elephants. And in less than ten hours, we'd be a part of it. No backpackers, no stench, no Donut King. Just uncharted territory. Well, at least no territory with a Chart Guesthouse.

Bäd Karma

"You know what, El?" I muffled through a mouth full of crumbs. "I'm so excited I could eat roadkill."

"That's pleasant," she said, delicately removing a spongy piece of gristle from her teeth. Two sandwiches and the horrific squeal of brakes later, it looked like I was going to have to eat my words. Not to mention roadkill.

"What the hell?" The abrupt screech had thrown us across the bottom bunk and had sent our food jiving through the air, giving Chicken Shake a whole new credibility.

"What was that?" I asked nobody in particular. Being a slight paranoiac and not yet completely to grips with travel in a so-called third world country, my mind flooded with images of train robbers. Unfortunately, the only train robber my brain could come up with was Phil Collins in his incarnation as Buster. And no matter if you're in a first, second or third world country, the last thing any person wants on their mind is a vision of a balding cockney dwarf.

"It's not train robbers, for crying out loud," El said when I relayed my fears. "We probably just hit a cow. C'mon," she rolled off the bunk. "Let's go and have a look."

Going nowhere in particular to have this look, we'd just burst into the restaurant carriage when we heard some type of lame moo noise and the train slowly began to clack into motion again. El turned to me. "See? A cow. As if there's going to be robbers. Or, God forbid, Phil Collins. This isn't exactly a wealthy tourist train."

She was right, judging by the fact that ours were the only foreign heads among a herd of people slumped over plastic bowls of soup and rice in the dining car. Actually, strike that. Amtrak Superliners have a dining car. The Nong Khai Express has a trough.

But none of that mattered to me. Beyond all the people spilling rice down their fronts, beyond a carriage full of clattering cooks, was a room full of smoke. To the average healthy person, a room full of smoke is cause for alarm. But not me. Smoke equals joy.

20

"Smoking!" I breathed, savouring the faraway perfume of toxins and noxious chemicals. "El, we can smoke!"

A shameful addict like myself, El's head spun around. "Where?"

"There! Oh, thank God!" Before bandits and bovines had distracted me, I had been chewing my sandwich and wondering what to do once it was finished. As they say in *Stand by Me*, "There's nuthin' like a smoke after a meal."

With the astonishing lack of manners particular to fervent junkies, we pushed and cursed our way through the melee of soup-sloppers and chefs, who proved that you don't have to be French to be temperamental in the kitchen. "Hey!" called a squat Thai chef, aggressively brandishing a catfish.

"Hey, yourself," I called back. Adroit repartee is not my forte when in the midst of a severe nic fit.

It's a strange thing about cigarette cravings. When I'm confined in one of those rude establishments, like an aeroplane or hospital, that absolutely forbids smoking, I can think of nothing else. The crackling noise of a just-lit fag, the glowing castles of ember and ash, the bittersweet burning of the blue smoke as it vanishes down my throat and coats my lungs in slime. Aaah. My eyes mist over, I start salivating and sucking on whatever cylindrical object is at hand. Thankfully, it's usually only a pencil.

But the moment I'm off that plane, or have been kicked out of the hospital for slurping on someone's IV, and have furiously lit up, the lust for arsenic, DDT and whatever else they put into tailor-mades these days, evaporates. The first drag is sensational, and if I haven't had a smoke in, like, fifteen hours, I am privileged enough to get a head-spin and I get to feel thirteen again. But after that, and the first hacks of an ugly emphysemic cough, which reminds me that thirteen is a long time gone, it's no big deal. It still tastes like I've given head to an old piece of barbecue charcoal and it makes me violently thirsty. So why do it?

Who knows and who cares? Talk to me when I've got a tracheotomy. All I know is that it's that first drag that means the world, and if I had kids, I'd sell them for it. It's pathetic to be so deeply smitten with a chemical cocktail, but there we both were, mooning with glazed, adoring eyes at our just sparked ciggas like lovelorn twits.

"Yum," El sighed.

"Ooh yeah," I slurred. "All I need now is a beer."

"Then get one," El said. "What are you, under age?"

I'd been so lost in my nicotine reverie that I had failed to notice we were surrounded by dozens of soldiers and extremely tidy policemen, all in the process of necking tall ales and looking slyly at one another. It could have been a coup for all the guns and uniforms flashing about but, to my knowledge, bacchanalian railway revolutions are not yet a prevailing means of rebellion.

"This is a bar!" I exclaimed, blatantly stating the obvious.

"No, it's a convent." El had resorted to the lowest form of wit to deal with my bottom-crawling standards of intelligence. "You went to a Catholic school, you know what it's like."

"Well, if Sister Marlene had taught English wielding a gat and a stubbie of Singha Beer, I probably would've gotten better marks. Want one?"

"But of course."

I slid through the phalanx of militiamen and cops, taking extra care not to accidentally slide their holstered machine guns off safety, and ordered a couple of tall beers. As he lugged two sweating bottles from an icebox, the bartender looked at me with vague surprise, most likely because I was toting nothing more lethal than a bad hairdo.

It dawned on me that we might have stumbled into a secret men-with-guns club, that the carriage may have been reserved for a cross-country meeting of the Thai NRA. "Are we allowed to be here?" I asked with a tinge of hysteria in my voice. If we were booted out now, being so close to completing our pilgrimage for beer and butts, I was liable to jump out the window.

The barman flashed me a famous Thai smile and he was suddenly gorgeous. Still too short, I mourned. "Of course, you are very welcome!" he cried. I sighed with relief. "The mens will love it!" The sigh morphed to resignation. Just what we needed. A carriage-load of jumped-up junta ogling El and me over uzis and whiskey chasers.

Which, of course, is just what they were doing by the time I got back to El. Her red hair and obvious lack of accompanying boyfriend had sent the upright guardians of the Kingdom of Thailand into a frenzy, and she was squinting from the glare of their grins.

"Jesus!" I said, pulling her away from a square-faced Thai soldier flashing his massive gun at her with pride. "Don't they have motorbikes or Ferraris to boast their penis size around here?"

"Somehow I doubt that gun is indicative of anything but his failure to get a real job." El nodded at the squat soldier's trousers. "I mean, come on."

"I shudder at the thought. Let's sit down before someone flashes us."

Ignoring the amorous gaze of the uniformed legions, we squeezed our way to a long table that faced out into the humid Thailand night. I took a long gulp of my beer, let loose with one of those annoying "aaaaah" noises that most people make after their first sip of tea in the morning, and El fired up a couple of cigarettes.

"This is bliss," I said, fondling my beer and staring out into the whooshing darkness.

"Ooh yes," agreed El, taking a little sip. Booze was never her strong point.

"I wonder if I have anything to play with," I said, rummaging through the grotesquely bulging handbag that I'd been lugging around for years. With a five-foot-five, round Buddha of a father and a gorgeous mother, I'd often wondered if I was adopted. And during my brother's pre-pubescent years, I'd certainly hoped I was. But if proof of my true bloodline were ever needed, my bag would prove beyond doubt that I am indeed my mother's daughter. From as far back as I can recall, my mum's purse or, as she rather obscurely prefers to call it, her "nosebag," has been a Pandora's Box of treats and surprises. She has whipped bras, bike pumps and bags of bait out of that sack of hers. Her bag is too small for a kitchen sink, but I distinctly recall finding a coiled-up hose in there once.

"There's got to be something in here," I gurgled through a gulp of beer.

"No shit," said El. "Look at that thing. What the hell have you got in there? A Bangkok street kid?"

"No," I said, lifting my head. "Even better!" Averting a minor disaster that would have seen the bar floor littered with tampons, a harmonica I can't play and a variety of toys, I skilfully slid out the Thai phrasebook I'd bought earlier that day.

"Hooray!" El clapped her hands together like a freaky little kid. We're both total word geeks, no matter the language. One time, we were nearly escorted out of a bank for loudly guffawing over a copy of *A Pocket Guide to Literature and Language Terms* while waiting for a teller. I can't help it if we find asides like "Hey fella, don't dangle my participle" incredibly amusing. Fat lot of good it's done though. I still speak in monosyllabic grunts.

"Let's see, hmmm," I flipped through the tiny book. "Would you like a ya ra-bai?"

"What's that mean?"

"It means laxative."

"No I don't think I need one. The Chicken Shake should be re-emerging any minute now."

"Charming. Now how about this?" I peered at the page and sounded it out. "Chuay ao bia ma hai khuat neung."

"My high cat?"

"Not at all. It means, go and get me a beer."

"Are you serious?" El hadn't even sipped down to the bottleneck yet.

"Khrap."

"Crap?"

"It means yes."

She sighed, put on her best Don't Mess With Me face and cut a swath through the tract of men, many of whom were staring with unabashed amusement at my slaughtering of their language. Forget love. Toilet humour is the universal language.

Half-pissed from swilling my beer so quickly and buzzing off the weirdness of the carriage, I flicked faster through the book to find something ridiculous. It wasn't too hard really.

"Fan khawng phom phoo," I read, as El plonked a beer before me.

"I await with baited breath," she said.

"You'd have breath of bait if you had this. It means, I have decayed teeth."

"Why," El asked, "do they put that stuff in these books? I mean, if you had decayed teeth, surely it would be fairly obvious. That book is useless."

Too right it was. For all its decayed teeth and laxatives, there was nothing in the book that instructed the bumbling tourist how to ask for the toilet.

"It gets better," I said. "How about this?" I laboriously read out a lengthy phrase, attracting the giggles of a nearby cluster of policemen. A giggling cop is something that must be seen to be believed. It's in the same league as a breakdancing school principal—high farce with a tinge of the creepy.

"What's so funny?" El asked over the snickering.

"It means, must I pay for her by the hour?"

"Jesus! The Thais that put out this book must think Westerners are a mob of perverted yobbos."

"Aren't we though? Listen to this. Phom tawng-kan thawn awk." The police were joined by an inebriated knot of soldiers in a chorus of titters, elbow nudges and snorts. "I want it pulled."

El cracked up and buried her face in her hands, nearly half the carriage slapping their thighs along with her. She snatched the book from my hands and, above starched uniforms and medals, the usually stern faces of the Siamese military were goofy with expectation.

"Right," she said, riffling through the pages. Sniggering to herself, El twisted her neck, stared forlornly down the back of her shorts and blurted out a jumble of sounds with dramatic melancholy.

Instantly, the carriage erupted into a frenzy of hee-haws and howls, with soldiers and constables wiping their eyes and dropping their beer bottles.

"What the hell was that?" I asked her.

She affected a prim and slightly mollified look for the benefit of the still helpless men. "All I said was, 'I had an accident. Please get me my underwear.'"

After that, it was on for young and old. Drinks were being flung at us with great alacrity, and the lads were wasting no time in throwing even more down their throats. The phrase book, now sticky with whiskey and beer, became the holy grail of Really Dumb Humour. Everyone, from the most stern commander to some guy in a turban who'd wandered in, was pawing at its pages and bellowing out moronic idioms. Of particular delight to the men was fan plawm, the Thai for false teeth. In all my years of root canals and fillings, I'd never considered dentistry to be among the comical arts, but it just goes to show that travel really does expand one's horizons.

Anyway, I was on my third whiskey and in the middle of causing a ruckus with my pronunciation of "Please wash these filthy curtains" when the book was plucked from my hands by an unusually tall Thai man in a blue uniform. For the first time in my life, I was frightened that a strange man harassing me wasn't carrying a weapon. In this carriage, people with guns were my friends.

"Go to bed!" he ordered.

"Yeah, right," El said. I nodded with her, and we looked at our rowdy gun-slingin' companions, ready to acknowledge their support. But none was forthcoming. The room was suddenly silent, and everyone was concentrating intently on their bottles or shifting in their seats like naughty schoolkids. Everyone but El and me, that was. She was giving the guy her best glare—the look we called "the bald eagle"—and I was slumped in resignation. Bald eagling would get us nowhere. Nothing would. This guy was a Train Nazi.

It had been a few years back, when I'd hooned across America on a jump-on-jump-off Amtrak ticket, that I'd first become aware of the existence of the Train Nazi. A jobsworth of the highest order, he (Train Nazis are invariably male, in my experience) is self-trained in the arts of anal retentiveness and pedantry and wears his daggy uniform with pride. A card-carrying member of the Fun Police, the Train Nazi is constantly on the lookout for people that seem to be enjoying themselves, despite having to sleep in cramped seats and eat cardboard food. Favourite catchphrases of the Train Nazi include: Get your feet off that seat. No drinks in the smoking car. No smoking in the drinks car. If you don't stop having sex in that toilet I'll throw you off in Jacksonville. And now this. "Go to bed!"

El was trying to plead our case, and she was, despite being quite unused to the effects of Thai whiskey, making a lot of sense. "Why can they stay and we have to go?" she demanded. "The bar's not closed." But it was all in vain. For whatever reason, the

Train Nazi had decided that we were having too much fun and it was, according to the code, simply not on.

With El's words bouncing off the side of his head, he started to walk away. With our book. Pathetically enough, reading out random ruderies from the phrase book turned out to be the sole reason we'd enjoyed any semblance of friendship with the drunken men and, without it, probably the only way we'd be able to keep on their good side would be to get naked. And that, no matter how many beers or whiskeys they poured down our throats, was not a possibility.

So we followed. Defeated and drunk, we staggered out of the bar to sheepish goodbyes. Those guys knew it, and so did we—you just don't fuck with a Train Nazi.

✳

After endearing ourselves to our fellow first-class passengers by slurring obscenities and illegally smoking out of the window, El and I had thankfully passed out by 2 a.m. By the sounds of her snores, El enjoyed a contented sleep, and I was so blind I didn't care that I was reposed in a pool of curry and Chicken Shake crumbs. Lying in food must be conducive to a sound slumber, though, because it wasn't until we were on the outskirts of Udon Thani that I finally dragged myself into consciousness.

"Ugh," I groaned to El, who was still lying in a daze in her top bunk.

"Ugh," she grunted down. Mornings, especially mornings kicked off with thick tongues and hammering heads, are not our métier.

But as the train shuddered to a halt at Udon Thani Station, we were suddenly revived. We may not have been prancing about and singing anything from *The Sound of Music*, but at least we weren't grunting any more.

"And away we go!" I called to El as we hitched on our packs.

"Nong Khai, look out!" she called back.

A well-dressed Thai woman, whom we'd no doubt annoyed senseless only hours earlier, looked up, startled. "You go to Nong Khai?" she asked.

"After Udon Thani," El answered.

"This train goes on to Nong Khai," the woman said in strikingly clear English. "You should stay on it." I don't know whether this woman was sado-masochistic and keen for another bout of obnoxious behaviour on our parts to liven up her day, or merely the voice of a premonition. "You should stay," she repeated.

With a cheerfulness idiosyncratic to idiot savants and clueless travellers, I replied, "Oh no, we're going to hang out in Udon Thani for a while. It sounds great." Actually, Udon Thani didn't sound great. It didn't sound like anything at all. For all our hours on the train, I hadn't once opened my guidebook to read up on it. But how bad could it be?

Chapter Three

Udon Thani: Byword for Hell (Part 1)

What a stupid question. I should know better than to ask "How bad could it be?" That joins the ranks of such doomed questions as "Does it bite?" and "What does this big red button do?" Of course it was bad. It was horrendous. Udon Thani became our byword for hell, and whenever El and I swear at people now, we damn them to Udon Thani. Fire and brimstone has nothing on that dump.

But the fact that we were standing in the bowels of hell had not yet occurred to us. All we knew was that we were outside, breathing fresh air from an atmosphere untainted by the presence of other backpackers. And, with our beer goggles still on from the night before, the place looked pretty good. Suitably exotic and appealingly scruffy but without the slime of Khaosan Road or the parasitical touts of Bangkok.

"Alrighty then," I said. "This looks pretty cool. Shall we get out of here and find somewhere to ditch our crap?"

"Brillo," El said. "This book reckons the Prachapkdee Hotel is alright, close to everything, whatever "everything" is in Udon Thani, and it's cheap too."

"Suits me. Let's go."

We wandered into the street and with a surprising minimum of fuss or attempted shakedowns, managed to find a willing samlor driver. While the gaily coloured seating cages of tuk tuks are just big enough for three people, apparently a samlor can tote entire families, plus whatever livestock they care to count as kin, for miles on end using only pedal power. Failing the presence of scrawny chickens or squalling brats, they're quite similar to open-air limousines—minus an engine, plush seats and free champagne. And, unlike tuk tuks where you're forced to practically drape your knees over the driver's shoulders, samlor drivers get only a limited chance to see up your skirt.

As we cruised along through the traffic of cyclists, cows and motorbikes, all lumbering along on whatever side of the road they chose, my spirits lifted once again. From all indications, Udon Thani was a "real" kind of town. Unlike showy Bangkok, Udon Thani looked as if it couldn't care less about pandering to overseas visitors with bright lights, street booty or rip-off souvenir stalls. Ugly, industrial and with its head up its own arse, Udon Thani seemed ripe for the exploring. As bleak as it looked, I loved Udon Thani.

∗

"I hate Udon Thani," I told El as we climbed back into the samlor.

We had pulled up at the Prachapkdee Hotel to the collective glares of loiterers and the growls of mangy street dogs. Considering the state of the hotel, you couldn't have asked for a more apt welcome. While Thailand has never been under the thumb of any Soviet regime, the architects of the Prachapkdee had obviously been in the throes of a bizarre gulag obsession. Depressingly stark with a concrete façade and almost totally windowless, the building made a fine poster child for a Prozac overdose. Nevertheless, we'd decided to check it out anyway on the premise that ugly and weird was better than postcard-pretty and interminably boring. You could meet a million gorgeously bronzed boys down at Le Meridien on Phuket, but only at the Prachapkdee were you liable to run into a lunatic in a stained undershirt, sprouting nonsensicals over a bottle of rice wine. I am still considering therapy on the grounds that the latter prospect thrilled me more.

With our samlor driver yukking it up outside, El and I had loped into the hotel, and I held my breath in excitement, waiting for the undershirt guy of my hungover imagination to come falling down the stairs. In the end, the only thing that came crashing down were our hopes of a bed for the night.

"No farang," the receptionist said.

"No what?" I asked. We hadn't even gotten around to asking for a room yet.

"No farang," she repeated, walking away with a light wave of the hand.

"What the hell is farang?" I said. "We don't want farang, just a room for the night."

The receptionist whipped around, her eyes suddenly ablaze with a wild death glare. "No farang! No farang! You must leave!"

"Jesus!" El said. "Someone's obviously forgotten to tell this chick that acid-style freakouts of the *Apocalypse Now* variety are supposed to be restricted to Vietnam."

"Farang!" We heard the banging of a door and, with images of some anti-farang bouncer crashing the scene, we bolted. Panting and wide-eyed, we hustled up to our samlor driver, who was obviously in the midst of some dodgy deal, and pulled on his sleeve. "Let's go," I begged him.

"No stay?" he asked.

"No way," I said.

"The woman said 'no farang,'" El told him. "What the hell is that all about?"

"Aaah," said the driver, nodding his head sagely. "Farang is you."

"Who?" I asked. "Me or her?" I'd known El for ten years and had never known her to display any farang tendencies. Whatever they were.

"You and you," the driver said. "Farang is," he stumbled over the word, "foreigner."

Behind the driver, a dwarfish halfwit sniggered. "Farang!" he giggled. Obviously these people didn't get out much.

"Right then," I sighed. "Can you take us somewhere they'll let farang stay for the night?"

"Try to," the driver said. "Is very hard in Udon Thani. Many places do not want farang."

I shook my head in disbelief, and absentmindedly reached down to pat a bony dog that was licking my knees. It bit me.

Hell sucks.

✳

After being booted out of another three hotels, we finally found refuge in a two-bit establishment called the Chai Porn, presumably only because there was nobody else staying there that we could offend with our blatant farang-ness. Modern Seedy seemed to be the theme, with an interior design scheme dominated by dim lighting, gloomy furniture and a sign reading "No guns." All it needed was a battered old boozehound collapsed in the corner and the place would be a Tom Waits song.

But what with getting blacklisted from every other dive in town, and me fretting about rabies, staying in an empty flophouse was the least of our worries. At least we knew, so long as we didn't pistol-whip the receptionist, that we had secured somewhere to lay our heads for the night. If we were game enough to touch the pillows, that was.

Despite the fact that we were the only two guests in the entire place, we were shunted into a third-storey corner room far from the prying eyes of whatever anti-faranger happened to be passing by on the street. The room, a box reminiscent of our cubbyhole on Khaosan Road, overlooked a jumble of slums and smelled like goat. And if that wasn't enough to ensure we'd be hauling our embarrassing, farang selves out of town tomorrow, they'd thrown in a sagging bed with grey, curiously stained linen to get us on our way.

I gingerly sat down on a corner of the shapeless bed and promptly slid to the floor. "Good grief, they really don't like us honkies around here, do they?"

"They certainly don't. And what the hell for? It's not as if we're out there eating their children or raping their bloody goats," El said. "It's weird, I tell you. This town feels freakish."

"Maybe it's just the hotels that don't like us," I tried hopefully. "Gimme that book." I reached for El's *Lonely Planet*. "Maybe it'll say something."

I flicked through to the brief entry on Udon Thani and scanned the page. "Oh shit," I said. "Of course they're gonna bald eagle us. This place used to be an American Air Force base during the Vietnam War."

"Christ!" El muttered through a cigarette. "No wonder it's such a dump. But really, what the hell does that have to do with us? I mean, look at us, do we really look like we're about to bomb the place and start groping their women?"

"We're just another couple of bastard farang as far as they're concerned. Coming in with our round eyes and long noses to tear up the joint. Jesus, the only thing I want to ravish is a plate of Thai food."

"That's it," El said, squashing out her cigarette. "I refuse to survive solely on belching up the remains of last night's Chicken Shake sangas. Surely the people in this town can't despise us so much they refuse us food."

"Yeah. Someone has to be nice around here. Hey, maybe we'll see some monks finally!" There had been a noticeable absence of Buddhist monks along the Khaosan Road. Saffron duds seemed to clash with dreads and dope. "Yeah, that's it. The monks will take care of us."

✳

Take care of us indeed. The only thing the monks of Udon Thani looked capable of taking care of was a low-grade smuggling ring. With filthy robes, stubbled chins and tattoos, it seemed that monastic life in this town was a condition of parole. They gathered on every street corner, seedy-looking men fidgeting and cadging smokes the way their more pious brethren would beg alms, while the lawless roads were made all the more dangerous with the appearance of a crusty monk screaming by on a beat-up motorcycle. God may be everywhere, but Buddha was playing rigged poker on Prachak Road.

With our hands jammed in our pockets and our wallets down our pants, we edged past a particularly scabby swag of monks, leaning against a ramshackle food wagon selling dried squid dangling from clothespegs. As they ooh-ed and aaah-ed over each other's knuckle scars, one of them, sporting an impressive dent to the skull, swung around to catch a glimpse of us and nudged his mates. "Hey, farang," he said, using a tone of voice usually reserved for men with Tom Selleck moustaches and open collars. "Hey, hey!"

And there was me believing that TV evangelists had the monopoly on sleaze in the name of the Lord.

"Just keep moving, El, just i-g-n-o-r-e."

35

"Does that spell "retch'? Because one of them, I swear, just went to lift up his robe at us. I feel ill."

Remembering Lot's wife, I refused to turn around until we'd rounded the next corner. Of course, Mrs. Lot never had to cast her gaze upon a curmudgeonly monk fondling himself between squid stalls, but I was taking no chances. As it turned out, we probably would have been better off staying for the striptease.

We ducked into the next street, a bustling corridor of beeping tuk tuks, open-front shops and itinerant shoe salesmen, and glanced around, SWAT team style. "No monks here," I said. "It's cool."

"That was just wrong," El said, shaking her head as we trundled along. "Buddhist monks are supposed to be lovely and divine and sweet. What is wrong with this place?"

"I'm traumatised," I said. "If only there was someone in this entire damned town that would smile, just be nice for God's sake."

"I wish."

Amid the begging, bartering and general brouhaha of the raucous streetscape, an evil Tinkerbell must have been lurking, waiting to pounce on every idiot who blithely tossed off an "I wish." The cliché "Beware of what you wish for" is only a cliché because it's been proven time and time again. We were just another two rubes about to be duped by bad magic.

"I don't bloody believe it," I said.

"What?"

"Over there, by the kerb. That old guy is actually smiling!"

Somewhere in a back alley, Tinkerbell giggled into her sleeve.

"Where? Where? I've got to see this." It is a sad day indeed when a smile becomes a tourist attraction. "Where is he?"

"There." I pointed discreetly towards a weathered old man, leaning back Fonzie-style on his parked motorbike. In a slouch cap and faded shirt, he looked just like every other guy on the block but for that one accessory. A smile. How lovely. Without really meaning to, we started walking towards him, drawn in by his grin, which seemed to be aimed directly at us. As we pushed past a frowning melee of newspaper boys, I noticed he was pointing at something with rapid, almost secretive movements.

"What's he pointing at?" I whispered to El. "All I can see is just more rubbish and grotty shoe salesmen."

El squinted in the direction of the old guy, whose smile was broadening with every step we took closer to him, then jerked back with a spasm. "Oh, shit!"

"What?" I cried, stumbling behind her. "What?"

"He's not pointing, he's bloody wanking!"

Why some people insist on masturbating in public has always been beyond me. It's bad enough that construction workers seem to genuinely believe that shouting "Show us yer map of Tassie!" will one day lead them into an encounter of the Penthouse Forum kind. But what do sidewalk self-stimulators hope to achieve? Do they really think that some girl is going to sidle up and purr, "Here, honey, let me do that for you"? I mean, has there ever, in the history of public wanking, been a successful love affair sparked off by a girl falling for a guy tugging himself on a city street corner?

"You depraved freak!" El yelled. "Put that hideous thing away!"

But he just kept on grinning and pulling away, oblivious to our shouts. If I'd known the Thai word for "little peanut," I could have perhaps shamed him back into his pants. Then again, maybe not. Judging by the impassive faces of the passersby, I guessed that spending time with Mrs. Palmer and her five daughters on the kerbside in Udon Thani was no less common than scoring crack under the bodhi tree. So much for karma.

We fled. Again. I was beginning to feel like one of Pavlov's dogs, but instead of drooling at the bell, we were bolting at the pervert. At least it was making for an innovative exercise regimen.

"I really can't cope with any more of this," I said as we stopped to catch our breath. "Racist hoteliers, demonic dogs, debauched monks and old men tossing off in the gutter. The *Lonely Planet* guy who recommended this dump must've been fucking lonely alright. Lonely in the bloody head."

"And as for that copy of Let's Go," El ranted. "They forgot to add 'to Hell in a Handbasket' after the title. Really, are these people insane? What could they possibly have seen in this place?"

I shrugged. "All they ever talk about are temples and shrines. What're they called? Wats and stupas."

"Yeah, well so what? I mean, sure, they're nice to look at and all that, but we're not here to look at buildings all day. The whole thing is supposed to be about bumbling around strange places, trying weird things and annoying the locals, not just gawping at some old building."

"Honestly, the only building I want to see right now is one that's housing food. The closest thing to food we've found so far is that guy hawking dried squid bits. And I'm sure these Udon Thaniites don't get the strength to flog their logs just by eating bait."

El stuck her tongue out and gagged. "Bugger eating bait. We are going to find some lush Thai food right now and don't even think about opening one of those guidebooks. They'll have us dining on salted cat in some dingy basement. This is Thailand, right? There's got to be coconut curry somewhere."

*

I'm sure that, somewhere, there was. For all we knew, somewhere in Udon Thani, some lucky bastards were burning their tongues on spicy chicken and rice. But not us.

We had pizza.

After scouring the streets for two hours, the only thing we'd found that even slightly resembled edible had been a shipment of dried onions in a busted-up warehouse. Sweating, starving and ready to devour the next small child that crossed our path, we had somehow suddenly found ourselves standing before the mammoth Charoen Sri shopping centre. In the Western world, shopping malls mean food courts. And food courts always mean Chinese food. Hell, if we couldn't eat Thai, at least we could use chopsticks for something.

But no. Amid the jumble of Hello Kitty rip-offs, spruikers hawking scratchy T-shirts, and still more shoe shops, the closest thing we could find to Asian food was a poster of Ronald McDonald with a slightly Eurasian countenance. In the end, we were faced with three options: Maccas, KFC or Pizza Hut. After figuring out that urban myths about biting into cysts and people doing rude things with mayonnaise seem to revolve around burger joints, we decided that even a weird fusion of Thai and Italian cuisines would be better than playing "Guess the Meat" anywhere else.

"It's pretty ironic, you know," I said to El as we scanned the menu. "The best Thai food I ever had was in New Jersey. And you know what New Jersey's famous for, don't you?"

"I dunno," El said, scowling at a No Smoking sign above our table. "Big hair, acid rain and glam rock?"

"Well, all that too. But no, really, it's pizza. New Jersey is Mafia central, meaning pizza heaven. So it'd be a fair swap, say, if the best Thai I had was in Jersey and the best pizza was in Thailand, hey?"

"Somehow I doubt that'll happen," El said. "Look at that." She nodded towards a nearby table, where a middle-aged Thai businessman was in the process of coughing up a misshapen glob of pepperoni onto his plate. "Now that's class."

Just as the choking guy was wiping a trail of dribble from his mouth, our voyeurism was cut short by the appearance of a waitress. Young and beautiful in the classic Thai way, she nervously hovered by our table, most likely hoping that the sight of a man retching up processed meat wasn't going to spoil our appetites.

"Sawadee kha," she said sweetly. "Take you order?"

"We're still deciding," El said. "But could we have some water to start with? We're very thirsty." She wasn't wrong. Not only had we not found anywhere to eat on the Udon Thani streets, but non-toxic liquid had also proven a scarce commodity.

"Water," the girl said. "Yah." She stood there, smiling down at us.

"Righty-ho then, thanks," El said, turning back to the menu.

"Yah," the girl said, in the same curious monotone.

"Um, just water for now," I ventured. "Still choosing."

"Yah." She didn't budge. El and I shifted in our seats and made a grand show of perusing the menu, only to peek up and find the girl still standing there, smiling to beat the band.

"Yah."

"Look, could we get that water now?" El asked. "It's hot and we're thirsty."

"We don't know what we want to eat yet," I added.

"Yah."

Half a minute passed in a roaring silence. Even the retching guy had stopped making gurgling noises, presumably to add to our feeling of discomfort. I knew that if I didn't get some water soon, I was either going to scream or start licking the perspiration off El's forehead. But I didn't really want to cause a scene. After all, maybe this was how it was done in Thailand. Order quickly or perish.

But El was having none of it. "Listen lady," she growled, slamming down the menu. "We don't know what we want to eat. Just, please! Get us some water!"

The waitress beamed even brighter. Maybe this was all part of a game, Pizza Hut employees competing against one another to see just how many customers they could frustrate into a temper tantrum. It sure beat flipping dough all day.

El freaked, and, like most horrible things, it happened in slow motion. Your car crashes and you get to see each sickening contortion of metal in what seems to take an eternity. You jump off a highrise ledge and, so I've heard, it takes about a day for the ground to hurtle up to you. And when El finally lost it, I got to marvel for an aeon at the first flush of her face, the flash of her eyes, the creaking open of her mouth. I even had time to wonder what she'd have to say. I should have guessed.

"Would . . . you . . . just . . . fuck . . . off!"

Echo, echo, echo.

We sat there in a stunned silence, me with my eyes popping out of my skull, El goggling back at me in horror. This was it, and we both knew it. This was when the citizens of Udon Thani–the monks, the hotel receptionists, the masturbators–all raced into the restaurant with their torches and nooses to lynch us once and for all. Bad enough that we had insulted them all by just being there, poking our pink foreign noses into everything. But we had really done it now and we were dead meat. I suddenly wished we'd just taken the plunge and eaten dried onions and bait. Amoebic dysentery was nothing compared to a public beating.

The waitress looked at us, an only slightly confused look crossing her eyes. "Yah," she smiled and tottered off into the kitchen.

"Holy shit," El whispered in a shaken voice. "I cannot believe I just said that."

"I know," I said. "But check this out." The waitress emerged from the kitchen, water jug in hand and an even brighter look on her face.

Profanity pays.

*

We'd wound up barricading ourselves in our hotel room the moment the sun went down, still fearful of reprisals from the locals after the Pizza Hut debacle. While we'd somehow managed to finally order and devour two medium pies without attracting the wrath of the staff, we estimated it could only be a matter of time until the waitress figured out that "fuck off" wasn't the usual, polite way to order a drink. And then we'd be in trouble.

Aghast at the idea of running into her on the street, her pearly whites bared in a murderous snarl, we'd run back to the Chai Porn at breakneck speed, stopping only to grab essential provisions. After all, you can't cower in fear without stale corn chips, cigarettes and beer.

But thankfully, the night passed without our being slaughtered and we'd managed to pass out fairly early, helped along by a few stubbies of strong ale and an even stronger desire for morning to arrive. And when it did, announcing itself with the bleating of an emaciated goat in the ghetto below, we were up and dressed in record time. Still traumatised by the Train Nazi debacle, we'd decided to make our way to Nong Khai by bus.

"My God, I cannot wait to haul arse out of this shithole," I said, hastily throwing on my rucksack.

"You think you can't," she said. "What about me? I told the village idiot to fuck off. People get very attached to their local dimwits for some reason. I'm dead meat if anyone sees me now."

"I think this entire place is populated by village idiots. Maybe this is where they send them from villages across Thailand, like idiot training."

"Well," El said, unlocking the door. "That chick will surely graduate top of the class. You can't get more idiotic than that."

Unless you count us, that is.

After hastily checking out at reception and realising we still had an hour before our bus to Nong Khai pulled out, we'd crept into the street for one last, hopefully uneventful look around. As

I stood in the hotel doorway staring at a boy throwing rocks at the traffic, El called me over in a resigned voice.

"Just have a look at this," she sighed.

"What is it?"

"Just look." She pointed at a sign hanging over the door of the building next to the hotel.

"Mandarin," I read. "A fruit store? So what?"

"Just look in the window."

I peered inside. Not even three metres from our hotel door, dozens of happy, well-adjusted locals were chatting animatedly over bowls of rice, seafood and what was undoubtedly coconut curry. A handsome waiter, raffish in a loose tie and with a wayward lock of hair, did a round of the tables, filling up glasses and piling more food before the obviously pleased diners. A sign on the door read "Open seven days, early until late."

Employment Wanted: Idiots seek village for random acts of folly.

Chapter Four

The Annoyance of Being Earnest

Maybe I was wrong. Maybe Udon Thani wasn't actually hell, just an extreme form of purgatory. According to my religion teacher in third grade, hell was impossible to leave. Once you were there, Mrs. Lombardi said, the devil liked to chain you up and burn you with hot sticks and never let you go. No wonder I slept with the light on.

But Udon Thani seemed quite pleased to see the last of us. There was no dead cow blocking the road, no bag snatchings or last-minute locust plagues to keep us from getting on board that bus. Not that a bunch of bugs or some barnyard roadkill would have stopped us. It was Nong Khai or bust.

It was raining as we climbed aboard the bus, and we waggled our now-trademark two-fingered salute at the miserable landscape of mud-splattered tuk tuks, drenched ticket huts and one hirsute monk who hadn't the sense to get out of the downpour. I was glad I, for one, was dry—who knew what was in the water around there.

But it wasn't until the last bedraggled passenger had hauled themselves aboard and the bus began to slide along the quagmire of a road that we finally allowed ourselves to relax. I leaned back as we swerved through Udon Thani's waterlogged streets, put my head on El's shoulder as we hurtled past random fringe developments and fell asleep as the bus splashed its way past tatty palm trees and green wasteland.

Two crusty eyes, a sore spine and fifty-one kilometres later, we were there. After twenty-four hours of melodramatic fiasco, I felt sure that in Nong Khai we'd find an oasis of sanity and relaxation. If someone could shut those bloody dogs up, that was.

"What the hell is that racket?" I asked El, wiping a trail of my drool off her shoulder.

"Sounds like a pack of wild mongrels," she answered, shifting around for a better look out the fogged window. "I can't see."

As the bus gasped its last and the driver swung open the door, the din rose to a cacophonous clamour. It sounded like someone was getting torn to shreds out there.

"Can you see?"

"Hang on," I said, smearing the grime off the pane. "It's, um," I squinted, rubbing the glass with my spit until it was clear. "Oh shit."

Just beneath our window, no fewer than fifteen Thai men were wrestling, shoving and generally flailing about like uncoordinated mosh pitters. The taller ones were jumping up and slapping our window, while the rest were busy trying to untangle their body parts in a mad dash for the open door of the bus.

"What on earth is that?" El yelped.

"I have no bloody idea. At least there's no rabid hounds waiting to chew us up."

"Oh yeah? Listen to that."

The rumble of voices crescendoed, the dissonant barking noise suddenly taking form in the shape of a single word: "Farang!"

I stared at El in horror. Had these people followed us all the way from Udon Thani in some twisted bid to drive us insane?

Or was all of northeast Thailand a hotbed of racial intolerance and xenophobia?

"They're going to kill us," I whispered.

"No they're not, you idiot. They're bloody tuk tuk drivers and touts."

"Do they have to travel in packs like savage timber wolves? Honestly, how did they know we were coming?"

"Who knows," El replied, pulling on her pack. "But they can get stuffed. I hate being pressured into things, especially when they're undoubtedly going to rip us off."

"Even more especially when they come barking up like the Hounds of Hell. Let's go."

For a brief moment, I knew what it felt like to be a rock god. With the appearance of our faces at the door, the crowd went berserk, and when we stepped down from the bus, the men mobbed us, tugging our arms and grabbing snatches of our clothes. All of this would have been fine and dandy, were we boasting leather trousers and bodyguards. But being pulled and prodded by men essentially calling us honky trash and looking to get paid for it was not quite Beatlemania.

"Get off . . . No! . . . Beat it! . . . Jesus!"

With a final heave, El and I tumbled out of the scrum, let loose with one last "No!" and tried to readjust ourselves. My bra strap was down over my left shoulder, El's backpack was hanging like a broken arm and, in defiance of gravity, one of my pigtails was sticking straight up like a unicorn horn above my forehead. Now we looked like rock gods. Or at least Courtney Love.

"Quick," El said. "They're regrouping. Let's bolt."

We strode quickly ahead, trying to look stern and purposeful. Which was somewhat difficult when I didn't know where we were going. "What's the name of that hostel again?" While under self-imposed incarceration behind the doors of the Chai Porn, we'd found what promised to be a "cheery, welcoming" guesthouse listed in the *Lonely Planet*. Which probably meant it was "dismal and rude."

"The Mut Mee, I think. They reckon it's popular, so that probably means it's a farang-a-thon."

"Who cares," I said, looking over my shoulder at the slow procession of tuk tuks not so subtly trailing behind us. "It's only for one night."

Despite the fact that Nong Khai, with its lazy location along the Mekong River, was billed as a magnet for travellers, we had already decided not to get too attached to the place. Laos was just a stone's skip across the Mekong and the temptation to haul arse into a country we could hardly pronounce was too great. We figured we'd just kick back, enjoy one last day in civilisation (Nong Khai apparently had an internet café somewhere) and catapult ourselves into the great unknown the next morning. And if we were surrounded by other backpackers, so what? It would take a lot more than boring travel tales and a room full of Birkenstocks to annoy me after the Udon Thani experience. Hell, I figured I could even handle the odd goatee or earnest recounting of a pot-induced conversion to Buddhism. I was ready for anything.

"One night, hey," El said. "Bugger this, it'll be nighttime by the time we find this place." She frowned down at her map. "It's supposed to be right on the river, wherever that is." We glanced around furtively, trying to look like eager sightseers instead of just lost. The minute those tuk tukkers figured out we had no clue where we were, they'd pounce. It wasn't that we were afraid of being ripped off. After all, the most a ride could cost us would be the equivalent of two bucks. No, it was a matter of pride. That same pride that would see every dad in the world getting lost on a family roadtrip rather than ask directions or consult a map.

"Let's keep going," I said. "It can't be that hard to find a river, for crying out loud."

Oh, but it was. The Mekong hid itself well behind a labyrinth of badly paved streets, fishy-smelling cafés and corrugated-iron bars done up in Buddha statuettes and Singha Beer flags. Unlike some rivers, which boast their presence with booming rapids and spray townsfolk in a fine, constant mist, the Mekong slipped quietly on its way, content to water crops, provide fish and carry boats. It was a very Buddhist river.

Perhaps we too should have followed the Noble Eightfold Path. Maybe we should have followed any path. Any path, that is, except the one that we kept stubbornly taking, the one that continually led us in circles, only to deposit us before some guy selling soft drinks beneath a broken parasol. "Fanta?" he would ask each time we came trudging around the corner. "No thanks," we'd sigh, plodding off again on our useless crusade, tuk tuks still hopefully tagging behind us.

An hour and six trips past the soft-drink seller later, we relented. We were dizzy, hot and were beginning to believe that the Mekong River, not to mention the Mut Mee Guesthouse, were simply two more products of a *Lonely Planet* writer's overstretched imagination.

"Fanta?" the guy asked.

"Yes please," we sighed.

"Tuk tuk?" came a voice from behind.

We looked at each other with weary eyes. "Yes please," we droned.

We were broken.

∗

The Mut Mee was more of a backpackers' resort than a mere guesthouse. Slouching right on the banks of the elusive Mekong River, the Mut Mee was made up of a handful of wooden cabins, a basic café, a timber bar and an abundance of chill-out areas, ranging from elaborately carved benches and tables to a tyre swing. Down a pebbled lane, travellers could resume contact with the outside world in a New Age bookstore-cum-internet café, while those wishing to preserve the dreamy estrangement from real life that Thailand offered could smoke joints and lie around under their mosquito nets.

"Right then, ladies," the incredibly named Bruce said in an embarrassingly nasal Australian drawl. "Here's ya keys. Cabin Three, all yours fer now." He leaned out of the small office which served as reception, kitchen and tour desk and pointed to a ramshackle but homey-looking shack behind the bar. "Just remember, no smoking, food or drink in there."

"Okay," we said. "Thanks heaps."

We climbed cautiously up a rotting staircase and creaked open the cabin door, revealing four large, surprisingly stain-free beds, each draped in sheer netting. The room smelled like incense and a gaudy sarong hung limply over a large window.

"Now this makes for a nice change," I said, throwing my pack on to one of the beds. "Very hippie, but nice."

"Too right," El agreed. "I don't smell a single goat and they didn't even want us to check our guns at reception."

We flopped on a bed and sighed happily. I shook out a packet of cigarettes from my pocket and held them out to El. "Butt?"

"Oh yes." She took a couple out, lit them and passed one to me with her bottle of still-chilled Fanta. "Drink?"

"Indeed." I took a gulp, and passed the bottle back. "Now if we only had something really greasy to eat in here." We were Class A obnoxious.

El laughed. "Well, stuff 'em. I don't think I could be fagged launching straight out there and mixing it up with the farang just yet. Anyway, if we want to smoke and guzzle Fanta inside, it's not like they're going to know."

"Maybe we should open the window just in case," I said. "Can you imagine getting booted out of here after five minutes?"

"We could always stay with the soft drinks guy," El said, getting up to open the window. "At least we know where he is."

El wrenched the window open and we both leaned out into the sunshine, cupping our cigarettes in case Bruce or some other fresh air fiend came strolling by. But it wasn't any Aussie yobbo we had to worry about. It was the New Agers.

"Check this out," El whispered to me. "Look in there." She nodded down towards an open timber hut just below our room. Inside, a thin white guy lay still on the floor, evidently meditating in a classic coffin pose, with his dreadlocked hair fanned out behind his head. A few feet away, another guy with matching dreads and an instantly irritating beard was standing on one foot, slowly raising his arms to an arc above his head.

"What's that," I asked under my breath, "Tai Chi?"

"Tai Chi, my arse," El whispered. "It's the Karate Kid." I spat out my cigarette in a spasm of laughter and we dissolved into a fit of snorts and giggles. The Ralph Macchio gone wrong looked up, a look of very un-nirvana-like anger crossing his face, and we rolled for cover underneath the mosquito net, laughing even harder. Not that there's anything wrong with meditation or introspection, mind you—it's just the people who insist on being so earnest about everything that crack me up.

We pulled ourselves together and, crouching low, peeped out into the hut. The meditating guy was sitting up, scratching his mop and looking around the room like a torpid bear just roused from hibernation, while the bearded guy was back at it, making languid, purposeful motions with his hands and trying very hard not to look rattled. I could almost read his mind: "I am calm. I am calm. I'm calm, damn it!" Naturally, we lost the plot.

Tangled in the netting and gasping for air, it took us nearly a minute to regain any sort of composure. "Oh man," El panted. "This is really harshing my karma."

"He's going to do irrevocable damage to his if he catches us," I said, still snickering away. "Like when he beats us to a pulp."

El stood up and straightened herself out. "We should get out of this room so we're not here if he does come up. If we're down there with all the others, he won't know it was us pissing ourselves at his fresh and funky moves."

"Maybe we should just get out of here, full stop. By the time we come back from loitering around town, he might have dharma-ed out and forgotten all about it."

"Sweet," El said, strapping her money pouch under her shorts waist. "Let's see if we can manage not to get run out of town for once."

✳

It was a tough call.

We'd been on the pavement for less than a minute when I copped the evil eye from a stooped old woman, presumably because I was gallivanting around town in a red singlet. Baring your shoulders was crime enough, as I'd learnt in Bali, but to be so brazen as to tart around in red seemed the ultimate in harlotry.

"Get thee to a clothing shop," El said, watching the old woman shake her head in disgust. "I'm not walking around with a whore."

Whoever decided that shopping is "retail therapy" has never gone T-shirt hunting in Nong Khai. Although a small town, it was lined with dozens of shops, while a large riverside market boasted everything from carved Karmic circles to fake Rolexes. Any sane person would reasonably expect to find at least one T-shirt among such an array.

But no. Besides flogging a wealth of tacky statuettes that would thrill any Franklin Mint devotee, the vendors of Nong Khai possessed an improbable eclecticism when it came to fashion. There were fleece jumpers and gimcrack blouses of hot pink lace with gold buttons. There were ski jackets and sarongs, raincoats and training bras. In one shop, most likely lit up at night with a red flashing bulb, there was an entire wall rack devoted solely to gossamer tank tops. But no T-shirts. Nong Khai had to be the only town on earth where you could buy the ceramic likeness of an electric-blue flute-playing duck without clapping eyes on a plain white Fruit of the Loom.

But, nearly two frenetic hours of shopping later, there I stood, my wanton shoulders finally covered. I was a whore no more. I was, however, looking more and more like a complete lunatic.

"I really can't go around like this," I said to El as we walked out of the Friendship Clothing Store, my sluttish red singlet concealed in my day pack. "Look at me, for Christ's sake!"

While Nong Khai may not have had any T-shirts in adult sizes for sale, there were plenty for kids. This would have been well and good, were I someone who shopped in the petite section of the local department store. But I was nearly six feet tall and had the vague beginnings of a beer gut, which didn't look exceptionally attractive at the best of times. Let it all hang out beneath an "Eight to Ten Years" T-shirt inexplicably emblazoned with the cartoon face of a tongue-wagging lime and what you get is definitely not Vogue material.

"Quit your whinging," El said. "At least now we can look around without fear of you getting whisked away to a harem somewhere. Where shall we go?"

I thought for a second, still self-consciously tugging the shirt over my belly. "How about the pub?"

El turned to me in surprise. "You spend all this time bitching and moaning about your so-called beer gut and now you want to go to the pub?"

I shrugged. "It'll make me forget about my beer gut."

El shook her head. "No way. We'll drink tonight at the Mut Mee, but now we should probably go and get whatever we need for Laos. Tampons, aspirin, film, all that shit. I have no idea how hard it'll be to get stuff over there. Laos sounds pretty two-bit."

"So you wanna check out the chemist?"

"I guess so."

I beamed, all thoughts of flab and beer pushed aside by the idea of going to the chemist. Not just any chemist. A Thai chemist.

El eyeballed me with ill-concealed suspicion and I answered with my own look of ill-concealed guilt. "You just want to get your hands on some Valium, don't you," she accused.

"Well," I began. "Um."

"For God's sake, let's just go." She started off down the road and I skipped merrily alongside, tunelessly singing "Valium, Valium" like an idiot.

Don't get me wrong. I'm not a pill junkie by any means. I've only ever tried Valium once in my life, and it, along with the aid of six Southern Comforts, led to a disastrous chain of events culminating in my passing out in an airplane toilet for four hours. Not that I remember any of it. I was filled in by my fellow passengers once the stewardess had broken down the toilet door and dragged me snoring back to my seat.

No, I just wanted to get some because it sounded like what you were supposed to do in Southeast Asia. Try new food, trek with some hill-tribe guys and pop illegal prescription drugs. With anchovy and pineapple pizza being the sum of my culinary experiences so far and no hill tribes in sight, it looked like smacking out on out-of-date Valium would be my one nod to the travelling norm.

Or not. As El loitered between shelves crammed with hair oil, tins of loose herbs and jars containing things reminiscent of Year 10 Biology, I nervously approached the counter with pen and scrap paper in hand. I hoped I looked less like a jittery drug fiend than an inherently nerve-wracked soul in desperate need of tranquillisers.

"Sawadee khrap," the chemist said.

"Sawadee kha," I replied, stunning him with my mastery of the Thai language. If only my teeth had been decayed. I could have really knocked him for six. "Do you have . . ." I paused, scribbling the word "Valium" on the paper, "this?"

The chemist picked up the paper and squinted at my shaky handwriting. "Ah! Valium!" he pronounced. "Yes. We have."

"Great! I mean, um, good. I'll have . . ."

"But no for you." He smiled at me and made a great show of crumpling my piece of paper into a tiny ball before tossing it on to the floor. In a voice designed more to humiliate than chastise, he boomed, "No Valium for farang! No more!"

Feeling like I'd swilled a bottle of whatever Alice drank to make her shrink, I fidgeted and hunched inwardly as everyone in the store turned to stare at me. While El just rolled her eyes and went back to the shelves, the rest of the shoppers continued to gawk and mutter among themselves, doubtless disgusted by the oversized drug addict at the counter.

"No Valium, not like before," the chemist continued, obviously taking great delight in my discomfort. "No . . ."

"All right, I get the point," I muttered. It seemed, in Nong Khai anyway, that the halcyon days of shelling out dodgy drugs to dodgier Westerners had come to an end. I wondered when this guy had twigged that the swarm of travellers begging for sedatives were not actually riddled with anxiety but were, in fact, looking for cheap thrills. Knowing my luck, it had been just as I walked in the door.

"Finish?" the chemist asked with an air of impatience. He had more important matters to attend to than lambasting would-be pill poppers—like selling what looked like a pickled ear to a woman waiting behind me.

I gave up. Trying to understand the vagaries of the Thais was beyond me. It was fine and dandy for some guy to wank away on a busy street but two decently clad women keeping their hands to themselves couldn't even get a hotel room. The charred visage of a pig was palmed off as a lunchtime delicacy but nobody would sell me a T-shirt. Chemists balked at selling pharmaceuticals but preserved ears floating in formaldehyde were presumably covered by Medicare. It was suddenly all too much.

I slumped on the counter. "Aspirin," I said.

Chapter Five

Haight-Ashbury on the Mekong

By the time El, laden down with bags of sensible purchases, joined me outside the chemist, it was late afternoon. With our shadows stretching into improbable stick figures, we sauntered along towards the riverside markets and watched vendors arrange their wares for the expected influx of night-time browsers. Along one aisle, sarongs fluttered in the gentle pre-dusk breeze above folded piles of gauzy fabric, while down another, brightly painted Buddhist icons cluttered sagging card tables beside kiosks of Chinese pottery. Small motorcycles were parked between stalls, their sidecar stands laid out with dried fish and bowls of chilli sauce, while on the fringes of the market, children stood guard over crates lined with bottles of sticky soft drink. The entire scene, replete with the occasional non-leering monk strolling by, looked like something out of a travel brochure. For the first time since we'd arrived in Thailand, life had an air of normalcy about it.

Inspired by the lack of calamity, we decided it was safe to return to the Mut Mee. The Karate Kid had surely forgotten us by now and the meditating guy on the floor would either be deep in a trance or pulling bucket bongs in the shallows of the Mekong. There'd be no worries there. As for the other farang, who'd no doubt be kicking off an evening of trying to outdo each other with bullshit travel stories, we'd just be nice. And if we couldn't do that, we'd ignore them. Just for once, we were going to be typical travellers, without sarcastic remarks, without disaster, without getting lynched.

For the first few minutes, all went well. Mr Macchio and Meditation Man were nowhere to be seen, and we managed to smile at a group of Canadians piled on the tyre swing, despite the fact they all had goatees and sarongs tied around their heads. We tolerated an Age of Aquarius mural painted above one of the café tables and only barely winced when we heard someone mauling Cat Stevens on the guitar. But when we saw the dinner menu, we went to pieces.

"Rat prik!" El exclaimed. "What the hell is rat prik?"

"Oh God," I groaned. "Anorexia here I come."

"I'm sure it isn't really a rat's prick, but couldn't they have called it something else? Or maybe this is part of the 'I'm down with this Thai shit' backpacker thing. It's cooler to ask for rat prik than chicken with rice."

I wasn't very down with the Thai shit, so when Bruce came out to take our orders, I opted for the Aussie alternative. "Beer please," I said. El, ever the patriot, ordered one too.

"Good bloody choice," Bruce said, cracking our beers. I took it that he had no say in the gastronomic offerings of the Mut Mee. "Youse want to go and drink that down by the river. It's lovely for the sunset."

It was sound advice. Hidden far enough away from the Mut Mee's chattering crew but close enough to stumble back up for more beer, we lounged on the bank of the Mekong, sipping our dinner and watching Laos turn on its lights across the way. All was well with the world; the river prowled by, rippling silver in the dusk, the sky was awash with pinks and lavenders, and the insects of the night were beginning to hum.

Unfortunately, they were also beginning to bite, despite repeated attempts to smoke them out, slap them down and scream them away. For some reason, bugs are always attracted to new blood. Maybe they go for the foreign taste, the way humans fall over themselves to get their hands on Belgian chocolates or French cheese. Whatever the reason, we grabbed our beers and fled back up the riverbank, breaking out into mammoth welts and trying to remember if we'd taken our malaria pills.

But back at the Mut Mee, mosquito-borne diseases were the least of our worries.

Chapter Six

Animosity Bridge

From all indications, there was a sixties party going on and nobody had told us to bring our flares; a German woman with hairy armpits and a turban was extolling the virtues of nude pottery to a group of serious-looking twentysomething girls in bellydance pants and sarongs, while two bearded guys, one of whom looked suspiciously like the Tai Chi guy, hunched over their guitars, belting out a Garcia-esque version of "Hello Mary Lou." A tall black guy in orange African robes and matching pillbox cap read poetry from a notebook to a tiny Japanese girl, who covertly dragged on a joint and nodded sagely. Towering above it all on a wobbly ladder, a heavily tanned blond man was dabbing paint on the mural, which, in his artistic wisdom, he had transformed into a cultural stew of Hindu deities, laughing Chinese Buddhas and topless purple women with unfeasibly large breasts. It was like walking on to the set of Hair, except nobody was naked. Thank God.

"What the hell is this," El muttered to me, "Haight-Ashbury on the Mekong?"

I shook my head and grimaced as the resident artiste brushed the word "Enlightenment" across the top of his masterpiece. I didn't know about anyone else, but I doubted I was going to attain any higher knowledge by staring at some hypothermic chick flashing her tits at Ganesh.

With nowhere else to go, we reluctantly sat down at the end of the table where the hirsute German woman held court. Nude pottery had given way to a lecture on auras, and as I glowered into my beer, I prayed fervently that she couldn't see mine. Sure, crystals were pretty, dreamcatchers looked cool hanging off car mirrors and yoga was a good excuse for not doing real exercise, but I'd never really gotten into the whole New Age thing. Rebirthing seminars, affirmations and $100-per-hour gurus irritated more than they irradiated. And Goddess help me if I ever heard the word "empowerment" again. If I wanted to get in touch with my inner child, I'd just play in the aisles at Toys R Us until someone called security.

While I, with my Old Age sentiments, may have been in the minority, I was not alone. El took a hearty swig from her beer and leaned close towards me. "If I hear anyone even mention The Celestine Prophecy, I'm going to lose it," she said.

In a startling concurrence that would have thrilled any good New Ager, a loud American woman at a nearby table suddenly grabbed her boyfriend's hands and cried, "My God, that's so Seventh Insight!"

El looked like she wanted to cry. "Seventh Insight my arse," she spluttered, suddenly forgetting our company. "Which one was that? The one where they all realise that, like wow, we're all connected? No shit! Did millions of people need a bloody book to figure that out?"

Evidently they did. While the American woman, oblivious to El's verbal rampage, kept on blathering about Macchu Picchu and hidden manuscripts, a stony silence descended on our table.

After a moment of pointed glaring at us blasphemers, the German woman rose from her chair and swanned, turban held high, to the next table. Her cronies followed and we were joyously alone. For about point three of a second anyway.

"Hi there, Aussies," came the voice. "Mind if I take a seat?"

We looked up at our guest and choked. It was the Karate Kid, in all of his earnest, unshaven splendour. Judging by the amicable glint of his teeth behind all those whiskers, we guessed he hadn't twigged that he was addressing the saboteurs of his earlier attempts at calm and grace. "Uh, sure," I said, mentally exhorting myself not to let slip with an identifying laugh. "Sit down if you want."

"Thanks, sis." He pulled out a chair and curled into it, arranging himself in what must have been a rather uncomfortable lotus position before giving us the once-over. "I noticed that you two are newbies here at Mut Mee and I just wanted to have a little chat to you both."

I swallowed hard and tried not to look at El. It was going to be hard enough not to break out into raucous guffaws if this guy kept using words like "newbies," but if I even glanced at El's face, I knew I would lose it. Luckily, she grunted at him before I could open my mouth. "Uh-huh," she said.

"Cool," he said. "Well, my name's Pancho and I'm from California." What a surprise. "I've been living here for, like, three months, sorta recharging my chakras, but I'm getting going again tomorrow. How about you two? What's your story?"

Grunts and non-committal shakes of the head wouldn't carry us through a question like that, so I told him our names. "We're just hooning around," I said.

He looked absurdly delighted. "Hooning! That's really cool man. Just hooning. Love it, real *On the Road* like. Anyway, what I really wanted to tell you about was some of the awesome things we've got going here, if you're planning on sticking around that is."

Sensing that a response of "I'd rather electrocute myself" would not go down a treat, I just shrugged. Not that he noticed.

With the obtuseness particular to people with their heads shoved up their own arses, Pancho raved on about life-drawing classes, guitar workshops and poetry readings, unaware that his audience's eyes were glazing over. "Yeah," he continued, "I've also been running classes in meditation and martial arts. Just today I was doing a session on Silat, an ancient Indonesian fighting art. Of course, I don't use it to fight, but I find its physical discipline really cleansing."

I bit my lip and stared at the "Enlightenment" mural like it was the most fascinating thing I'd ever clapped eyes on. El, however, had had enough. "So that's what you call it, hey?"

Pancho stared at her. "Whaddya mean?" he asked, finally beginning to cotton on.

She opened her mouth, but I got in first. "She means, uh, that we've been trying to remember the name of Silat for days now. Just slipped our minds, y'know?" I smiled weakly and hoped that his brain really was just a big lentil squash. Getting in trouble with normal aggro people was one thing, but the beration of a Sensitive New Age Guy would be just too much to handle. We'd probably have to beat bongos in repentance.

"Oh," he said, unfolding himself from the chair. "That's cool." But it obviously wasn't. Pancho quite clearly wanted to get away from us but didn't know how to leave in a politically correct manner. Telling us to "Get fucked and lay off my trip, man" wouldn't do. So we made it easier for him.

"Cigarette?" I asked.

"Shit no," he said, clearly alarmed. "That stuff is . . ."

Ignoring him, I passed one to El. We drew deeply, belched out a factory's worth of smoke and ash and smiled at each other. By the time the air cleared, he was gone.

Blissfully shunned again.

✳

The organic crowd nurtured its grapevine well, and it wasn't long before everyone at the Mut Mee was informed that El and I were not to be approached. We were dangerous, we weren't "into it," and we certainly wouldn't be joining them for a nightcap of wheatgrass and celery juice. All of which suited us to the ground. Hanging out with a bunch of woolly Europeans or West Coast undergrads bumming it on daddy's credit card was hovering somewhere near "Eat dog" on my list of Things to Do in Southeast Asia. So it was with little consternation that we passed out in our cabin at 3 a.m., having talked to nobody since Pancho except for two dorky Japanese guys just back from Laos and wanting to practice their English.

Morning arrived in silence. With no guitar strumming or heartfelt renditions of "Morning Has Broken" clogging the air, we decided the coast was clear to beat our hasty retreat, and quickly gathered our things.

"I'd love to have this as a beach wrap," I said, eyeing off the sarong-cum-curtain hanging off the window frame.

"Don't," El said. "I hate to Pancho out on you here, but can you imagine the karma?"

I guessed she was right. I didn't want to be dragging a piece of the Mut Mee around with me wherever I went. Besides, that sarong might once have been draped around the arse of some Pancho-type person of questionable hygiene. I'd stick to nicking hotel towels.

Packed and ready, we traipsed down to the office and handed a very hungover-looking Bruce our cabin keys. I hadn't seen him since he served us our first beers, and figured he must have spent the night holed up in his cabin with a carton or two. Bruce had all the good ideas.

"Would youse ladies like some breakfast before ya go?"

We looked at the menu board, still advertising last night's speciality, and our stomachs churned. "Um," El said, clutching her guts. "Maybe just some coffee." If this rat prik trend kept up, it would be a long time before we touched solid food again.

Over sugary coffees and cigarettes, we chatted excitedly about the day ahead of us. Laos was, according to the Japanese boys, an easy trip across the Thai–Lao "Friendship Bridge" and we could pick up our visas for a pittance. Everything, they assured us, was dead cheap in Laos. I couldn't wait. It would be like starting all over again, this time in a place almost completely uncorrupted by Western influence.

"This book reckons that Laos is 'the place to listen to the rice grow,'" El said, thumbing through my copy of Let's Go. "They say there's 'a dramatic change in the pace of life' from Thailand."

"Thank God," I said. "I like Thailand, but I'm not sure it likes us very much. I can't wait to get to Laos—I can almost hear the rice growing now."

El made a pretence of straining her ears then sadly shook her head. "If that's rice growing, then I'm refusing to step foot in Laos. Check it out."

I put down my coffee and turned on my eardrums. Like so many people, I find it difficult to engage two sensory receptors at the same time. If that sounds like the hallmark of a purebred idiot, think about the last time you turned down the car stereo while trying to find a house number. "What is it?" I listened harder then choked. Pancho.

Loaded down by a patched rucksack, embroidered duffel bag and a guitar, Pancho was obviously clearing out. While the relief shone clearly out of Bruce's eyes, ours twinkled with fear. Whatever bad things El and I had done in this or any previous life, they surely weren't so horrendous as to warrant sharing the same travelling trail as Pancho.

"Well," coughed Bruce. "Enjoy the north." El and I looked at each other with frank relief. "The north" meant Chiang Mai and hill tribes and jungle, surely enough to keep Pancho and his misplaced idealism busy for a while.

"Thanks, man." He took Bruce's meaty paw between his two delicate hands and, instead of shaking it, merely held it and looked into the big Aussie's eyes. "Brother," he said in galling earnestness. "We'll meet again in this world, I can feel it."

Bruce released his hands with a scowl. "Bloody oath we will," he rasped, pointing at Pancho's cargo. "You've got my guitar."

※

For the second time in as many days, Pancho's cool was well and truly shattered by our raucous guffaws. "So much for soothsaying," I choked, watching him slink through the gates of Mut Mee. "Meet again indeed. C'mon El, let's get out of this country before we wind up reincarnated as Pancho's jocks."

"Yeah," El said, distractedly flicking the pages of the guidebook. "There's just one thing we should really check out here first. It's called Buddhist Park and they say it's one of the most bizarre temples in the country."

"Bizarre, hey? That would make a change."

"Want to?"

"Sure, as long as it's nowhere near Chiang Mai," I said. "Maybe we'll pick up a bit of religion along the way."

We didn't, but the mystic who built Buddhist Park back in the late 1970s certainly had, along with a good dose of acid to boot. Guarded by a skyscraper figure that appeared to be a four-storey gas chamber with a constipated-looking Buddha's head perched on top, the complex was less of a temple than a science experiment gone hideously wrong. Accessible only by crawling through a yawning dragon's head, the park was littered with weird cement statues of hybrid Buddhist and Hindu characters, dogs playing poker and seven-headed serpents, all of whom supposedly represented the cycles of life. How on earth the likenesses of a moustachioed clown, Hanuman in drag or a smarmy-faced mermaid doing a Bangles "Walk Like an Egyptian" impression symbolised birth, death and taxes, I'll never know. But to someone out there it did, and whatever he was on, I think I'd like some too.

We were raring to go by the time we were regurgitated out of the dragon's mouth. Having dutifully recorded the perplexities of Buddhist Park on our cameras and even buying a couple of postcards from a bamboo stall in the shadow of the looming Buddha edifice, we felt we'd finally done our bit for tourism in Thailand. Besides, if we didn't leave quickly, we'd probably wind up deported. We were Laos-bound.

From all indications, Laos was going to be the most easy-going place on the planet. The bucolic country had only just opened its doors to the first trickle of foreign visitors after twenty years of insularity, and what they found was a nation on the nod. It's not that the Laotians were lazy good-for-nothings. They had crafts to make, rice to listen to and, when the mood took them, the occasional minority hill tribe would fire off a mortar or two just to keep things interesting. For the most part, the locals lived by sanuk-sanuk, a concept which roughly translates as "having a good time" and, apparently, nearly all of them wore big smiles more often than they wore shoes.

They simply weren't interested in following the lead of Thailand or the emerging Vietnam in their quests to be the new "tigers" of the Asian economy. And with the bleak claim of having been the most heavily bombed stretch of dirt in history, all the Laotians really wanted was a good snooze. Pyjamas were their national costume. Even the money was called kip.

But actually getting into this mellow haven was another story. While the Friendship Bridge separating Laos from Thailand spanned less than a kilometre, we were forbidden to walk across it. Instead, border hoppers were forced to sample an array of overpriced transportation: tuk tuk from Nong Khai to the bridge's Thai edge, absurdly plush coach for the dozen or so metres to the visa-issuing office and finally, songthaew—a ute adapted to carry passengers—to the other side. These people were clearly stoked with the invention of the wheel.

Despite the fatuity of having to shell out every time we moved more than an inch, El and I went along with it. We were the only farang on the way to Laos and we didn't want immigration to give us any hassle–if they didn't like the look of us, they could easily send us packing back to the Mut Mee. With the thought of death by pottery quite vivid in our minds, we quickly cultivated an innocuous air and widened our eyes in the classic manner of Dumb Tourist. Just like the Mounties always got their man, harmless dweebs always got their visas.

In keeping with our new look, we took our time stepping down from the bus and bumbled, elderly American tourist-style, over to the immigration box. A burly Thai security guard was busily chatting up the visa girls inside and we meekly hung back to wait for a break in the courting. We waited. And waited. And. Waited.

"I don't know if I'm going to be able to retain this composure," El said after about twenty minutes of being ignored.

I nodded, worried. Our cheery countenances were beginning to droop into impatient scowls in the late afternoon heat and I felt a vague foreboding welling in my chest. It was approaching five o'clock, and what if they decided to shut up shop for the day? There was no way, I thought, panic rising, that I was going back to the Mut Mee. I imagined I could hear the strains of "Kumbaya" carrying over the river, and I broke.

"Excuse me," I said, rapping on the office window. "Hello?"

The guard started at the knocks and hastily stood to attention, while the girls picked up pens and began scribbling nonsensicals in a too-late attempt to appear busy. But when they saw our two sunburnt faces mooning hopefully at the window, rather than the castigating glare of an irate boss, they all relaxed and resumed their conversation.

"What the hell?" El said. "Hey! Hey! Excuse me!" She pounded on the window, agitation usurping any remnants of moronic tolerance on her reddening face. "HelLO!"

The girl closest to the window sighed visibly and rolled her eyes and, with what looked like the most supreme of efforts, slid the glass open. "Yah," she said, bored out of her tree.

With what must have been images of the Udon Thani Pizza Hut roaring through her mind, El struggled to get herself under control. Forever after, the bleating of that simple word "yah" would be like a red flag to Elissa. She inhaled deeply. "Right. We'd like our passports stamped." She looked at the woman. "Please," she added.

The woman stared at El as if she'd asked for the first twenty-eight digits of pi. "Visa?" El persisted. "For Laos? God," she sighed, turning to me. "How much clearer can I be?"

But there was no response—the woman wasn't even looking at us. The uniformed Valentino was bidding them farewell and she was flirting her goodbyes. El and I tapped on the window again. "Please?" I begged.

With lover boy out of the office, both the women turned their world-weary eyes on us and sighed in unison. "You have kip?" the one farthest from the window asked.

El and I looked at each other. The two Japanese boys had given us the remainder of their kip the night before, but had told us it was illegal for them to do so. Transporting the currency over the border was a crime, perhaps because the Lao People's Democratic Republic didn't want outsiders having a good chortle over the worthlessness of the bills. We had nearly two thousand kip secreted away in our money pouches, which would have gone a long way if we ever ran out of toilet paper.

"Um, no, no kip," I said.

"You cannot enter Laos without kip," the first woman said.

"But you can't get kip anywhere in the world but Laos," I cried. "It's illegal! It's impossible!"

"Kip, there." She nodded towards another small box about four metres from the office. "Change money, get kip." With that, she slid the window shut.

We waited for a second, sure that a unicycle or some other amazing form of wheeled transport would be required to shunt us over to the Bureau de Change, but it seemed that footslogging was acceptable in this case. Aussie dollars, however, were not. The woman behind the desk, a bored doppelgänger of the visa chicks, took one look at our fluoro-coloured notes and cracked up, shaking her head. I'd always thought that Australian cash looked like Monopoly money, and now it seemed the world, even backwaters like Laos, agreed with me. Nobody trusts money that glows in the dark, so we mournfully peeled off some of our emergency greenbacks and were handed a wad of bills the Mafia would have been proud of.

"Hey, nearly eighty grand here," I said, counting the kip as we walked back to immigration. "I feel loaded."

"I'll feel loaded when we're actually inside Laos," El said. "Till then, this is just a load of fish and chip wrappings."

The window was still jammed shut when we got back to the office, and we tapped lightly on the glass. It slid open and the woman who'd asked us about the kip stood there gawking at us. "Yes?" she said, her voice giving no clue that she'd ever laid eyes on us before.

"Visas?" El said. "We have the kip now."

"I cannot help you. I no do visas," she said, sucking the end of a pen.

"Where's the other lady?" I asked, trying to keep the agitation from creeping into my voice.

The woman made a tsk noise and called over her shoulder. Half a minute later, the original woman appeared from a back room and moved languidly to her desk. "Yes?"

I squeezed El's hand in an effort to calm both her and myself. These easygoing Laotians were beginning to make me agitated. "Visas," I said. "Please."

"You have kip?", she asked.

"Yes!" we chimed.

"I see please?" We pulled out the bundle of kip and flashed it at her. "Okay," she said. "Visa for two weeks is thirty-two dollars."

We looked at our kip, which, for all its volume, was only worth twenty US dollars. "We have to change more into kip then," El said. "We only have twenty's worth."

"No, no. Is thirty-two dollars. Dollars, no kip."

"Why did we have to get kip then?" I asked, totally at sea.

"At shocking rates," El added.

"Kip to enter Laos, dollars for visas. Is policy."

Shaking our heads, we dug back into our pouches for more money. "Wait a minute," El said, looking at the window. "Your sign says visas are thirty bucks. What's the extra two for?"

"Is past five o'clock. Overtime pay." She smiled triumphantly and turned her attention towards opening a waxy paper bag.

"What a scam!" El exclaimed. "There's no sign saying anything about that!" She looked to me for support but I couldn't do much more than retch. Instead of searching for a list of night-time visa rates, the woman was sucking hungrily on what appeared to be the inside-out, ironed-flat carcass of a long-dead chicken. On a stick.

"Not again," I said woozily.

El looked at me beginning to turn green then back at the woman, who was gnawing happily on a giblet. "What's the fascination with impaling farm animals around here?"

70

The woman grinned through a mouthful of chook innards. "Firty-two," she muffled.

"This is such a rort," El moaned to me. "That extra money is probably going towards the funding of her next serving of tripe on a spike. It's only two bucks, but it gives me the shits."

"We have no choice," I said, hanging back from the window to avoid becoming violently ill. "I don't think there's a consumer affairs board anywhere in the vicinity that we can complain to either. Let's just shell out and get off this bloody bridge."

So we did. We swallowed our pride the same way the visa woman swallowed a particularly chewy piece of offal, and we gave her the extra two dollars. She stamped our passports and we found a songthaew to take us off Animosity Bridge.

＊

Wedged between eight nattering Laotian women, we careened through the twilight on our way to the capital city of Vientiane. Judging by the dozens of clothes-filled plastic bags they had wedged under the benches of the songthaew, the women, unlike me, had found Northeast Thailand to be a shopper's paradise. And judging by their faces when a cop pulled us up for a random search, such smuggling wasn't looked upon too kindly in this neck of the woods. Then again, if they'd looked at our faces during the raid, they probably would have got the impression that we were bringing smack, guns and hardcore porn into the country. El and I were among the multitudes who suffered severe attacks of angst at the very sight of a policeman, even when we were on our most angelic behaviour.

But the cop was a Laotian first and an officer of the law second. With the laid-back attitude that characterised his countryfolk, he lethargically waved us all out of the back and took a quick look inside, studiously ignoring the badly-hidden bags bulging from beneath the bench seats. His duty complete, he reeled off something in rapid Laotian then lit up a handful of smokes and shared them with the relieved women on the side of the road. He even managed to flash an unthreatening smile at us. People who say Australia is the Land of No Worries have obviously never been to Laos. Last time I tried to bum a fag off a Queensland copper I was nearly done for soliciting.

The rest of the journey was made in silence. We couldn't see much in the darkness, and the dilapidated villages on the outskirts of Vientiane were either without electricity or had been abandoned. All we could make out were the dim silhouettes of thatched huts and the cadavers of junked-out cars. Nobody passed us on the road. So far, Laos was chicken guts, cops and moonlight.

Vientiane arrived like a hungover morning. Without warning, we were ripped from the sleepy, contemplative shadows and plunged into a dizzy headache of honking buses, short-circuiting neon signs and a million spluttering mopeds. Old men pushing trolleys heavy with snacks, soft drink and plastic toys waited on craterous pavements for a break in the relentless traffic while women swept out their shops and waved at passersby. Despite the bustle, the city felt like a dream where everyone moved underwater. Where Bangkok jerked in an amphetamine spasm, Vientiane was a Wall Street trader on Quaaludes. It looked busy and made a lot of noise, but it beeped and blurted through a thick fog of stoned torpor.

But just as quickly as they had appeared, the lights and the buzz of downtown suddenly gave way to darkness once again and we found ourselves bumping down a dirt track that skirted the Mekong. Was that all Vientiane was? A strip mall surrounded by mud? "Where the hell are we?" I asked El. "Where's the city gone?"

She squinted myopically into the night and shook her head. "No idea," she said nervously. "Driver?" she called. "Where are we going?"

"You want Mixai Guesthouse?" he asked.

I shrugged and looked at El. She rifled through the *Lonely Planet* to see where she had marked. "Yeah," she called, finding it.

"Is here now," he said, pulling up into a mammoth dirt ditch. "You like okay?"

We poked our heads out of the songthaew and looked around. The Mixai slumped on a dusty street corner, a bland concrete block reminiscent of the communist style of architecture that had so enthralled the hoteliers of Udon Thani. In the throes of a flashback, I anxiously blinked at what passed as a pavement, certain a grotesque contingent of deadbeats and rabid mongrels would be waiting to greet us, as they had in the city we now called Hell. But there was nobody there. All we could see was a sign: "Farang welcome."

We liked it very okay.

Chapter Seven

Begging to Differ

After checking into our fluorescent green room, we still liked the Mixai, but not enough to want to starve to death in it. According to our guidebooks, the guesthouse had once boasted a restaurant, but now all we could get were bottles of Cherry 7-Up and packs of Marlboros. Unless we wanted to beg for scraps at the next-door monastery or see what we could drag out of the Mekong, there was nothing in the neighbourhood to chew on.

"Go into town," the girl behind the counter suggested. "All near the Nam Phou Fountain is many restaurants."

"Town?" I cried, waving my arms out into the dark, silent night for effect. "Town must be miles away!"

The girl studied me like I was some new breed of idiot. "Town is around the corner," she said. "Two minutes walking is Nam Phou, the very centre."

She, of course, was right. After less than five minutes of stumbling past boarded-up buildings and into potholes invisible beneath broken streetlights, we found ourselves blinking in the glare of busy Nam Phou Square. By the looks of things, Vientiane had to be the only capital city in the world that had never heard of urban sprawl.

"This is unreal," I said, goggling at the many eateries that cluttered the square. "Restaurants galore and not a Pizza Hut in sight."

"And I don't see anyone eating anything on a stick, either," El said. "Look at all this. Laotian food, Indian, Vietnamese, veggie. Jesus, we're spoiled for choice."

We strolled past a few restaurants, savouring our hunger in the face of so much food. After not putting anything but booze, coffee and our feet into our mouths for aeons, there was no way we were going to settle for just any cheap tripe. We were going to schnarf up big. If our teeth could remember how to chew, that was.

"Look at that place," I said, pointing at an outdoor brasserie lit up like a birthday cake. "Now that is flash. I'd love to eat there."

"Maybe it's cheap," El said, squeezing her stomach wistfully. "Laos is supposed to be even more of a bargain than Thailand."

I doubted it. Encircling the fountain that gave it its name, the Nam Phou Garden Restaurant was the epitome of class. A diner's Camelot, its elegant table settings shone under golden lights while discreet waiters fussed over flower arrangements in crystal vases. Background music piped gently through concealed speakers, complementing the low murmur of privileged guests clinking their silverware.

But this was Laos, not the Upper East Side, and anyone who could pronounce "chablis" and knew how to use cutlery could live like a king. For the price of a Happy Meal back home, a patron of Nam Phou could order a jug of beer and a feast to satisfy the most ravenous sybarite. The only thing missing was a cheap toy.

"Whaddya reckon?" I asked El, trying desperately not to drool on myself. The chance to shove copious amounts of unsuspect food into my face for less than the cost of a VB stubbie was too good to pass up. There was just one problem: guilt. To us, blowing three bucks on a whopping feed was laughable. Score one to the bargain hunters. But to the kids and cripples lurking in the shadows of Nam Phou, three bucks could mean the difference between life and death or even a blackmarket prosthetic limb. I wasn't sure whether I could cope with devouring the economic equivalent of someone's leg. So I did what any normal person would do when their conscience plays tug-of-war with their roaring belly. I passed the buck.

"So, El? It's up to you."

"No," she snorted. "I want to see if I can find some offal impaled on a splintery old stick. Are you kidding? Let's get in there!"

I secretly sighed with relief and allowed myself to be led to a table by the fountain. The decision had been made, the pressure was off. I decided I would just enjoy my meal and forget about guilt and plastic body parts. Besides, I thought, looking around, nobody else looked guilty about being there.

That's because they were bastards.

We'd just finished chowing our way through an absurdly heavy meal of cheese ravioli and lager when we spied her. Surrounded by the glitz of the restaurant, the little girl, with her ragged dress, dirt-streaked face and clumped hair stood out like a boil on a high-class hooker's arse. Her wispy legs looked as if they were ready to collapse as she hovered around the tables, saying nothing aloud but telling a pathetic tale with her vacant eyes. A tidal wave of guilt crashed over my head and I suddenly felt like I was going to vomit up my enormous meal. Not that puking on the pavement would do her much good. This chick wanted kip, not secondhand pasta.

She wobbled up to a table of Americans, bowed her scruffy head and extended her hands, palms up, like a hungry Oliver Twist. But the Yanks were obviously unschooled in Dickens. It took them nearly a full minute to even realise the girl was standing there.

"What's this, our new waiter?" one of them exclaimed, giving her the once-over.

"Honey, if ya wanna tip, ya gotta freshen up. Bitta makeup, somethin'," laughed another.

"Hey!" cried the first guy, enlightened by a sip of whiskey. "I think she's one a them beggars. You want some money, hon?" He reached into his pocket and pulled out a wad of kip and waved it in her face. "Want some a this?"

The girl just stood there, totally stiff, her eyes glued to the floor.

"C'mon, say somethin'," he said, clearly enjoying himself. "Say please!" When it became obvious that the girl wasn't going to utter a peep, the guy grew bored of his game. "Ah, take it," he spat in disgust, throwing a 500 kip note to the ground. She scrambled for it then straightened herself up, bowing solemnly to the man.

"No problem," he bellowed. "Hey," he said, nudging one of his mates. "Next time, bring your older sister!"

As they guffawed and clapped each other on the back, I felt my gorge rise. "Those rock apes!" I yelped. "I wish I could go over there and shove that kip down his throat."

"Well, it's either down his gob or in her pocket," she said, motioning towards the beggar. "Here she comes now."

I watched as the girl shuffled towards us. "I'm giving her some," I said, reaching for my bag. "Aren't you?"

"Oh God, yes. Looking at her with my distended gut full of lard makes me feel so evil and wrong. Here you go," El said, handing her a couple of thousand kip. The girl took it and made a soft mewling sound before turning to me.

I folded up some notes and passed them to her. "Be well," I said, feeling like a supercilious moron. Be well? What the hell was that? Was I suddenly the great white saviour because I shelled out a few measly kip? "How humiliating," I grumbled as the girl bowed and ducked out of the restaurant.

"What?" El asked, lighting up a smoke.

"Me. 'Be well,'" I said, putting on a gravely important voice. "What am I, bestowing my almighty blessings with some spare change now? As if it's going to do anything anyway."

El puffed away. "I thought it was nice," she said. "At least you've helped one person's life get maybe a little easier."

But when it comes to beggars, there's no such thing as one person. The paupers' fraternity has a grapevine to rival any knitting circle, and when word gets out that you're handy with the dosh, it's big news. In a feat almost inconceivable without the aid of mobile phones or networking cocktail parties, the panhandlers of Vientiane had rallied en masse outside the restaurant within moments of the girl's forlorn departure. And they were heading our way.

The painfully thin guy toting a limp infant came first, and with our bellies busting out of our shorts, we felt obliged to slip him some kip. A blind granny led by a child of indiscriminate gender arrived less than thirty seconds later, followed in perfect synchronicity by a granny leading a sightless child. The boss-eyed old man whose shorts kept falling down tugged at our heartstrings, and how could we say no to the midget wearing nothing but faded underpants?

As he toddled away on his misshapen legs, El and I looked at each other, exhausted. While the other diners were left to chat unhampered over their meals, we'd been shaken down by every ragtag scrounger in town. Some of them, like the girl, just stood in front of our table not saying a word, while others groaned and wheezed. A few of them lurched, some wobbled and one tripped over his own cane. It was a carousel of tragedy, an endless parade of misfortune and woe. But there was nothing else we could do about it. We were nearly totally skint.

"I can't stand to do this, but I'm going to have to say no to the next one," I told El.

"Me too," she said, counting her money. "After all, we can't be expected to shell out to every beggar in town."

"Yeah, really," I said, becoming indignant. "Why doesn't the bloody Laotian government do something to help them? What are we, UNICEF?"

"And anyway," El continued. "Why only us? Do we have big dollar signs on our heads? We're probably the least well-off in this whole restaurant but they only come slithering up to us."

In hindsight, it was a poor, yet grossly apt, choice of words. No sooner had El shut her mouth than it was wide open again, this time in a silent scream. I looked down and nearly fainted. There he was. No arms, no legs, just a head, a few stumps and a torso moving along the ground on his stomach. He was grinning up at us. He was slithering.

Our emotions went into frenzied overdrive. Battered by shame, profound sorrow and intense fear, we somehow managed to shove our remaining kip into his gravel-worn shirt pocket without wailing or passing out. With our jaws agape, we watched as the man wriggled out into the square. I turned to El slowly, in total disbelief.

"Man," she sighed. "Twin Peaks has nothing on this place."

*

From the little-girl-lost to the limbless man, the procession of Vientiane's unfortunates grew progressively more wretched, and we weren't planning on sticking around for the finale. We bolted into the balmy night, keen to restock on kip and surround ourselves with upright people who didn't make us ashamed of having all our limbs intact.

But it wasn't that easy. Whereas in most cities the setting of the sun wheedles prostitutes, wannabe vampires, palefaced clubbers and insomniacs out of their holes, the dimming of the lights in this backwater served only to draw every dispossessed have-not on to the streets. The disabled, disease-ridden, insane and deformed lingered on every corner, making the nighttime streets of Vientiane read like a casebook of human misery. Even the few bars there had an air of tragedy about them. But at least the Laotian government had banned karaoke, which must have eased the suffering of the populace somewhat. Being a beggar must have sucked enough without the added insult of being forced to endure some drunken yodeller mauling "Copacabana."

Despite the proliferation of indigent misfits lining the pavements, Vientiane wasn't completely given over to the totally kipless. Men in suits buzzed by on motorcycles, some with a local beauty clinging on behind, while kids in Chicago Bulls caps raced in and out of dodgy fast-food joints, blathering excitedly over bags of hot chips. The more prosperous businesses proclaimed themselves in illuminated Laotian characters, the extremely well-to-do going so far as to translate their names into English. Although with epithets ranging from "Dorking" to "The Ho," I guessed it would be a long time before any of them made their mark on the international business community.

El had just finished taking my picture beneath the "Dorking" sign when we spotted the most obscure placard yet: "Fred's Down Home Fried Chicken." I've seen a restaurant called Hicks in a fashionable English suburb, a fish and chips shop in the Simpson Desert and a non-smoking café in Amsterdam, but for some reason, Fred's Down Home Fried Chicken in the middle of Vientiane struck me as outstandingly peculiar. It wasn't as if the Laotians didn't eat chicken. It was obvious they loved a good chook as much as anyone else, even going to the bother of putting sticks through them for the sake of portability. But there was something so dixie, so collard greens and grits about Fred's Down Home Fried Chicken that it baffled me. Somehow, I found it almost impossible to picture some dyed-in-the-wool confederate singing rebel songs over cornbread and gravy in Laos's "City of Sandalwood."

"El, we've got to check that out," I said. "Doesn't it strike you as weird?"

"Yeah," she replied, staring across the road at Fred's. "What Laotian worth his pyjamas would eat fried chook when they can have its innards raw?"

"Let's have a look. Fred's bound to be a farang, and we can ask if he knows where we can change some money while we're at it."

Fred's Down Home Fried Chicken was about as down-home as a cardboard box on the interstate. Sickly lit by a dying yellow bulb and the blinking neon likeness of a crowing cock, the shop was empty bar a card table, stool and cashier's desk. It smelled more like stale cigarettes than grease and burnt skillets, and even Fred looked less like a good ole boy than he did a pale, British accountant. He looked like a Trevor.

But despite his Trev-ness, Fred spoke like a true southerner. "Hey y'all," he drawled, looking up from a mound of kip on the counter. "Kin I help ya?"

"Um," I said, looking around the empty room.

"If y'want some chicken, I'm sorry but I'm all through for tonight," Fred/Trev said.

"We're actually wondering if you know anywhere in town we could change money at this time of night," El said, staring at Trev's bundle of cash.

"Weeeell, lookie here," he said, snapping a rubber band around a pile of thousand-kip notes. "Y'all're in luck. See," he said, leaning towards us, "I happen to offer very good rates m'self."

"You?" I blurted. "You do chicken and kip?"

He laughed. "My rates on kip are really what I'm best at. Let's just say the chicken is more of a hobby."

More like a front, I thought, looking to see if Trev had anything on the wall certifying him as a registered bureau de change. All I could see were faded pictures of chicken.

"Just a sec there ladies," he said, crossing the counter and locking the shop door. "Now," he said, returning to the desk. "I can give you 3500 kip per greenback, which is the best rate y'all will find in this town."

El and I looked at each other, astounded. When we'd changed money on the Animosity Bridge, we'd gotten under 2000 per dollar. Either we'd been seriously grifted or Trev was dodgy as fuck. Given that the bridge straddled a recognised international border and Trev was dealing in threadbare kip beneath a flashing rooster, I decided the latter was more likely. I'd always wondered what the black market looked like, but had never thought it would resemble a KFC for anorexics.

"Done," El said to Trev, gouging some American dollars out of her bag.

"Me too," I said, whipping out my wallet. "Give us thirty bucks worth."

He attacked his calculator and counted out the notes with the precision of a merchant banker or perhaps a sleazy Vegas croupier. Clandestine financial transactions were so much more fun than doing it by the book.

"All done, ladies," he said, tucking our dollars into his shirt pocket. I couldn't believe it. We had our kip, he had our dollars and we were on our way. No CIA busting in the door, no gypping, no hired thugs slipping into the shop to bash us and give Trev back his kip. The black market was not quite the cliché I'd imagined it to be.

But Trev/Fred was. "Y'all come back now," he called as we pushed into the street. "I got some chicken cookin' real good!"

We never did get to try his chicken, but we did return over the next couple of days to shake down Trev for some more kip. For some reason, he never ripped us off and we wondered how he made any sort of profit. Vientiane was hardly a tourist hotspot and the few farang we did see could hardly have known that Fred's Down Home Fried Chicken was the place to come for that extra value meal deal. Minus the meal, of course.

Chapter Eight

Pills, Thrills and Green Around the Gills

As the pleasure-pain maxim would have it, things went rapidly downhill on our way back to the Mixai, when we were nearly run over by a samlor, pinched on the bum by a familiar-looking midget and driven to fits of apoplexy by a shady monk who sprang out at us from a gloomy alleyway. Back in our room, the lightbulb burnt out and I wound up stubbing out a cigarette in El's pot of expensive moisturiser. And after a restless sleep plagued by ravioli-induced nightmares and mosquitoes, I could only hope Lady Kismet would be a bit kinder in the morning.

But Fate's a bitch. We spent the entire morning battling it out with everyone we came across. Our waitress at breakfast threw a spoon at me after I asked six times for milk. The cleaner at the Mixai yelled at us for smoking in our room. And on our way to register our presences with the Australian Consulate, two kilometres away, our songthaew driver took us on a 45-minute junket before charging us ten bucks for the pleasure.

"I think I've had it with city life," I grouched as we pushed open the doors to the consulate. "Even a little pit like Vientiane is getting too stressful for me."

"We should go up-country," El said. "A city is a city anywhere, but we'd get a real feel for Laos if we headed north."

The doors of the consulate slammed shut behind us and we leaned on the unattended front counter. "I reckon. What about that town we read about, the one with the bouncy-sounding name?" As usual, we had no plans and I had no clue.

"I think it's called Luang Prabang. It sounds utterly brilliant and really gorgeous. Hey, is anyone even in here?"

"On my way!" came an Australian voice from behind a heavy office door. The voice was saddled with a less strident ocker twang than Bruce's had been back in Nong Khai, but I cringed anyway. Back in Australia, where we spend so much of our time poking fun at the flat whines of the Yanks and the bizarre vowels of the Kiwis, it's easy to forget we have an accent at all. But spend some time overseas, preferably somewhere they don't broadcast *Home and Away*, and it hits you like a ton of bricks. We sound like freaks. Even in their rare moments of calm, Australian women sound constantly hysterical, and the men manage to give the impression that their words are suffocating somewhere between the glottis and their last meat pie. All this while hardly moving our lips at all.

The door swung open and a well-dressed woman approached us. Apart from the fact that she wore shoes, she looked like a typical Queenslander: blonde, tanned and hungover. But despite her bloodshot eyes, the woman was polite and efficient, negating my theory about her Queensland origins.

"G'day girls, I'm sorry to have kept you. My name's Louise. How can I help?"

I stared at a framed copy of the words to "Advance Australia Fair" on the wall while El explained that we wanted to register ourselves. "We were told we had to," she finished.

"Well, you don't have to," Louise said. "But it's a good idea. At least then we have an idea of where Australian citizens are when they're in Laos. That way, if anything happens, it makes it easier to identify you."

I winced. "Isn't that a bit dramatic? I mean, what's the worst that could happen?"

"It's just a precaution," Louise soothed. "If you play it safe, you'll be fine. But if you start wandering off into certain areas, you could find yourselves in big trouble. Laos can still be a very dangerous, unstable country."

"Well," El said, "it's not like we're going to wander into the opium fields and start harvesting, if that's what you mean."

Damn, there went all my plans.

"Of course there's that," Louise said. "But that is a bit dramatic. What I mean is that we have posted a traveller's advisory for Australian citizens on a few areas up north where there's been some trouble. If you steer clear of them, you should be just fine."

"Up north?" El asked with a twinge of anxiety. "We were planning on going to Luang Prabang."

"I'd give that a miss if I were you," Louise said. "The highway is too dangerous."

"Why?"

"This actually hasn't come out in the press yet, but in the last week, there's been missile attacks on tourist buses by Hmong bandits."

"What happened?" we gasped.

"Well, these rebels fire at the buses, y'know, blowing them up, and then come and raid what's left for valuables."

Apart from our lives, El and I didn't have anything of value with us. But how were these gun-crazy hill tribers supposed to know that? Strike bus travel. But we were still desperate to get out of Vientiane and into Luang Prabang.

"How about along the river?" El asked. "Can't you take a boat up there?"

"You can," Louise nodded. "But again, we'd advise against it."

"Why now?" I whined.

"For a start, it's the dry season and the river is incredibly shallow. The speedboats that travel up it wind up hitting mudbanks and crashing. There was an accident just a fortnight ago."

"What about a slow boat?"

"I was getting to that. This is very much under wraps still, but there was an Australian citizen shot off the top of one of those slow boats only a few days ago."

Jesus. And there I was thinking the worst thing that could happen in Laos was being forced to drink black coffee.

"That's a disgrace," I said, shaking my head. "But hey, what about a plane?"

El nodded at me and looked at Louise, who in turn was staring at us like we were lunatics. "You guys really want to get up there, eh?" she said.

"Yeah, we really do," I said. Five minutes ago, I hadn't known where I wanted to go. But now, despite, or maybe even because of, the warnings against it, I was chomping at the bit to get to Luang Prabang.

"Well," Louise continued, "let me give you some friendly advice. Don't fly in this country. Don't even go near an airport. Jesus," she shook her head. "It's totally off the record, but listen. Most of the planes in Laos are ancient Russian junkheaps. They're supposedly maintained by the French but I wouldn't go within a bloody mile of them."

We considered our options in silence. We could stay in Vientiane, bored senseless but safe, the able-bodied envy of every cripple in town. Or we could risk life and coveted limb on the airborne equivalent of the Lada for a chance to see the "real" Laos. Ennui versus a fiery death. It was a tough call, but my completely warped sense of logic kicked in and I had my decision. We'd fly to Luang Prabang. At least if we died in a plane crash, we wouldn't be bored.

"I say we do it," I told El, whose smile told me she'd made the same decision. I hoped she'd used a different system of reckoning, though.

"Well, I think you're both nuts," Louise tutted. "But it's your choice. Just fill these in," she handed us our identification papers, "and let's hope we don't need to use them."

✳

"What melodrama," I said to El as we strolled back out into the sunshine. "Old planes fly all the time, no big deal. Look at all those air shows, with planes from like World War Two."

"Yeah," El said, hailing a samlor. (We figured if they had to pedal, they'd be less inclined to rip us off.) "But have you noticed how nobody ever goes to an air show these days without a video camera? People who don't give a shit about old planes go, just to sell their film to the TV stations in case one of the aircraft explodes in mid-air. You see it on the news all the time."

"Oh come on. Is our plane going to loop-dee-loop? Are we going wing-walking? It's totally different. Besides, don't you want to go?"

"Of course I do. I'm just nervous about getting on some crusty old Russian deathtrap."

"I'm not." And I wasn't either. I'd been to a psychic years before who'd told me I'd live till I was ninety-one. I was in the clear. She hadn't mentioned anything about El though. "Anyway," I said, as we climbed into the waiting samlor, "we should remember Helen Keller's famous quote."

"What's that?"

"'Life is a daring adventure or nothing.'"

✳

That's the last time I ever take advice from a deaf, dumb and blind woman—especially one who lived in a time before they invented malfunctioning ex-Soviet bomber planes. It was all well and good for Helen Keller to go around shooting her mouth off about daring adventures, but if she'd seen the rustbucket that we were supposed to spend an hour in at six thousand feet, I daresay she would have taken dibs on that "or nothing" option.

Cracked, lopsided and balancing on what appeared to be a pair of deflated tyres, Lao Aviation Flight 643 looked more like a warning to pilots about the dangers of flying under the influence than any recognisable means of passage. Slouching beside a sparkling Thai Airways jet, our plane looked like the town drunk hitting up a society lady for some spare change, or at least directions to the nearest flophouse. It was not the most comforting imagery to spring to mind before taking to the skies.

Airport security didn't make us feel much better. After ditching our luggage, we ducked through a metal detector, beeping all the way. The guard took one look at us, scratched his head and moved us along. No emptying of the pockets, no once-over with the electric wand. We could have been weighed down with twenty pounds of gelignite for all that guy knew. Maybe encouraging terrorism was their way of phasing out old planes.

Security on the tarmac wasn't exactly watertight either. Smoking was forbidden in the lounge, so we were sent out onto the runway to puff. Made sense to me. Why choke up a bunch of passengers inside when you can explode a few fuel pumps on the airstrip outside? But it wasn't just smokers wandering around out there. Uniformed men, who I guessed were maintenance crews, lazed in the shadows of baggage trucks, while random people in civvies strolled aimlessly around, examining the underbellies of planes and jumping up to smack the wings. A skinny dog trotted by, sniffed one of the flat tyres of Flight 643 and kept going, eventually stopping to relieve itself on a median strip of grass. What a wasted opportunity, I thought. If I'd been allowed to cock my leg in public, I know exactly where I would have been aiming.

"This is just great," I whined, squashing out my butt. "Not only is our plane a total piece of shit, but look at this airport. Anyone could go straight up to our plane, chuck a bomb in the engine and wham! A few thousand feet up and we're screwed. If we can even get off the ground, that is." I lit another fag and exhaled nervously. "Don't they normally have mechanics checking out the plane before boarding? Jesus wept, we would have been better off getting shot off the top of a boat."

El turned to me, her sunburn vanished behind a pall of grey. "Where's that Valium?" she croaked.

The day after we'd registered with Louise, we'd gone into town to shake down Trev and buy our tickets to Luang Prabang. By the time we'd gotten to the Lao Aviation office, we were beaming like kids getting ready for a trip to Disneyland. But when they'd charged us double the local's rate for our return tickets, all hell broke loose. El screamed, I glared, but to no avail. If we wanted to go, we had to pay the farang fares. So we did. Anything to get up-country, I'd told El afterwards. It'd all be worth it once we were there. But my soothing words hadn't been enough to calm her ire, so we'd marched into a pharmacy and demanded a strip of Valium. It was out of date and crumbling inside its bubble pack, but it would have to do. I'd stock up on the real stuff later.

"El, are you sure you want some?" Despite my yearning for the pills, I was holding off until I could get some not marked "expiry August 1997." Besides, if the plane did go down, I wanted to be alert enough to get out my camera. El was right. There was big bucks in this plane crash stuff.

She nodded, growing paler by the minute. Judging by my overwhelming sense of nausea, I'd say I wasn't far behind her, but I had my psychic's prediction to fall back on. Granted, this was the same psychic who'd told me I'd have eleven children by the age of twenty-eight, but maybe she was speaking figuratively. If I was going to cark it in a plane crash, I'd know about it. I hoped.

"Here y'go." I passed El two blue pills and my bottle of tepid water and she gulped them down like a woman possessed.

"Aaaah," she said, as I eyed her cautiously. Well, at least she wasn't dying of chemical poisoning—yet. Things were looking up. If only the plane would stay in that general direction, we'd be fine.

A few moments and a last, rushed cigarette later, our boarding call came through over the scratchy speakers. "Well," I said, giving El a hand up. "This is it. Let's meet our maker."

*

People always carry on about wanting to die with dignity, but to our fellow passengers on Lao Aviation Flight 643, this was obviously not an issue. With only about fourteen people on board, death would indeed be a private affair, until the networks got hold of the footage, but there was no way one could hope to expire in a courtly or ennobled manner. Resplendent in peeling wallpaper and greasy windows, the cabin was suffocatingly small, which I suppose was appropriate as it matched the seats. Only just big enough to squeeze into, they had neither reclining lever nor room to stretch out, leaving us to sit bolt upright with our legs crossed tightly. We somehow managed to look both stricken with diarrhoea and as if we had poles jammed up our arses at the same time. But the Laotians seemed happy enough, relaxing their tiny bodies in the burlap chairs and chatting easily among themselves. If I'd had enough room to comfortably exhale, I would have sighed in relief. Sure, I told myself, these people probably fly all the time. If they're not concerned about the tatty state of the plane, why should I be?

"I'm definitely not scared now, El," I whispered. "The Laotians look cool with this whole plane business, and they should know the score."

El just grunted and I looked over at her. Her eyes were jammed shut and she was biting her lip to a new shade of white. "El, you should open your eyes. It's fine, check out all the happy people." She just shook her head and continued to gnaw her lip. "El, truly, just open your eyes. The first thing you see will be a bunch of chilled-out people, same as on any normal flight. It's a good omen, I swear."

With her eyes still clamped, she stood up to stretch and then carefully lifted her lids, staring towards the front of the plane. "Jesus!" she yelped, slapping her hands over her eyes and collapsing awkwardly back into her seat. "Thanks for the omen," she barked. "Great portent."

"What?"

"Just look up the front then give me another Valium. Omen, my arse."

I unbuckled myself and peered up the front of the plane. Whoops.

Wedged between the cockpit and the front row of seats, an old man lay gasping on a hospital stretcher, with dozens of tubes stuck into every available bit of loose flesh. He looked like a dying fish. He looked like death.

"Oh shit," I said, strapping myself tightly in. "Okay," I muttered, scavenging through my bag for the pills. "I retract every statement about omens. That guy is not an omen."

"Just give me another pill," she said woozily. I handed her one and she swallowed it dry. "Whoa, yeah," she sighed. "Now that really is better."

As El went back to devouring her lip in silence, I busied myself by plaiting my hair into Princess Leia hoops and looking out the window. I hoped I'd see something more auspicious than the dying old man, but all I could see was that same mangy dog pissing on everything.

"Lady and gentleman, please fasten seatbelt. We will take off soon." I tightened my belt until it nearly cracked my pelvis and grabbed my knees, a mix of fear and strange exhilaration coursing through my veins. Unfortunately, exhilaration made a rapid departure with the starting of the engines, the violent trembling of the plane paving the way for total domination by fear.

If you're one of those women who gets their jollies by sitting on an operating washing machine, then Lao Aviation has a treat in store for you. You want vibrate, they got it. Thanks to the roaring shudders of the old engines, we vibrated so wildly that I could feel my nostril hairs curling as my spine went numb. Sadly, so did everything else. I never was one for cheap thrills anyway.

"Hold on, El," I shouted above the din of the engines. "Here we go!"

She looked at me through the narrow slits her eyes had become. I must have looked like a psychopath with my juddering head, bug eyes and braids bouncing all over the place, but I suspected anything would look good to El after her last venture into the realm of the open-eyed. Besides, she was finally, blissfully, stoned. "Princess Leia! You look so cute I could punch you," she said with a dopey smile, and promptly passed out.

Hanging on for dear life as we began convulsing down the tarmac, I felt about as cute as Chewbacca, and nearly as eloquent. Between low moanings, I unconsciously dished up a word salad of curses, blasphemies and vague promises to a long-neglected God that would have thrilled anyone researching the phenomenon of speaking in tongues. At least Chewie always kept a firm grip on his vocab.

Then, somewhere between a particularly vulgar string of obscenities and a since-forgotten vow to lead a more chaste life, the plane took off. It panted and heaved like a huge asthmatic bird, but somehow, we actually became airborne. I peered through the grimy window and watched as Wattay Airport began to shrink below us.

"El! El! Wake up! We're in the sky!" I shoved her arm but it just fell limply on to her lap. If expired pharmaceuticals could knock out a panicking person sitting in the world's most uncomfortable chair, I might have to rethink my policy on superannuated medication. After all, 1997 wasn't that long ago.

But I decided to stay awake. It was a lucky thing I did. Otherwise, I never would have seen the cabin fill up with smoke ten minutes out of Vientiane. Or felt the grating of the plane's wheels as they came down mid-flight. Or watched the dying old man get beaned by falling hand luggage as we banged down in Luang Prabang. No, if I'd taken Valium that day, I wouldn't ever have become the neurotic freak that I am today. And what a shame that would have been.

Chapter Nine

Get Off the Monument

It was Friday, which meant Clean Up Day in Luang Prabang Province, and as our tuk tuk bumped along Phetsarath Road towards town, we were greeted by scores of schoolchildren waving sacks of stinking refuse from the wayside. But they could have been hurling the inevitable contents of chicken sticks and old fag ends at us for all I cared. All that mattered was that we were alive and on the ground. I had a gravel rash on my lip from kissing the tarmac to prove it.

El had snapped out of her pill daze after the plane had skidded to a whiplash halt and, despite feeling a little bit groggy, was back to her old self again. Chainsmoking and bald eagling the driver, who had adjusted his rear-view mirror for a better view up her cargo skirt, she was rattling on at the speed of light, trying to coax the gory details of the flight out of me. I wasn't saying a word. We had to get back to Vientiane somehow, and unless she graduated to pure morphine, there was no way El would get on a plane that malfunctioned and smoked more than we did. Besides, I wanted to forget all about it. Particularly the part where I promised God I'd give up all my vices in exchange for another day on earth.

"Forget it, El," I said, waving at a screaming mob of kids. "There were no worries at all." She stared at my scratched lip accusingly. "I always kiss the ground after a flight," I explained. "It's all part of my Pope complex."

Thankfully, she just shrugged and flicked open her Lonely Planet to the section on Luang Prabang. I sighed gratefully, lit a cigarette and pulled out a copy of The World's Most Dangerous Places, stolen from the Cairns City Library. So much for abandoning vice.

"It says here that Luang Prabang is part of the Kingdom of a Million Elephants and the serene spiritual centre of Laotian culture," she read.

"That's nice," I murmured. "My book's section on Laos is headed 'Bombies and Zombies' and goes on to say that this part of the country is littered with unexploded cluster bombs left over from the Vietnam War."

"Oh, lovely," she huffed. "Just what I wanted to hear. Now does that book of yours list places to stay, or just those not to on pain of death?"

I glanced down at it. "Nup, just vague locations of guerrilla camps. Maybe we could catch up with those trigger-happy Hmongers Louise was telling us about."

El was about to comment, no doubt on my poor choice of travel guide, when the driver nearly veered off the road. "Hmong?" he screeched. "Hmong bandit?"

"Shit," I mumbled. "No, no. No Hmong bandits, it's okay." He glared at me in the mirror and carried on towards town at top tuk tuk speed, shaking his head in disgust.

Next time I'll steal a *Fodor's*.

✳

All was forgiven by the time we pulled up outside the Viengkeo Guesthouse, but I made a resolution never to mention jungle-dwelling insurgents in the presence of a Lao citizen again. Unlike in Australia, where we revered our outlaws, I got the feeling that the Laotians weren't too big on crime-worship. Maybe if they wore metal buckets on their heads or came up with catchy nicknames like Chopper, it'd be a different story.

While Luang Prabangers may not have been too into the rebel thing, they sure dug farang. As we stood on the pavement hitching up our backpacks, children of all ages emerged from nearby buildings to giggle and wave shyly, while motorcyclists bipped at us from the busy street. And the lady of the Viengkeo house was positively rapt. She'd bolted outside the moment our tuk tuk had spluttered to a stop and was making a great show of our custom.

"You come inside Viengkeo? You come now? Is special price for you, only for you. Come, come." Shrugging, we followed her inside and she beamed triumphantly at the crowd that had gathered on the pavement. We were obviously a great catch. If only someone would tell that to the eligible men of this world.

From outside, the Viengkeo looked pretty much like any other building on the street. The colour of bleached sand, it crouched at a modest two storeys beneath a sagging roof and had big open windows that gaped as if in surprise. The only thing that distinguished it from any of the surrounding shops or apartment blocks was an expansive balcony that seemed to be holding on to the structure for grim death. But behind its one-of-the-gang street persona, the Viengkeo was like a faded beauty living her last fragile days in antiquated tropical style. Cooled by slate floors and open passageways leading to a back courtyard, the ground floor was dotted with bright flowers and framed paintings, while a short stumble up an ancient stairwell revealed a breezy sitting room softly scented by the ghosts of old joss sticks. And the balcony, far from being the deathtrap it appeared from the street, was a peaceful outdoor haven of stuffed sofas and Buddha statuettes. Even the traffic noises from below seemed to be filtered in such a way that they sounded calm. I imagined myself slumped on one of the couches, drinking beer and watching the street scene, and the thought appealed to me greatly. It looked like bliss, and El and I smiled our approval.

Our admiration was not lost on the woman, and she hastened to show us our prospective room. "Only if you like, then you stay," she added. One look at it and we dumped our bags. As airy as the rest of the place, the room was furnished simply by two slim timber beds, a heavy ashtray on a three-legged table and a creaking ceiling fan. No art was hung on the walls, but a giant window opening on to the garden provided all the ornamentation we needed. It was lovely, and with a tariff of just seven thousand kip per night, it sent the word "bargain" rocketing into a whole new sphere.

Only in a country really big on karma would we have been told by a guesthouse proprietor to put our money away until the day we checked out, whenever that might be. But this woman had faith in us and, even more importantly, in the power of destiny. Under her belief system, it was incomprehensible that we'd voluntarily be horrible to someone who'd treated us so well. After all, if we grifted her, we'd wind up copping it bigtime. Rip me off, huh? See you in the next life, worm.

Our wallets stuffed back into our pockets, we scribbled our details in a tatty guest registry and went back to our room to claim our beds. Grabbing the one closest to the door, I lay down and lit a couple of cigarettes. I passed one to El, sprawled on her side directly beneath the creaking fan, and puffed happily. "This really is getting better all the time," I said. "Look at this bloody place. Anywhere else, it'd be considered a resort. No pool, no room service or any of that shit, but it's gorgeous!"

"It is lush," she agreed. "I could definitely hang out here for a while, and just chill. I love it."

"Uh-huh," I said, lifting back the thin sheets on my bed. "But I bet you don't love it as much as the last guy who slept in my bed though. Check this sick shit out." Directly at crotch level, someone had bored a hole into the flimsy foam mattress, giving it a suddenly obscene appearance. "Someone's been screwing my bed."

"No way!" El leapt up and examined the mattress. "That is so fucking perverse. Do you think it's what it looks like it is?"

Too revolted to lay back down, I mentally measured the bed and the position of the hole. "Oh yeah," I said. "Forget inflatables. The way of the future is foam. And no stupid-looking blow-up bimbo's face staring accusingly at you the whole time. Bed-fucking is the here and now for the modern desperado."

We cracked up laughing, trying to imagine the love-starved Romeo pursuing his holiday fling with a ratty slab of foam. We wondered if the goodbyes had been tear-jerking. "I need a photo of this," El gasped, racing for her bag. "This is something sick that could really catch on in Japan—right alongside schoolgirls' undies vending machines and pubic wigs. Maybe I could start pimping out mattresses to supplement my income."

I crouched by the bed and pulled a lewd face, ready for the camera. "C'mon," I called to El, frowning at her turned-out daypack. "I can't stick my tongue out forever."

"Fuck," she said, looking up from the pile of bus tickets, sun creams and books. "My camera's gone."

Oh no. The dreaded sentence. Anyone who's ever travelled further than their city limits has blurted out this sentence at least once, and is familiar with the unconditional horror that accompanies every syllable. And everyone who has ever travelled with someone who can't find their treasured camera has come out with the infuriating, "Have you checked?"

"Of course I have," she snapped, still following the script. "I've turned my bag inside out."

I furtively glanced over to my open pack and was relieved to see my Pentax wedged between my journal and a carton of Indonesian cigarettes. Thank God. At least now El and I didn't have to whinge competitively as to who was worse off without their camera.

"I know I didn't put it into my backpack," she said, tipping the sack on to the floor in a frenzy. "I always keep it on me."

"You never know," I said hopefully, scurrying over to help sift through the rumpled clothes and assorted crap. "Maybe in the rush this morning you shoved it in here."

"Nup," she announced, flinging dirty laundry across the room. "It's definitely not here. Some fuckwit has nicked it." Her face grew scarlet and I leant back against my ravished bed, waiting for the explosion. But none came. Instead of unleashing her notorious temper by wrenching another leg off our already incapacitated table or cursing the place down, El simply collapsed on a pile of her clothes and motioned despondently for a cigarette.

I passed her one and shuffled around, not knowing what to say. I can expound at length on just about any topic, no matter how imbecilic or disgusting, but when it comes to comforting people, I'm thoroughly useless. "It'll be okay" is a ridiculous thing to say unless you're peering into a crystal ball, while "I know how you feel" is just a tangent that invariably leads to your own story of woe. And the feeble "There, there" is nothing more than an admission of your conversational worthlessness.

So I decided to be inventive.

"Hey El, figure it this way. The prick that stole your camera is going to get karmatised so badly for this. They'll probably come back as a rock or something and when we're reincarnated, you can smash them with a hammer."

The redness went out of El's face and back into her temper. "I don't want to smash a rock with a hammer! I want my camera, you idiot!"

The word "idiot" echoed around the concrete room, and we stared at each other in stunned amazement. Since we'd become friends in Year 11, we'd never once had an argument, and while we often used "idiot" as a term of endearment, it had never been whipped out as a damning indictment of the other's low ranking on the intelligence ladder.

"Jesus," El whispered. "I'm sorry. I can't believe I yelled at you like you were some moron at Udon Thani Pizza Hut."

"That's okay," I said.

"I'm just so pissed off about this camera. It had all my pictures on it, everything. Maybe I'm pre-menstrual or something. I'm so sorry."

A tear slid out of her eye and I patted her on the shoulder. "There, there," I said.

✳

After turning out both of our backpacks and scouring the Viengkeo for anywhere El might have unwittingly dropped her camera, we gave up. It had well and truly vanished. Alas, the same could not be said for El's foul mood. Tears long dried up, she ranted and raved, pacing the floor of our room and kicking the odd inanimate object. Better it than me, I thought, as her journal went flying out the window, and decided to keep my mouth shut. I didn't fancy being called an idiot twice in one afternoon.

But when she started throttling her pillow, I decided enough was enough. She'd lost her camera, alright, it sucked. But that was no reason to seek revenge on the soft furnishings—I began to wonder what it was about the Viengkeo that made its guests start treating its sleeping accessories as living objects. Besides, it was one thing for a guy to hump his mattress, but to murder a pillow was beyond the limit.

I calmly pried the misshapen lump from her hands and dropped it on the floor. "C'mon El," I said. "Let's go have a look at the town and see if we can find another camera. If new ones cost too much, we can always get you a disposable one. Let's go."

Giving her no time to embark on another rampage, I grabbed my daypack and opened the door to the hall. "Coming?"

Still sighing and cursing, El shoved some of her junk into her bag, flung it angrily over her shoulder, and stormed out of the room. Great, I thought, an aggro redhead let loose in the spiritual centre of the most laid-back country on earth. This is going to be a real treat.

Surprisingly, it wasn't as bad as I'd expected. Sure, El swore at a leprous-looking moneychanger who kept touching her bag, but he didn't understand English anyway, let alone, "How'd you like a rap in the mouth, you putrid schmuck?" Yeah, she slammed her fist down on a glass display case at the Kodak store when told a disposable camera would cost an exorbitant thirty US dollars. And okay, while she did throw a lit cigarette at a smug-looking American couple claxoning by in a tuk tuk, it never really had a chance of actually hitting them. But the moment we clapped eyes on a small crafts market crouching in the shadows of Luang Prabang's famous Mt. Phousi, El's aggression evaporated immediately. All it took was one look at the dozens of card tables, each strewn with tapestries, woven indigenous garb and multicoloured knick-knacks, for the hostility in her eyes to be usurped by a joyful spendthrift gleam. There might be something to this retail therapy after all.

Anyone who has ever sat on the loo flicking through old copies of *National Geographic* would have a pretty good idea of what this market looked like. There was something strangely familiar about its wrinkled old women sipping at jars of mysterious black stuff, piles of rainbow-hued handicrafts and naked babies squealing happily in the dirt, exotic as it was. I almost expected the trademark yellow square to be framing the scene.

But the sense of conversancy evaporated when we approached the tables. I'd never, not in all my days loitering on the toilet reading magazines, seen anything like it. What had looked, from afar, like a jumbled heap of piebald, cutesy native rags was actually exquisite tapestry. Detailed scenes from local life came alive on ragged pieces of bright fabric: miniature farmers sowed seeds, hemstitched women raised sticks to pesky birds, and fancywork oxen trundled before a backdrop of needled-in trees and an ever-present embroidered sun. Even the rumpled stacks of handmade clothes looked like they'd be more at home on a museum wall than draped over someone's spotty back. God help the Versaces of the world if these Luang Prabangers ever got the catwalk in their sights.

We learned later that this type of craft—called pa ndau by those who could pronounce it—was actually a measure of a woman's marriageability and, for the first time in my life, I wished I'd been born male. I'm sure I could handle lugging around that extra appendage, if it meant being kept in tapestries and beaded frocks.

But for now, being both female and without the language skills necessary to propose to any of the old women behind the tables, we had no choice but to pay for the goods. That is, if you could call trading the cost of a pack of gum for a sublime work of art "paying." It has always struck me as perverse that haggling prices down to ridiculous levels is the etiquette of trade in a region where, to the foreign visitor, everything is so dirt-cheap anyway. No matter how paltry their asking price, you are impelled to laugh in the vendor's face, shake your head and insist on paying just enough to ensure their family continues to starve in the manner to which it is accustomed.

If the world made any sense whatsoever, tourists travelling on any currency that doesn't feature cows on its bills would beg local merchants to take their money, while bartering would become standard procedure in overpriced department stores. But just try waving your arms and letting loose with your most scornful guffaw over a $250 pair of Nikes. The price won't go down but you most likely will—on a blacklist of nuisance shoppers at the local mall.

So, as much as it pained us to do so, we bargained. In the process of "saving face," we completely lost respect for ourselves. Closely following the rules of haggling, we pointed out imaginary flaws in the merchandise, declaimed the usual tripe about being poverty-stricken travellers and scoffed at their "special price." To us it was hideous, but the locals loved it. After a particularly fiery exchange over an embroidered pom-pom bag with what appeared to be a 300-year-old woman, she leapt from her spindly chair, smiling to beat the band and pumping my hand vigorously. She even grabbed my cheeks and pinched them in the time-honoured manner of grannies everywhere. I was stoked. No matter your age, or how tough you mistakenly believe you are, nothing makes you feel better than a surrogate grandma, even if she only adopts you for point three of a second.

$*$

By the time the sun began its journey westward, El and I had nearly bought out the entire market. The camera debacle forgotten, we babbled merrily in a post-shopping frenzy, comparing our stashes of wall hangings, accessories and clothes we wouldn't normally wear in a million years. People say LSD expands the mind's horizons, but it's travel that really alters the brainwaves. Trippers may be given to hallucinate that they're wearing a handstitched jewel headdress, rainbow sack-dress and bell-tipped elf shoes, but it's only travellers who haven't seen a pair of Levi's in a while who come to believe that this really is a good look. If I, in my new tricolour beanie (tassel and all) and Hmong patchwork bag, was not living proof enough that visitors to fantastic, far-flung places should bring along a copy of The Gap catalogue to remind them of where their fashion loyalties really lie, then the Euro contingent atop Mt. Phousi tipped the balance.

Europeans, in my eyes, are not really the fashion gurus most glossy magazines would lead us to believe. Rather than leading the world in glamour and style, the majority of continentals seem to have been left behind in an era when proto-mullets, moonwalk loafers and white socks were right up there with Pac Man and rollerblades. Jumpers are XXL, and their ironed stonewashed jeans are hitched up below the armpits to achieve the Where's-the-Flood look that keeps their ankles constantly cold. Far from jet set, I believe this look is called Jerry Seinfeld.

But even a tucked-in puffy shirt would have been an improvement on the spectacle that awaited us atop Mt. Phousi. After cramming our market purchases into our bags, we decided to keep on playing at tourists and wheezed our way up 329 tortuous steps to reach Wat Chom Phousi, the rugged mountain's revered golden stupa. Our guidebooks informed us that the lofty temple was the spot for watching Luang Prabang's dramatic sunsets, and we were looking forward to ending our hectic day with some eye candy.

Our eyes got liver and onions instead. Rather than focussing on a sky awash with oranges and reds, our tired retinas were involuntarily glued to a dozen Eurogeeks clambering over the sacred edifice clad in their finest outsized hill-tribe gear. We gasped as a French matron, decked out in a lurid blue kimono-type thing, stood triumphant atop the stupa as if to annex it, and we grabbed each other in horror as a Dutch girl in a multicoloured Hmong balloon skirt stubbed out a cigarette on the temple wall.

And when some Czech guy, wearing a woven pink sash as a bandanna (which amplified his already alarming afro-mullet), squatted over a cement Buddha's head, I nearly hurled myself over the mountain's edge.

But while I quietly contemplated my protest suicide, El was getting vocal. Focusing on a motley group of hirsute Italians doing their best to shinny up a holy mound, she let loose with a torrent of vitriol. "What the hell do you freaks think you're doing up there? Have some fucking respect, you rock apes, and get off the monument! I repeat," she ordered, "get off the monument!"

It was an impressive performance and, for the first time, I could imagine El before the blackboard—without the swearing or demeaning references to physical stature, that was. For a split second, she was no longer My Mate El, but was transformed into Sensei Rutherford, dominatrix of the Saitama Board of Education's languages department. Christ, I thought, if this is El getting crazily PC over a shabby temple, imagine facing her wrath in the playground. But Wat Chom Phousi wasn't a jungle gym, much as the assorted Eurojocks seemed to treat it as such, and they weren't listening to her –or anyone without an orange sash and a shaved head. Or carrying a violin case. It looked like respect went only as far as their nearest Godfather.

"C'mon El," I said as I watched her face reddening. "They have no regard for anything and you're not going to do anything about it."

"Can't they see how incredibly rude and offensive that is? How'd they like it if we carved our initials on the Sistine Chapel? That's about the equivalent of what they're doing to the poor bloody Buddhists."

"Let's just go to the other side and watch the sunset away from everyone. Next time we're in Rome we can tapdance on the catacombs. A bit of," I did the world's worst Brando, "revenge."

I could almost hear the violins wail.

✳

As karma would have it, we didn't have to indulge in any displays of necrodancing. Buddha took care of it for us. As we picked our way down the now-dark 329 steps, we heard a howl as one of the Italians went arse-up on the stones, dragging down two of his mates in the process. As they flailed and fangulo-ed on the dim path, we gingerly stepped over them with a smug "scusi." Buddhism may be a peace-loving religion but it tops the lot when it comes to revenge.

Chapter Ten

The Kip Kid and the Queen of Whatever

Our second day in Luang Prabang kicked off with the most gentle hangover of my life. We'd stayed up late the night before, buggered as we were, drinking Beerlao and puffing my smuggled Indonesian cigarettes at a splintery bar on the banks of the Mekong. Having muttered the jinxing, "We'll just have the one," we wound up totally intoxicated by both the stunning view of the moon on the water and the most fantastic ale we'd ever quaffed. Even El, who I usually have to force into having two pieces of brandy cake at Christmas, managed to guzzle down four big bottles. My brain blanked out on my eighth, but by no means last, bottle, and remained that way on the subject of how we got back to the Viengkeo.

Maybe it was some unique local brewing process or perhaps the overall tranquillity of Luang Prabang had somehow seeped into my subconscious, but when I gingerly raised my head, I felt healthy and calm. Normally, after any decent night on the turps, I wake in trepidation, waiting for the dreaded jitters and nausea to hit me. Once these have become firmly established, I usually

107

move on to self-pity, self-loathing and finally to panicking about what idiotic things I may have done at the height of the night's carousals. The hangover is made complete by rampant irritation at everyone and everything and most times closes with a Hair of the Dog, which in turn eventuates in yet another plonk-up. Repeat endlessly.

But on this morning, not even the incessant squeaking of the ceiling fan, nor the endless trilling of the birds outside my window could launch me into the expected state of agitation. It was a Prozac hangover.

"G'day there, missy," I called out to El, who was just beginning to show signs of life. "How art thou this fine and dandy morn?"

"Ugh," she replied. "I'm too scared to get up. Aren't you dying?"

"It's no worries, look," I cried, leaping out of bed to prove it. "Beerlao is some kind of elixir. There's no hangover!"

As I moonwalked across the bedroom, mauling the lyrics of "Thriller," she rubbed her eyes in disbelief. I couldn't blame her– if I'd woken up expecting to have to bitchslap my best friend out of a coma and instead found her sliding across the room yodelling an appalling pre-surgery Michael Jackson medley, I too would have been startled.

"C'mon, get up!" I cried, contorting myself into a terrible attempt at The Worm manoeuvre. "I feel great! Whoo!"

It's a very good thing that El felt as robust as I did. Any decently hungover person would have taken me down with one hurl of a heavy ashtray. Breakdancing is vexing at the best of times, but when your head has a locomotive crashing through it, it becomes grounds for justifiable homicide.

Thankfully, she just doubled over and cracked up. "You're a freak! Let me sleep some more!"

"Don't you feel good today?"

"I feel fine. But I want more sleep, just another half hour."

I shook my head and gyrated my hips. "No chance, honey. It's time for the electric boogaloo."

She buried her face in the pillow she'd tried to murder only half a day before and convulsed with laughter. "Sleep!"

"Get up! Get funky!"

She didn't get funky, but at least she got up.

∗

It was a beautiful sunny day, and there was nowhere better to spend it than inside a dank, claustrophobic grotto. And who better for company than thousands of little wooden men?

The Pak Ou Caves, a 25-kilometre boat trip from Luang Prabang, are hugely famous in the Buddhist domain for their galactic collection of statues of their enlightened leader, and are just as unknown in the Western world. So when El, nose in book, suggested we pay them a visit, all I could think of was spelunking. To a confirmed agoraphile, the idea of willingly stuffing oneself through tiny dark passages was akin to getting zipped inside a gimp suit. I hated latex and I hated caves.

"No chance, no way, no how," I said. "You want to make like a snake in some black hole, you go for it. I'll stay here and throw things off the balcony."

El looked at me in disgust. "Don't you even want to hear what they are?"

"Nup. I know what they are. Black, cramped and terrifying. The only time I ever want to wear a lamp on my head is at a frat party, thanks very much." I lay back down on my bed and lit my breakfast cigarette nervously. No caves. Nuh-uh.

She sighed in frustration and picked up the *Lonely Planet*. "For your information, Miss Conclusion Jumper, the Pak Ou Caves are nothing like that. Yes, there are two caves, but they're not the squirming around, lamp on your head type. They're just hollows on a mountainside crammed full of zillions of Buddha images. According to this, you just catch a lift with a fisherman in town here, climb a staircase and you're in them."

I looked at her with suspicion. "No stalactites piercing your scalp? No bats clawing your head or holes to get stuck in?"

She made a great show of reading intently and shook her head. "Nothing. It doesn't even advise against pregnant women or old people going up there."

That did it. If nauseous women and the clichéd frail could do it, so could I. The balcony would have to wait.

*

Despite the fact that the boat-hire place was supposed to be right next to the bar we'd drowned our joys in the night before, we were bollixed if we could find it. We were wandering around like the proverbial Jew. Until we ran into one.

Tanned, husky and over six feet tall, he looked like he'd be better acquainted with a soccer ball than one of the matzo variety. His athletic build, shown off in a daggy yet effective singlet, was no doubt achieved by months of enforced service in the Israeli Army, while his long tousled mop was obviously a result of getting the hell out of it. With an air of well-deserved confidence, he looked nothing like the Jewish people I'd known back in the States, who faithfully donned their yarmulcas at sunset each Friday and juggled their neuroses like hot potatoes. Apart from the Star of David pendant glimmering at his desirable throat, this guy looked like a practising pagan—or that's what I, with my filthy mind full of salacious heathenish rituals, wanted him to look like anyway.

I stood there ogling him as he nonchalantly picked through a bin of fruit outside a grocery store and nudged El to attention. "I know," she whispered. "He's lush, alright."

Morphing into a thirteen-year-old schoolgirl, I whispered back, "Spunk-o-rama. To put a creature like that on earth, there is indeed a God."

"No, I think this proves there definitely is no God," El replied. "If there was, he'd have put two of them down here." With that, we cast sideways glances at each other and, without realising we were doing it, puffed out our non-existent chests. Competition between our A-cups was fierce, and I suddenly wished for a cold snap. I just knew my nipples were bigger than El's.

Busy fondling melons, the object of our attention took no notice, but we were transfixed. The closest we'd come in recent days to anything resembling sexually attractive had been my bed at the Viengkeo, and that was just through the eyes of some departed sicko. He was mesmerising.

Eventually he sighed, dropped his fruit and called into the shop. "Roni! Let's go, man." Oh yes, we thought in unison—a clone. With no need to compete, we deflated ourselves and waited for the second god to emerge.

A shout and a couple of hairy legs later, he was out. Tall but skinny with a crop of black tight curls and bony limbs, this Roni was the antithesis of the fruit fondler. We re-inflated.

And just in time. "Hey," Adonis said, walking up to us, "how's it going? You new in town?"

For a split second, we allowed ourselves the indulgence of believing he had targeted us for our incredible good looks and obvious charisma. But Luang Prabang was a small place and to any normal, sociable backpacker, making friends with other out-of-towners was the natural thing to do. Unless you prided yourself on avoiding them, like we did. Or had until now.

"Yeah," we chorused, giving each other the sharpest of glares. We'd spent the early stages of the previous night's drinking session bagging men as mongrel bastards and now here we were competing to answer one in the affirmative. I know why men say women are hard to understand. Venus? Try a galaxy far, far away. I don't get us myself.

"We got in yesterday," El added smugly. It was ridiculous. If we could have, we would have been elbowing each other out of the way. Sadly, it had been done before.

"We've been here three days," the Almighty One said.

"Bussed up from Vientiane," the Roni one said. "What a trip."

"Isn't that supposed to be really dangerous?" I asked, feeling like a lame weakling the moment I did. "I mean, we heard there was a lot of bandit activity on Route One." Phew. If in doubt, throw in the name of a provincial highway. At least I could pretend I was down with it.

"We had no problem," Roni said. "The only thing in danger was our arses. Talk about potholes!" He rubbed his bum comically and we laughed. "What was the plane like?"

Screw it, I thought, and launched into an exaggerated account of the smoky cabin, the dying guy, the faulty wheels. They gasped and guffawed in all the right places, while El's eyes grew wider and wider. Until I opened my big trap, she had still been none the wiser about our aerial misadventures. It was going to take a crate of out-of-date pills to get her back to Vientiane. But to two people who didn't even know where their feet would fall in the next five seconds, things like return flights were an impossible eternity away. I'd deal with drugging El when the moment called for it. For now, there were other matters at hand. Like little stick men in a cave.

I turned towards the boys, studiously ignoring El's ill-concealed wrath at my deception. "Anyway, now that we've survived a Laotian plane, we're going to try our luck on a Laotian boat."

"You going to the caves?" Roni asked.

"Attempting to," El said, the colour returning to her cheeks. "But someone hid all the cave-bound boats."

"Well, ladies," Roni said in his most gracious voice. "It so happens that we are on the way there ourselves. Shall we?" He held out his hands, and in a vague daze, we took them. We were almost drooling in shock. Being addressed as "ladies" when we were clearly mangy travel pigs was surprising enough, but the fact that after all our griping and determined insularity we had actually hooked up with other backpackers was stupefying. We were part of a team. And nobody had gotten New Agey yet.

"With you girls and your dodgy plane, I just hope this bloody thing doesn't break down," laughed Roni as he led us towards the river.

It wasn't celestine, but it was prophecy enough.

$$*$$

There are times while travelling in third world countries when your entire being suddenly becomes über-aware of the squalor, the chaos, the contradictions and the decrepitness of your surroundings; times when you become possessed with longing for things like bus timetables, price tags and only slightly suspect hamburgers. These mini-frenzies can be brought on by anything from finding feathers in your soup to gagging on the mingled aromas of shit and squid in a rotting alleyway. More often than not, victims will find themselves standing in a pile of old bananas, furiously wondering why they didn't go to Eurodisney as their travel agent advised.

But those very same moments that lead to irrational cravings for Health and Safety Boards and dancing mice can also occur in the contrary. The drunken, lecherous samlor driver becomes a champion of the downtrodden, the hole in the ground a fantastic aid to your digestive system. All is seedy romance and the gritty "reality" you came here for in the first place, and you wouldn't trade it for all the Goofy souvenirs in Le Kingdom Magique.

The Luang Prabang "boat launch" could have swung me either way. On the one hand, the much-lauded "launch" was nothing more than a haphazard sprawl of firewood, while our potential skippers loitered around half-naked, quizzically staring at piles of tangled fishing nets. But on the other hand, the entire scene was a quintessential Mekong River tableau, unchanged through the centuries. These people weren't putting on a show for us and I doubt they could have cared less whether we saw the Pak Ou Caves or not. Hell, there was string to unwind here. Having grown up in a tourist trap on the Great Barrier Reef where you're more likely to get a pineapple shooting fireworks out the top of your pina colada than ignored at a marina, I was quite enamoured of their grotty disinterest and decided we should pick the pilot who ignored us the most profoundly.

It was a hard choice. Whereas the crippled of Vientiane couldn't get enough of us, the fisherfolk of Luang Prabang couldn't give a stuff. We waded through the Mekong mud from boat to boat, taking it in turns to mispronounce "Pak Ou" at the various mariners, who responded with vague shrugs and grunts. Had my mood swung the other way, I would have found myself wishing for some ruggedly handsome old sea dog and his crew of nubile first mates to hand me a laminated ticket and a mango dacquiri, but I was loving the rejection. Thankfully, so was everyone else.

"This is deranged!" chortled El after we were yawned off by yet another boatie. "It's actually hilarious that, for once, nobody is clambering all over us."

For almost the first time since his more vocal travelling companion had arrived on the scene, the shy demigod who had first commanded our attention opened his mouth. "Speak for yourself," he announced, looking pointedly down at a grubby boy tugging at his hand.

Adorable in that alienesque big-head, small-body type of way, the scruffy imp peered up at us, his mouth opening and closing like a just-caught fish. While we squinted stupidly down at him, Roni knelt beside the child. "What's that, little man?"

His mouth moved again and it wasn't until Roni shoved a giant, hairy ear into the boy's face that he finally peaked at .07 of a decibel. "Kip, kip," he said. "Kip."

We looked at each other with a mix of exasperation and weary pity. "This kid must be a mega-desperado," I said. "We're the only farang slopping around in the mud down here. What," I peered down at the kid, "you get booted out of town?"

"Kip," he answered. "Kip, kip, kip."

"Well, there's someone who knows what he wants," Roni said, lifting himself off the riverbank and reaching into his pockets. "Here you are, you little–"

The kip was nearly in the boy's waggling hand when the voice of authority boomed from behind us. "No, no, no!" We froze, shuddering in recognition. It was the voice of an irate father, and we were momentarily transformed into humbled children. We may have been four independent wayfarers, but the threatening tones of a pissed-off parent are enough to make even the toughest street fighter regress.

"Sorry 'bout that," Roni muttered as the boy's dad, himself little more than a wrinkled version of the alien-boy, hovered rumbling over the child. With a snare of fishing nets slung over his shoulder and all his limbs intact, it was clear this man was no beggar. And, in the same way my own dad had once glowered at my safety-pin-pierced ears and declared "No goddamn kid of mine is gonna be a punk," so too was this kid copping it. "No goddamn kid of mine is gonna be a beggar" may have sounded like high-pitched warbling to my foreign ears, but I got the message. Kids want ripped clothes and those bastards always say no.

With the boy looking suitably chastised, we all nodded sorrowfully at him and started to walk away when El had a flash of brilliance. "Hey," she said, turning to us, "he's the only boat guy who's paid us a scrap of attention. Let's hound him into giving us a ride to the caves."

"What about the kid?" Roni asked.

"It's pure psychology," El replied. "The dad'll feel bad because his brat tried to gyp us and will feel obliged to take us down the river."

"Either that," I added, "or he'll think we're such idiots for falling for his kid's act that he'll be delighted to relieve us of our kip himself."

"Whatever," El said. "Either way we get to those bloody caves. It can't be that much kip, anyway."

In the end, she was right. While he shrugged at our request like all the other boat guys, it was a shrug in the affirmative. And when it came to ripping us off, the man either couldn't be bothered, or was as yet unschooled in his offspring's forte. After only the briefest of haggles, he wearily resigned himself to a four-hour return trip up and back the Mekong for about five bucks.

We handed him the cash and he led us towards his boat, a long contraption that resembled a waterlogged banana. The driver, his kipping son and whatever farang happened to bumble on board were protected from the fierce Laotian sun by what appeared to be two chequered tablecloths swindled from the local Italian restaurant. With our combined lard shoved into the four plastic children's chairs provided for our ultimate discomfort on board, the wooden boat bobbed just high enough to keep the murky waters of the Mekong from lapping over the sides. Despite the lingering stink of rotten fish and a ten-minute effort to get the motor revved, the boat was quite the score.

"Well, yee-bloody-ha!" I said, adjusting my girth in the tiny chair as the boat pulled away from the shore. "We're finally doing something besides getting pissed and bitching."

"We're not exactly normal tourists," El explained to the guys.

"No shit," Roni said.

"Hmm," said the deity.

"Kip," said the boy.

＊

For two languid hours, we puttered upstream, and the excitement of the voyage made us chatty and curious. We discovered that Roni was from Tel Aviv, had recently finished his military service and, with his partner in crime, was combing the weirder parts of the world in a search of great hash and, in between smokes, a few decent shags. The god-man, introduced as Tamir, was rapidly losing my interest with his litany of shy "hmmms," but when he yawned at the word "shag," that settled it. Visual Viagra was one thing, but you had to turn the lights out sometime. I deflated my chest for good.

"And how about you two?" Roni asked. "What are you looking for?"

"Looking for?" El asked. "I have no idea. It's not hash or shags . . ."

"Although they wouldn't go astray," I butted in.

"Yeah, whatever. Um, I don't know. Just having a look and annoying the world, really."

"Annoying?"

"Sure," I said. "Annoyed yet?"

"Nope," Roni said.

"You will be."

"Well," he sighed. "It's good to know we all have our quests. Good luck."

Grilling complete, we settled in for a lethargic cruise down the Mekong. El trailed her hand lazily in the water, Roni and Tamir closed their eyes and I slid out of my Lilliputian chair on to the floor of the boat to stretch my legs and cop a better view of the strange paradise gliding silently by.

Cutting a swath through the watery outskirts of Luang Prabang, the Mekong lolled past soft knolls of wild palms and sandy jungle

117

before giving way to a mountainous netherland. For what seemed like a humid infinity, we hummed past high slopes fuzzy with undergrowth, occasionally catching glimpses of villages tottering above the brambles. The odd fishing canoe, usually half-submerged with either heavy catch or low maintenance, passed us every now and then, and those feeling energetic enough waved whenever a rainbow-painted houseboat clamoured by with the shrieking of a million kids on board. Everything else was haze and stupor.

By the time we reached the caves, we all felt completely stoned. No breeze was blowing and the heat sat heavily on us like a pregnant wrestler. Keeping our eyes open was difficult enough and, as much as we all would have liked to, nobody had the energy to tell Kip Boy, who'd kicked in with his monosyllabic litany again, to shut the fuck up. It was too hot, our surroundings were too surreal, and the trip was too dreamy to inspire any action whatsoever.

But that was us slack honkies. Our driver had other ideas.

"Out!" he commanded, and after a flare of mutinous anger flashed through my heavy head, I instantly felt the added weight of guilt. It wasn't really his fault that he didn't know how to say, "Ladies and gentlemen, we have arrived. Please disembark from the rear of the vessel." Curtness can be an issue with hooning around countries whose languages bear absolutely no resemblance to English. When you don't know the local lingo, and the locals have but a fleeting grasp of English, it is all too easy for both parties to find themselves glaring each other down with "You rude prick!", in whatever tongue, screaming through their minds. I mourned the demise of Esperanto and heaved myself out of the boat.

It was worth it. From the narrow, rotting plank that served as a landing, I cast my eyes over an *Apocalypse Now* landscape of brooding ranges and darkly beguiling inlets meandering around mysterious rock formations. I imagined Colonel Kurtz holed up in one of the sinister coves I could barely make out across the river, and pictured him polishing his big bald head. Surely it was too hot to be bothered with slaughtering sacrifices.

As I stood, rapt in fantastical daydreams, El came up and pinched me. "Hey, drongo," she said, "you're looking the wrong way."

"Huh?"

"Up."

Reluctantly turning my overly imaginative head away from the river and up towards the Pak Ou Caves, I went quickly from "Oh" to "Whoa!" This kicked the arse out of any movie I'd ever seen. Set back into the stained stone gorge was a yawning black gape fringed by what looked to be a sparkling white picket fence. I couldn't see any Buddhas yet, but the effect of having a symbol of the American domestic idyll ringing an evil-looking black hole was tremendously weird. It was like Beaver Cleaver meets *The Twilight Zone*.

By the time we paid some ancient cave guardian two thousand kip for the pleasure and slipped our way up a dodgy stone staircase, the fence had warped back into what it really was; a miniature whitewashed temple wall. But the cave still felt creepy. And after clambering through a small crevice for a better look, the feeling only intensified.

The Pak Ou Caves are a place of worship for the Laotians, who go so far as to flock to them every New Year for mass prayer. But to me, a devout non-believer in anything, the echoing chamber looked like a secret outdoor doll's house assembled by an obsessive child. Hundreds upon hundreds of Buddha statuettes stood, crouched, lounged and sat in the shadows of the cave, all staring doe-eyed at the Mekong. Gold, copper, wood and clay, it didn't matter. If it looked like Buddha, it was here. It reminded me of my bedroom when I was fourteen years old and infatuated with Michael Hutchence. Obsessive child indeed.

"Hey, El!" I called, my voice bouncing off the walls of the cave. "Isn't this slightly freaking you out?"

"Ssssh!"

"No really, I mean, can't you imagine all of their little eyes following you, like those scary portraits of—"

"Hey!" she shout-whispered. "This is a holy place! Keep it down!"

Ooops, sacrilege. Being unused to boat rides and mountaineering as normal ways to get to church, I had forgotten that the Pak Ou Caves were a shrine, not an adventure. "Sorry," I whispered.

"Cool. Hey, really, think about it. Imagine the devotion of whoever it was that set this cave up. I mean, that's real belief."

"Are you Pancho-ing out on me here?"

"Kind of. But seriously, even if not for religion, then for art, it's incredible."

She, again, was right. I squinted deeper into the gloom and studied the statues individually. Everything, from the kindly vacant eyes to the curled-up toes on each figure was exquisitely carved and even the seemingly haphazard layout of the statues had a beautiful, almost purposeful randomness to it. Whoever did this must have been a huge fan of Buddha, maybe even the macdaddy of the fan club. This was love.

I had just gotten over my feelings of being creeped out and was big into the appreciation stage of the proceedings when I heard a low howl. Being creeped out was instantly the In Thing again.

"Jesus!" I yelled. "El!"

"Oh shut up," she muttered. "It's just those idiot boys being moronic."

I sighed in relief, having completely forgotten that Roni and Tamir even existed. They had raced up to the top cave first, and were now scrambling down to us with a cacophony unmatched by any potential statue-spook.

"Hey," Roni announced, jumping down to the fringe of our cave, "that's some pretty weird shit, huh?"

El and I spun around to him and shhh-ed him our most

violent shhh. While I was inwardly relieved that I wasn't the only blasphemous buffoon in the cave complex, there was no need for everyone else to know we were on the same thuggish level. I tutt-ed him again for good measure before turning haughtily and walking up to the top cave. Scapegoats are highly unappreciated members of society.

⚹

The top cave was much the same as the bottom one and, as we walked out half an hour later, our feeling of déjà vu was intensified by the same crotchety cavemeister hobbling up to us to collect another two thousand kip.

"Oh no," I said. "That was for both caves."

"Huh?" the old man grunted.

"Don't even try it, mate, I know you can't charge us twice." I was quite the smug spelunker.

"Kip," he said, fixing his narrow eyes on me.

"Hey, if you want to take a break, I've got just the replacement for you." I pointed down to the boat, where the ET kid was looking groggily up at us.

"Kip," he demanded.

"Oh, for God's sake!" El said. "I am so not surprised, but screw it. Let's just pay again."

As she thrust her money into his hand and I, shell-shocked, did the same, I marvelled at the calm that had settled over El since entering the caves. The Righteous Defender of the Kip had vanished behind a new persona, the Queen of Whatever.

"Very Buddhist of you," I remarked as we trod carefully down the steps.

She shook her head. "Buddhist indeed. I'm just too bloody hot to argue." This was a first. "Where can we get a drink around here, anyway?"

I'd been wondering the same thing. The heat had dehydrated me to the point where I was ready to start slurping the scummy froth from one of the many rockpool puddles near the caves. Well, nearly ready. "No idea, baby, but I'm parched. Let's just get back on this boat and hit Luang Prabang for some beers."

"Bliss and joy," El moaned. "Beer is good."

It was a breakthrough. The delights of Beerlao had finally turned El into a drinker, and I was keen to get to town before her usual sensibilities kicked in and robbed me of a steady piss-up partner.

"Full speed ahead," I cried, running down the plank and crashing into the boat. The boys, already wilting in their kiddie chairs, looked at me with tired curiosity. "Luang Prabang ahoy!"

"What's your rush?" Roni mumbled. "Chilling in this boat is fine with me."

"You'll be chilling in it for another two hours, anyway," I said. "And I don't know about you, but we want to get a wriggle on and sink some beers back in town."

Beneath his heavy lids, his eyes sparkled and he licked his lips. "Beer?"

"Aren't you thirsty? Can't you just feel that cool goodness sliding down your throat? Can't you just taste it? Can't you just . . ."

"Alright already!" Tamir cried. We all stared at him, agog that he'd opened his trap for once. "I'm dying of thirst!"

"Me too," Roni echoed mournfully. "I want some beer."

"Well, let's hit it," El clapped. "Go, go, go!"

Our driver obviously had "Go!" stored away in his English collection along with "No!" and "Out!", for two seconds later, the engine was kicked over and we were puttering slowly down the river.

"Yay!" we chorused. Our throats may have been dry as dust, but the idea that beer, or any liquid not swimming with intestinal tapeworm for that matter, was less than two hours away was cause to celebrate. And while two hours may be a long time to the conscious, thirsty soul, it was nothing to a catnapper.

"Wake me when it's beer-o-clock," I mumbled to nobody in particular, and lay down on the floor of the gently rocking boat. I'd read somewhere that the ancient shamans had used the steady beat of drums to regulate their heartbeats and send themselves into deep trances, and decided to try the same. An outboard motor was no set of bongos, but with its steady putt-putt, it seemed to do the trick. Putt, inhale. Putt, exhale. Putt, inhale. Splutter, exhale. Gurgle, cough, silence. What the hell?

Chapter Eleven

If One Intestinally Ulcerates

I pushed myself up on my elbows and looked around foggily. "Where's my drums?" I burbled.

"The bloody boat's broken down," El spat.

"What?!"

"Broken boat," she pronounced loudly. "Do you see us going anywhere?"

Fully awake, I sat up straight and watched the landscape slowly circle our drifting boat in an eerie, motorless silence. "Nowhere but hell in a handbasket," I sighed, slumping back to the floor. No sleep and, more importantly, no beer. No good.

The pilot, pulling furiously at the motor cord, barked something to his son, who had been curled up at the back of the boat, doubtless dreaming of kip. He ran to his father and, looking like an extra-terrestrial tag team, they tugged and kicked the motor as we gawked idiotically at them. But neither their systematic whupping of the dead engine nor our moronic stares was getting the boat anywhere but further downstream.

"Holy shit," I whispered to El. "If this keeps up, we're going to wind up sleeping back in those caves." I shuddered at the idea of all those Buddhas keeping a glassy watch over me all through the night.

"I'm not scared of that," she whispered back. "I'm more scared of dying of thirst."

"Me too. Do you think you die quicker when you're actually surrounded by water you can't drink? Like go nuts or something from the temptation of it all?"

The conversation having reached its usual peak of idiocy by means of my excited imaginings, she turned away from me and lit a cigarette, shaking her head at the boys. I lit one, too, and waited for either death or a saviour to come.

*

Our messiah came in the form of a very long stick. We'd been drifting aimlessly for the better part of an hour, and our exasperated driver was scratching his head in confusion, when shoals of driftwood began banging against the boat. In a moment of either divine inspiration or primitive logic, he scooped up one of the larger logs and began pushing us, gondola-style, towards the shore.

"We're saved!" I cried, as the land drew nearer with each push on the stick.

"By what," El asked grumpily, "a big Coke machine just behind that palm tree there?"

"Nooo," I drawled, "look up there." I pointed to half a dozen roofs sticking out from behind a scrabbly hill covered in broken weeds and charred trees. "Hill tribers!"

To many visitors to Southeast Asia, hill tribes and their villages are the rough-and-tumble Disneyland of the East. People pay good money to go on "Hill Tribe Adventures," which invariably wind up being torturous group hikes through malaria-infested jungles, a quick ride on the back of a malnourished elephant

125

and some aimless floating down a river on a bamboo raft before arriving in the "Hill Tribe Village." The "authentic" village is indeed a bona fide settlement of true-blue tribespeople, but in many cases, has been so warped by the constant stream of rubbernecking, camcorder-wielding Westerners as to become more of a theme park. Poverty World, Primitive Land, step right up. The elephant walks fill the need for amusement rides, while scrubby little hill-tribe kids, their teeth already falling out from the lollies dished out to them by the last lot of gawkers, tail tourists just like funny Mickey and Goofy. Culture consists of an overpriced handwoven scarf, and genuine interaction a bribing with sweets for a group photograph outside a lopsided, woven hut. While such ventures might bring the villagers a welcome influx of cash, it seemed to me like a tragic loss of innocence.

There was the romantic in me talking again, but the thirsty realist quickly booted her out of the way. "They'll have drinks," I salivated.

El, who was under the same impression that every village from Thailand's self-proclaimed "Hill Tribe Capital" of Chiang Mai to Vietnam's trekking destination of Sapa had been dragged into the 20th century by tourists and their whining, agreed. "You're right, y'know," she said. "Let's get up there and shake them down."

Roni and Tamir needed no encouragement, and were already knee-deep in the murky water dragging the limping boat to shore when El and I hopped off into the mud.

"Hey," I breathed, as we scampered clumsily up the hill. "There's probably a group of tourists up there right now, and we can get a lift back with them."

"Mmm," pondered El heavily. "But where's their boat?" I looked back down the hill and spied nothing flasher than a handful of suspect-looking craft docked on the shore.

"Maybe one of those is a tourist boat. I mean, look at what we rocked up in."

She nodded, and we kept on climbing through the dead grass until, breathless, we met the boys at the top. "I think you guys were wrong," Roni said, his eyes fixed forward.

"How d'ya mean?" I asked, still gasping for air and bent over my knees.

"Have a look," he said, his voice quiet for once with awe.

I did. In the large clearing was a jumble of top-heavy, frond-roofed shacks. Perched atop precarious timber beams and steps, they creaked and rustled as a slight breeze ruffled the hilltop. Completely unaware of the four out-of-shape intruders panting on his doorstep, a lone man in a faded pair of shorts furrowed his brow over a small fire while a chicken strutted impatiently by an empty lean-to.

"Where's all the tourists?" I whispered.

We looked at each other.

✳

If the lack of smiling natives bearing expensive souvenirs didn't prove my Every-Village-is-a-Theme-Park theory wrong, then the shrill screaming that nearly sent me hurtling back down the hill certainly did. Piercing and haunted, it was no cry of welcome and it sure wasn't the call of the drinks vendor. It was the sound of pure fear.

Terror breeds terror, and we found ourselves breathing shallowly and unable to move. I didn't know if this village had been struck off the Hill Tribe Ratings Guide for refusing to give up human sacrifice or if horrific ululating was part of day-to-day life, but I knew it was time to get outta town. If only my legs would move.

The wailing grew more insistent until even the man in the tattered shorts snapped out of his fire-building daze and looked around hesitantly. As his eyes silently probed the crannies of every tilting shack and behind every blackened tree, it could only be a matter of seconds before they came to rest on us. And then, God only knew. If they can make each other scream like that, I thought with more than a touch of panic, imagine what they'll do to us. I squeezed El's hand and, for the second time that day, waited for the end.

A million agonising years later, he spotted us. With a wiry, agile grace, he lifted himself off the ground and approached us slowly, the background howls a fitting soundtrack to my impending demise. He mumbled something to himself, scratched his head. And smiled.

Not the evil, drooling smile I, in my melodramatic way, had expected, but the kind smile of a harmless stranger. I dropped El's hand and felt the life come back to my frozen legs. Only now I didn't want to run anywhere.

He stopped in front of us and nodded his head in greeting. We were about to chorus hello, when we were interrupted again by another shriek. A mild annoyance crossed the man's face and he hollered something towards a nearby house where, for the first time, we saw signs of life beneath the run-down stairs. With the universal shrug that's shorthand for "Kids! What can you do?" and a wink at us, everything suddenly became crystal clear. Us. They were afraid of us. They, with their spindly, secret little village, were screeching in blind terror over us four twerps. I could have pissed myself in ridiculous relief.

"Hello," Roni began. "We don't want to bother you, but our boat is broken and we're stuck. We're also dying of thirst."

"You're also rambling," muttered El, subtly nodding her head towards the very confused-looking man. "Water?" she pronounced loudly. Still baffled and most likely wondering if those kids had made a good judgement call with their unnerving screams after all, the man looked quizzically at us.

"Drink?" Roni said, holding an imaginary cup to his mouth and making grotesque gulping noises.

"Ah," the man said, breaking out into another smile. He grunted something incomprehensible and beckoned us with a wave as he started walking into the village. With our throats and curiosities afire, we followed.

✳

As we trailed behind the man like rats to the piper, so too were we leading a parade. The kids who had been wailing at us from the fringes of the village now obviously saw us to be the harmless fools that we were, and had decided to get a better look. It seemed we were the first white people they'd seen in ages, if ever, and I heartily wished there'd been a better representation of the Caucasian race than us four rejects. But the fact that we definitely belonged to the lower echelons didn't faze the kids at all. Giggling and gasping, they tottered just behind us, calling out to other kids who were crouching behind trees and bundles of dried fronds along the way. With each step, their hoots and squeals grew louder and more intense, and when we finally reached the hill tribe village equivalent of a town square, they went berserk. El was nearly toppled as the kids attempted to touch her red hair, Tamir was groped by two little girls in matching faded floral cast-off shorts, Roni's abundant leg hairs were pulled by a yelping cluster of boys and one determined soul tried to shinny up my leg for a better view of the proceedings.

No matter the country or the culture, the raucous racket of kids having too much fun is enough to bring any parent running, and this little village—address Nowheresville, Mekong Heights—was no exception. Dads who'd been keeping a quiet eye on us from their shacks strode over, while mums came bearing down out of nowhere, a couple of them nursing incredibly tiny infants. From the quarter-acre suburban block to the remote jungle village, parents just will not tolerate mayhem.

But there was one slight difference. As the disorderly midgets were plucked, pulled and cajoled off us, the parents seemed to crumble behind their façades of serious intent and before long, were laughing shyly right alongside their kids. We were the day's, if not the week's, entertainment and damned if they weren't going to have a giggle as well. Between filling caves with dolls and eyeballing stray round-eye-long-nosed farang, the Nintendo-free world could amuse themselves, thanks very much.

Meanwhile, we circus freaks were getting thirstier by the minute—until eventually one of the women who had forgone all the thigh-slapping approached us with an indescribably filthy plastic pitcher in her outstretched arms. We stared blankly at her for a second, until she raised the jug to her mouth and made the same repulsive noises Roni had when calling for a drink. We nodded a wary thanks and reached for the jug.

When I was little, my mates and I would gross ourselves out by playing the "How much would you pay me if . . ." game: "How much would you pay me if I ran down the street naked?", "How much would you pay me if I ate dirt?", "How much would you pay me if I put a spider in my mouth?" But "How much would you pay me if I swilled wormy swamp water out of a filth-encrusted jug in a native jungle village?" had strangely never come up, so I couldn't put a value on what I was about to do. I reckoned about half a mil should just about cover it, though.

But there was nobody in the vicinity with that kind of cash and, unless we wanted to risk the villagers' wrath, there was nothing to do but neck the so-called water. I wondered if my insurance covered typhoid fever. "Knees up, Mother Brown," I said, with a bravery I did not feel, and took a hearty swig. With my eyes squeezed shut and my teeth clamped down to prevent anything with body mass from slipping down my throat, the water, unseen and unchewed, actually went down all right. Bacteria be damned, I thought, and had another gulp.

As I lowered the grimy ewer from my wet, hopefully worm-free lips, the others watched me closely for any signs of nausea, insanity or the sprouting of a second head. When none was forthcoming, they all lunged for the drink and passed it among themselves, gulping noisily. Ah well, I thought, if one intestinally ulcerates, we all intestinally ulcerate. Maybe there was something to this group travel after all.

The jug finally emptied, we passed it back with more positive thanks than when we'd received it. We weren't vomiting, our shorts weren't stained by dysentery and our collective thirst was quenched. Suddenly, life was very good, and I looked at the village in a new light. It was definitely dilapidated, with its pitching huts and earthen floors, but I'd lived in worse sharehouses. Sure, the denizens were covered in dirt and cast-off shirts emblazoned with badly reproduced images of the Smurfs and Big Bird, but kitsch was in. And while there seemed little else to do but chase tatty chooks and weave yourself a new house, that was definitely a better option than getting carpal tunnel syndrome in an office block. It seemed an envious lifestyle.

"Yeah," said El when I told her, "and I also envy them for having no medical care, having to chew their water and living in mud and fear for generations. Shall we talk landmines?"

"Oh sure," I grunted. "Bring reality into it, just when I'm contemplating life as a noble savage."

"Noble I doubt, but if we don't get back to town soon, I'll show you savage. It's getting late and I don't think quaffing Mekong ooze has filled my need for Beerlao. Remember beer, Little Miss Hill Tribe?"

I certainly did. "Right, that's it. Let's go. Guys, whaddya say?" I looked around for Roni and Tamir, but they'd decided that chasing squealing children was more entertaining than staccato communication with the oldies. It was up to us.

*

By the time we'd explained our predicament to the perplexed cluster of villagers by means of sound effects and mime, the bright afternoon sun had begun to wane. The shadows of the huts stretched over us and a sweet smoke from outdoor ovens curled temptingly through the air. It was a primordial scene of village bliss and the food sure smelled good, but no amount of chicken-head stew or whatever they were boiling up could have persuaded me to stay. I had convinced myself that Luang Prabang was the pinnacle of civilisation, and I wanted in. After a day steeped in antiquated idolatry and a feral-style modus vivendi, I was beginning to have my doubts that the wheel had been invented, let alone beer. I wanted proof and I wanted it now.

The soprano howls of children announced the presence of Roni and Tamir, who'd been chasing them around the village with their teeth bared in mock-scary snarls. "Okay, Nosferatu," El said, grabbing a growling Tamir. "If you've had enough of terrifying the children, we're outta here."

It was a motley parade that made its way down the scrubby hill. Led by the sure-footed village men, El and I stumbled over tree roots and undergrowth while Roni and Tamir engaged in a play-war with the nearly hysterical melange of kids that tumbled behind them. The women, waving us serene goodbyes from the top of the embankment, were going to have one hell of a time getting them to bed that night.

Down below, the driver and his son were collapsed in a spent heap by the side of the boat. Beating the shit out of the motor with the stick that had gotten us to shore obviously hadn't done the trick, and it had been repaid for its efforts by being broken in half. Now I'm no mechanic, but no tool box I'd ever seen housed a wet stick for emergency situations. I just hoped the village men had a tad more expertise.

They didn't. After rousing the driver and engaging in a spot of country mouse/city mouse banter, they peered at the motor and proceeded to prod at it with the larger half of the broken stick. When that yielded no result, the kids stepped in and threw sand at it. Astonishingly, this also met with no success. The only thing left to do was kick it. They did.

Sapped by the earlier heat and the events of the day, El and I slumped onto the boggy sand and chain-smoked as we awaited our fate. Surely there were worse things than having to sleep at the village, but with our demonic cravings for beer and civilisation reaching a frenzied peak, I couldn't think of any. I'd gone from wannabe wild girl to city slicker in a matter of moments, and something had to be done soon before I went through paved-street withdrawals.

Calling again on his vast knowledge of English, our driver addressed us with a commanding "Go!", and pointed to a bedraggled boat covered in palm fronds. With no motor and no plastic kiddie chairs, this boat really did look like something out of a bygone era. Considering the time warp we were loitering in, I guessed it was more than apt. Heaving and squelching through the shallows, we lugged the boat into the water and climbed awkwardly inside. One of the village men, presumably the proud owner of the vessel, hopped on board and pulled out his sophisticated navigational gear—another stick, only much longer than ours had been. This was a real upmarket cruise.

"Up, up and away!" I cried, as the stick propelled us away from shore. "Beer ahoy!"

"Wait!" yelled El. "What about the driver and the kip kid?"

"Shit!" we chorused. In all the stick-prodding excitement, we'd forgotten about getting them home as well. Surely the driver was as keen as we were for a belt of booze, and no doubt the kid had people to pester back in town.

"Stop!" we cried. The stick-guy wheeled around at us and we pointed frantically at the man and his son, staring forlornly at us back on the shore. He glanced at them, shook his head and went back to pushing us along.

"Bloody hell!" El fumed. "Hey! Hey!" The stick-guy turned around again, exasperated, and we pointed furiously again.

"No!" he barked, and pushed on. We gave up. Maybe kidnapping random outsiders was the isolated village's only means of hopping out of their inbred gene pool. We waved slowly at the two figures until they disappeared from view. Who were we to say no to a break in sister-shagging?

Chapter Twelve

Boogie à la Rama

"Here's to sticks!" Clink.

"Here's to drinking slime!" Clink.

"Here's to inbred kidnapping!" Clink.

Over a million orgasmic beers, the four of us recounted the happenings of the day in the first bar we'd come across since bumping to shore at sunset. The stick-guy had turned down our offers of a shout, so we'd showered him in kip and raced like the devil to this hole in the wall. A tiny place just across from a nightmarket, it was crammed with local booze artists and smelled like fish, but it sold Beerlao at twenty cents a pop. For that, you could shove your Savoy.

Three hours into the swilling spree and we were all pleasantly delirious. Tamir had come out of his shell and was enthralling us with a narrative, punctuated by Roni's smart-arse comments, on life in the Israeli Army. El was knocking back the beers like a pro and getting up every five minutes for a trip to the hole in the ground. I, in the meantime, had donned my beer goggles and was looking dreamily at Roni. From being a skinny, cactus-legged goofball, he had been transformed into a ruggedly handsome humorist, his hirsutism a nod to his masculinity. Maybe ugly people should forget about plastic surgery and spend their cash getting other people pissed instead. It really works wonders.

Although El was half-rotten herself, she knew my drunken leer when she saw it. She'd been forced to pull me away from all sorts of dweeby misfits in the past and, at the first sign of danger, she went to work immediately.

"Snap out of it," she whispered furiously through her beer. "He's foul." I gave her my best innocent look, which is a difficult manoeuvre when alcohol inhibits full control of the facial muscles.

"And that's just sick. Get up." She pulled me to my feet and dragged me to the shitpit out the back. "Listen," she slurred. "He's a bloody rock ape, so don't even think about it."

"He's funny," I protested, peering back into the bar for another look. All I could see was a fuzzy bunch of heads.

"And he's also a primate. If you think he's funny now, just imagine the uproarious laughter when he gets his kit off."

"Mmm."

"Come on," she pushed me back into the bar, "let's get some food."

No chance. I knew there was a steak and two veg inside every bottle of lager, and I'd had a feast. She wasn't going to pull this clever ruse on me.

Oh yes she was. "See you guys later," she called, shoving me into the street.

"Meet you later at Rama!" shouted Roni.

Enthralled by the sound of his voice, I staggered back to the doorway. "Huh?"

"Rama," he said, eyes swimming in requited love. Or beer. "It's a disco up the road."

My mind flooded with images of jiving hill tribers and monks caught up in Disco Fever. Even without the hint of drunken romance, I wouldn't miss this for the world. "You're on," I said. "Boogie-o-rama here we come."

∗

More like retch-o-rama. After shuffling reluctantly away from Roni, El dragged me to Luang Prabang's renowned Talat Tha Heua marketplace to line our stomachs by sampling the local wares, an experiment which nearly resulted in said stomachs winding up splattered across the pavement.

I'm not so naïve as to believe that every ingredient that goes into my usual Western diet is created by nature for consumption. They say bull semen is what makes jelly beans so chewy and who hasn't heard the story about cyst burgers? But, in most cases at least, our food is so processed that, to me anyway, it doesn't really matter what goes in there. If it looks like a hamburger and smells like a hamburger, then it's a bloody burger. If there's sheep anuses in there, I can't see 'em.

But what we found at the markets was a different story altogether—everything you never wanted to put near your mouth and more. Under glaring streetlights, stall after stall boasted the most revolting things Mother Nature had to offer: steamed giblets, foot soup and crusty things that, if they weren't insects, did a pretty good cockroach impression. Even the vegetables were scary. For all I know, this was the stuff that went into those roadhouse microwave hot dogs, but there is such a thing as Too Much Information.

But we were there and we were drunk. There are, of course, different types of drunk. The Unhappy Drunk. The Singing Drunk. The Fighting Drunk. Unfortunately for us, we had reached a hybrid state, the Hungry Drunk meets the Adventurous Drunk. That's fine for drunkards who, say, have to race across a busy street to get to a somewhat hygienic kebab shop, but to be

137

in this frame of mind surrounded by half-dead, unidentifiable things dished up in secondhand plastic bags, well you just know there's gonna be some gagging.

Unable to name our pleasure in the midst of so much weirdness, we simply charged through the market, pointing at whatever wasn't squirming at the time. Without knowing whether we'd picked up flora, fauna or flat-out freakshow, we took our purchases to a dark gutter just down from the market to begin the gorgefest. Alas, we wound up doing less eating and more releasing of our dinner back to the wild.

"I can't take any more of this," El groaned as she spat out yet another mouthful. "I think I've only actually swallowed twice, and that was by accident."

"Tell me about it," I said, coughing up a chunk of what I'd foolishly believed was chicken. "This entire scenario is repulsive to the extreme. This tripe makes pig's head on a stick look appetising."

"My kingdom for a pigsicle," El moaned, clutching her stomach.

I stood up and surveyed the landscape of oozing plastic bags and regurgitated mouthfuls that even the usually undiscriminating scavenger dogs were steering clear of. It was clear that any attempts to eat like a native had been in vain, unless local gourmandising usually bordered on bulimia. There was only one thing for it.

"More beer?"

*

By the time we found the Rama, we had sobered up considerably. The realisation of what we'd just put into our mouths had shocked us out of our beery stupor, and we'd drowned what booze we hadn't retched out with our dinner by guzzling day-glo cordial sold on the streets in the ubiquitous plastic bags. With my beer goggles well and truly off, any romantic inclinations towards weedy furballs had definitely evaporated, but not so my curiosity. The promise of the quiet, Buddha-fearing folk of Luang Prabang shaking their pa ndau-clad good thangs beneath a disco ball had "must-see" written all over it.

From the street, the Rama looked like any suburban disco in the Western world; ugly, tacky and littered with the loitering bodies of the staggering inebriated and the barfing under-age. Dodgy deals went down in the adjoining alleyway and the pissed-off screech of a drunken woman scorned echoed down the street. Apart from the fact that there were no jumped-up bouncers thugging it up by the door, it was a scene reminiscent of any club from Cairns to the Cross.

But any Australian analogies stayed on the pavement with the broken bottles and hiccuping kids. From the instant the heavy door swung shut behind us, it was third world chaos all the way. People who say the nouveaux riches don't know how to comport themselves should get over to Laos and have a good look at the nouveaux liberated. It really isn't pretty.

The cavernous room, dimly lit by blinking Christmas lights and a spotlight on the verge of imploding, did a fair to middling impression of a real nightclub and was stocked with all the essentials: an understaffed bar in a hard-to-get-to corner, overflowing toilets and mirrored walls to check your style. There was even a hanging lamp covered in flammable tinsel posing as a glitterball. But no amount of hazardous pyrotechnics could hide the fact that *Saturday Night Fever* was as yet unreleased in Laos.

Now, I've never been one to trip the light fantastic with any inklings of grace or even style, but the hundreds-strong contingent of seemingly epileptic Laotians on the dance floor inflated my usual writhings to Travolta status. Decked out in their finest Western cast-offs, they jerked, they flailed and they beat their chests wildly. By the looks of things, these people needed the Heimlich manoeuvre, not a night on the town. But it wasn't entirely their fault. The Laotians are traditionally a graceful people, but then tradition doesn't usually involve trying to keep time to five screaming grease monkeys mauling off-key electric guitars.

It was beyond abominable, and this is coming from someone who once thought The Cramps had a refined, lyrical quality. From a stage just out of my bottle-throwing range, this quintet from somewhere-beyond-hell managed to mutilate every musical note in the known range, while still finding time to create some new ones before mangling them as well. Sure, Celine Dion does it all the time, but even she doesn't employ the added horror of cacophonous feedback. Whichever misguided metal geek had taken it upon himself to bring rock and roll to this innocent country has a lot to answer for.

In the midst of all the squalling and spasms, El and I frantically shoved our way to the bar in an attempt to steady ourselves with a few bracing pints of their strongest spirit. As nightmarish as it was, we felt it our strange and compelling duty to stick around and observe the hell that was the Rama, but there was no way we were doing it without the aid of something over 25 per cent proof. Or then again, we could just have Fanta.

"No!" I cried as the barman pointed at the icebox of soft drink. "Whiskey?" He shook his head. "Vodka?" No go. "Beer?" He peered suspiciously at us through the smoke, trying to discern whether or not we were those wild farang chicks with a penchant for drunken bar-trashing. While *Saturday Night Fever* may not have been on the blackmarket yet, *Dusk till Dawn* obviously was.

But the few minutes we'd been inside the Rama had left us looking more like stunned mullets than psycho babes, and the barman forked over the beers. Four of them. I wasn't pushing back through that crowd until I was at least half-cut. We sequestered ourselves in a corner as far away as possible from the caterwaulings of the so-called band, and sucked desperately at our drinks, each of us hoping that beer earmuffs were as easily attained as beer goggles. "No end in sight," I called above the din. "These guys are worse than Queen with their epic sagas."

"Yeah," El yelled back. "And we know what happened to Freddie Mercury."

After more than five ear-bashing minutes, the racket came to an abrupt halt, with nothing but speaker static and the polite applause of the dancers filling the gigantic room. "Peace at last," El said in a voice husky from screaming. "Set break."

With the band silently slouching in the spinally-disfigured stance made popular by bad MTV videos, those that had been twitching it up on the dance floor filed neatly towards the back of the Rama. Finding their seats at long tables strewn with half-drunk Fanta bottles and giggling shyly into their sleeves, the scene was more reminiscent of a seventh birthday party than any hip cabaret.

"That's really quite cute," El remarked. "I can't believe these are the same people who were convulsing out there five seconds ago."

"I know," I said. "It's like the band is one of those Japanese cartoons that makes everyone have seizures."

El laughed and opened her mouth to comment further when, like an announcement from hell, the vexing twang of the guitar cut her off. "Tuning up," I mouthed over the noise. "It's about time."

But all it was time for was another ear-bashing. Over the top of the guitar, the drums crashed in and the frontman yowled into the microphone, signifying the introduction to another session of aural rape.

As we gawked in disbelief, the kids at the tables widened their eyes in misled joy, plunked down their Fantas and filed, ever so neatly, back on to the dance floor. By the time the singer had howled his way into the first chorus, the Rama again looked like a safe haven for the collectively possessed. It was bizarre, even by Laotian standards. A set break that lasted twenty seconds?

It was no set break. As we soon learned, to our chagrin, there was no such thing as a set break. Those twenty-odd seconds of blissful silence were merely pauses between songs, the gasping moment in normal clubs when girls fidget flirtatiously around their handbags and guys hoot loudly at the band. But the Rama was more sub than normal, and to club patrons, the dance floor was for dancing. Only. Besides, nothing went so well with a fidget and a hoot than a nice drop of Fanta. At a table, please.

And so it went on for hours. The band continued to lay waste to our auditory sensibilities, pausing only for the few seconds it took the crowd to parade off the dance floor, make contact with their chairs and march back again. Back and forth, back and forth. It was like everyone in the club was engaged in a warped game of musical chairs. I got the feeling that rock gigs and party games didn't enjoy a very successful crossover into the third world.

At one hazy, nine-beers-down stage of the evening, El and I decided enough was enough. If these kids were so desperate to adopt Western nightlife, then they were going to have to learn to stand around gormlessly in the breathing space between songs. In the logic peculiar to foreigners with a booze-inspired missionary complex, we figured we'd be doing them a favour, and took to the dance floor. It took several minutes of getting knocked around like pinballs by thrashing Laotians and the impending onset of deafness, but our chance to pass on our talent for standing still eventually arrived. As the band signalled the end of a song by assuming their usual rock-god-gone-wrong positions and the crowd began to shuffle back off for another five-second hiatus, we held our ground, loitering unsteadily just below the stage, trying to look cool.

It wasn't easy. We looked like twits at the best of times, and trying to act the trendsetter while getting stared down by hundreds of bewildered Asians on a silent dance floor wasn't proving to be our forte. Even the band was looking down at us with naïve perplexity and refusing to pick up their instruments although at least thirty seconds had ticked by. But while I was ready to slither under a speaker in humiliated failure, El wasn't giving up. "Whoo, yeah," she cried out in an insanely false tone of fun. She turned from the increasingly flummoxed crowd of kids to the band. "Bring it on!"

"Uh, yeah," I joined. "Whoo, I love standing on the dance floor between songs." Screw it. If these kids didn't pick up on our subtle invitations to emulate, I'd have to ram my agenda down their throats.

"Play s'more," El called. "We're ready! Whoo!" She launched into a horrid, head-bopping, hip-swaying routine that I recognised from dancefloors back home, the one people with nobody to talk to pull out when there's no music going. "Let's go, yeah!" She clapped her hands and signalled to the lead singer. "Uh-huh!"

But the band were still frozen in some kind of shock, and the would-be dancers were beginning to titter. Out of the corner of my eye, I could see the bartender pointing at us. It was suddenly very warm.

"El," I muttered, tapping her on the shoulder. "Let's quit while we're ahead."

She stopped bopping and looked at me dejectedly. I nodded my head towards our now openly guffawing audience and the barman, who'd moved from pointing to staring at us with showdown eyes. "C'mon," I said, "before they shoot the messenger."

With a sigh, El let me lead her off the dance floor and we both winced as the guitar wailed back into action. We shook our heads sadly and headed for the door. It looked like pointless milling was a gift that would go with us to the grave.

*

We found out the following morning that we hadn't been the only revolutionaries at the Rama that night. Over a highly inappropriate breakfast of chilli squid and noodles, we were interrupted at our chopstick fumblings by the sheepish likes of Roni and Tamir creeping up behind us.

"Hey," we grunted in a hungover chorus.

I glanced at Roni's unshaven grizzle and booze-dried lips and shuddered. I could've woken up next to that? Thanking God for small mercies, I mumbled through my sizzling seafood, "You didn't show up last night."

"We did," Roni muttered. "We just got, ah, sort of invited to leave."

"What the hell for?"

"Standing on the dance floor."

We were a wild and crazy bunch of kids.

Chapter Thirteen

Hello to What Unfortunately Is

El and I hung around Luang Prabang for the next few days doing nothing much apart from avoiding returning to Vientiane. With Roni and Tamir in tow, we lazed around in cafés and bars, strolled along the river and took a day trip out to the beautiful Khouang Sy Waterfall. It was an idyllic break from our usual dramas, made even more agreeable with the discovery of a back village "pharmacy" which sold unexpired Valium at ten cents a sheet. I made, and surprisingly kept, a vow not to indulge in narced-out bliss during the day, but night-time was a different matter entirely.

And so were plane trips. After four days of doing sweet bugger all, Roni and Tamir had packed their bags and ventured off to southern Thailand to resume their hunt for smoke and sex while we, inspired by their move and Lao Aviation's growing annoyance at us for continually changing our flight date, decided it was time to face the inevitable. We decided it was time to haul arse out of Laos. We'd been lucky so far, we figured. We hadn't been bazooka-ed out of existence by any rampaging hill tribes. We hadn't been riddled with internal parasites after drinking sludge supplied by a definitely non-rampaging hill tribe. We hadn't been lynched for changing our money on the black market and nobody had tried to hack off any of our limbs to replace their own. We'd even survived a Laotian disco. But it was only a matter of time before our luck ran out, and we'd decided it was time to start afresh. But that meant we had to get back to Vientiane, if only to pick up visas for our next destination and piss off again. And to get there, we had to conquer the infamous fear of flying. I guess spontaneous sex with strangers worked for Erica Jong and I intended getting fucked too. By about four hits of Valium.

*

With an early-morning slug of the local moonshine and a mouthful of pills, for all I knew I could have been going to the moon by the time we checked in at the Lao Aviation counter. Nothing could faze me, or a drugged-up El, for that matter—not even a blurry awareness that we'd be flying out on the very same rust bucket that we'd flown in on. All I wanted was somewhere to sit and drool, and if that place was hurtling dangerously close to treacherous mountaintops, so be it. Just let me slobber in peace.

It was the best flight of my life. By the time we landed in Vientiane, I wasn't even aware that we'd left Luang Prabang. Stressed-out housewives have definitely got the right idea.

*

It took us a while to collect both our wits and our luggage back at Pattay Airport, but by the time we staggered out into the furnace of Vientiane, we had at least regained the knack of speaking without salivating. While blathering inanely and chain-smoking were the full extent of my Valium-inspired talents, El enjoyed the added ability of remembering just what the hell our plans were for the day.

"Right then," she slurred, "find a tukkity tuk and then it's visa time."

I squinted stupidly, wiped the sweat from my brow and spoke—all at the same time. It took some effort. "Huh?"

"Passports. Visas. Remember?"

Dragging on another fag, I tried to think but it was all I could do to peer out of my pill-induced haze. Rational thought was within my reach, but it would be a few more moments till I got a good grip. "Nup," was the best I could do.

El's eyelids drooped then lifted in a monumental effort to pull herself together. "Visas," she almost shouted. "Visas for Vietnam. Today, remember?"

"Vaguely." I was coming out of the fog.

"We're going to Vietnam. Today. But we need visas. Jesus!" she slapped me lightly upside the head. "Snap out of it."

I snapped. Just a hint of El's wrath was enough to act as a psychological stomach pump, and my mind cleared. Enough for me to remember what we had planned for the day, which was almost enough to send me scurrying for the pill sheets again. We were going to Vietnam. Today. On a very shitty bus. Oh God.

But before we could even begin to dread the discomfort and hassle that inevitably awaited us on our cross-country odyssey, we had to get our entry visas. According to our nearly completely useless guidebooks, it takes up to four days to get a visa for Vietnam, but these are the same books that would have you believe Udon Thani is a traveller's delight and air travel in Laos is a respectable means of transportation. Besides, waiting was for suckers. We were going to march straight into the Vietnamese Embassy and march straight out with our visas. Surely all it would take was a handful of greenbacks and a convincing air of urgency, and we had both. With only a few precious hours before our bus hit the road, we were more than ready to present a portrayal of necessary haste.

We'd learnt that the way to get overland into Vietnam was by catching a bus to Savannakhet, a town in southern Laos some 200 kilometres from the border town of Lao Bao, the only legal land crossing between the two countries. The leg between Savannakhet and Lao Bao supposedly entailed a six-hour, spine-wrenching hellride along an unpaved mountain range, a trip which sounded like luxurious bliss after the horrors of Lao Aviation. But while we were prepared to risk partial paralysis on a bus that was most likely 400 years old and with a driver to match, we weren't ready to chance winding up in a Vietnamese gaol.

It was well documented that Vietnamese customs officials were nitpickingly meticulous when it came to searching the bags of any Westerner who entered the country at Lao Bao, often taking up to five hours to go through the grubby laundry of a whole busload of honkies. If you didn't mind waiting, and we certainly did, and you didn't have any contraband, and we hopefully didn't, then this was no problem. You bored yourself to tears all day in a grotty border compound then hopped back on the bus. But from the rumours we'd heard, tedium wasn't restricted to the fidgeting traveller. Customs officials, apparently weary of finding nothing to report among the crusty socks and mouldy towels of the average backpacker, had started planting drugs in the luggage of random voyagers and arresting them on the spot. This may have brightened up the otherwise ho-hum day of the man with the badge, but it didn't do much for the life of the accused. There were better ways to glimpse the "real" Vietnam than getting raped in a rat-infested Saigon big house.

But there was a loophole. For some reason, the Lao Bao guards apparently left alone anyone who crossed the border on foot, perhaps believing that any Westerner who couldn't afford a bus into Vietnam was too poor for bribes and too idiotic to smuggle. If we hopped off the bus before it crept into the compound, we could simply flash our visas and keep on walking. After that, it was thumbs out for the lads.

"So are you ready or what?" I blinked out of my reverie and stared at El, who was obviously quite lucid now—and well on her way to livid. "The bus goes at three and it's already eleven-thirty. Fuck, I don't know how we're going to make it."

I threw her a groggy smile and flagged a tuk tuk. "We'll make it, El. I guarantee it."

✳

With guarantees like that, I should've been a used-car salesman. By the time we got to the Vietnamese Embassy, it was already after midday, which to primary schools and government agencies can mean only one thing. Lunch.

"Oh, you bastards!" El howled as we rattled the locked embassy doors. "Open this goddamned door right now or I'm breaking the bloody thing down, you fuckers!" So much for the long-lasting effect of sedatives. "Open up, you fat pricks!"

Trying to recall the last time I'd seen an obese Vietnamese, I strolled around the side of the building and peered in an office window. As far as I could see, the entire place was deserted. What a waste of obscenities.

"Hey El, there's nobody here," I called. "They're all out stuffing their faces." I waited for another blast of vitriol, but there was only an eerie silence. "El?"

Fearing she'd been dragged away by security, I bolted back to the front of the building, only to find her silently but furiously kicking the wall, her face growing redder by the second. "What, El, what now?" Without saying a word, she pointed to a sign by the side of the door. Although it was written only in the unfathomable hieroglyphs of Vietnamese and the equally confusing slurs of French, you didn't have to be a linguist to figure out that this was bad news. A little paper clock had its moveable hands positioned at 2:15 p.m. and, while this almost certainly spelt our doom, I couldn't help but admire such dedication to inactivity. News of a two-hour-plus lunch break would give even the bludgers back home something to aspire to.

"Oh Christ," I muttered. Only a worker fuelled by dutiful alacrity and jet-propelled efficiency would be able to issue our visas in half an hour. Call me blinkered but, to my eyes, anyone who spent a quarter of their working day on the nosh was probably not a recognised model of customer service. "We're rooted."

El looked at me, her face suddenly glowing more with a sense of purpose than just crimson hostility. "No chance," she said, giving the building one last boot. "We're staying here till these lards get back from their extendo-feast and then we're going in there and demanding our visas."

I shuddered. I loved travelling with El and I loved how she never took any shit from anyone, but when she started using the word "demand," I couldn't help but think of security guards and manacles.

"Okay," I said. "Calmly demand, how's that?"

"Sure. Calmly, but forcefully. I mean really, it shouldn't even be such a drama. All they have to do is take our cash and stamp our passports. How hard is that?"

*

Until I got a look at the underachieving sloth that jockeyed the visa desk, I wouldn't have thought it hard at all. But to those weighed down by a long lunch and an unswerving commitment to making other people's lives a misery, everything bar acting the goat requires great effort.

We entered the embassy bang on 2:15 p.m., rejuvenated after a short snooze in the surrounding gardens, and headed straight for the counter marked "Visas." At first, it seemed like everything was going to go down a treat; there were no other applicants to be seen and we had what appeared to be the undivided attention of the visa issuer.

"Okay," El breathed, thrusting our passports, money and dog-ugly photographs across the desk. "Here's everything. We need to get these visas now, like right now. Our bus to Savannakhet is leaving in half an hour." She paused for a response. "Hello?"

As if suddenly realising where he was, the visa guy blinked twice then looked at us for the first time. I met his vacant eye and wondered briefly if he'd just returned from a liquid lunch or if this embassy, like so many government institutions the world over, made it a policy to hire only the most incompetent of its citizens.

"Help?" he said with a vacuity that left me unclear as to whether he was proffering assistance or begging it.

El drew a deep breath and began again, ". . . and our bus is going really soon," she finished.

"Visas, fine," the guy said. "Passports, please."

We nearly collapsed with relief. "Okay, but quick, please. That bus is going," I said, pushing the documents across the desk.

"Yes, quick. Fill these forms and please come back on Friday to pick up visas."

Bollocks to that. By Friday, I planned on having a wallet full of dong and turning down all the dog I could eat. "No, listen. We need the visas today."

"As in now," El growled, grabbing the forms. "Give me a pen, two pens. Quick!" Calm may have fallen by the wayside, but El was making good on the demanding part of the deal.

"Is okay," breezed the increasingly infuriating man behind the desk. "Fill in later and back by Friday." Either they didn't get many redheads back in Vietnam, or this guy had totally underestimated the fury of a carrot top with a bus to catch.

With creepy composure, El leant slowly over the counter. "Listen, mate," she hissed. "We are going on a bus to Vietnam. Today. We need those visas now. Not Friday. Now." Her tone sent chills up my spine, and I wondered if bunging on her Tarantino-villain voice had perhaps pushed things too far.

But, as it tends to do, even the slightest hint of imminent aggression worked wonders. After bugging his eyes out in stunned shock, the guy passed over two pens and opened a drawer containing visa stickers. "Yes," he whispered. "Visas."

"That's more like it," she said, drawing herself up. "And make it quick." She looked at the clock, which read a fearsome 2:35 p.m., and smiled grimly at me. "I still think we could make it."

But thick is thick, no matter how terrified it is, and our man was a plank. While he did manage to pick up the pace as he rushed off to make photocopies of our passports and tremblingly collected the inflated visa fee of seventy dollars each, he wasted precious moments writing in careful script on the entry documents, and even paused to admire our horrendous photographs. By the time we finally raced out of the building and found a tuk tuk to take us to the bus station, it was 2:50 p.m.

∗

There are few times in life that you actively notice a parallel universe sliding by before your very eyes. Despite the fact that we alter the course of our lives every moment of every day by doing ordinary things like leaving the house later than usual or even choosing to turn left rather than right, it's not something most sane people think about too much. If you did, I doubt you'd enjoy the pleasure of that sanity for very long.

But there are those rare moments when you can actually see your destiny veering off in a totally new direction, and at 3:01 on that hot Vientiane afternoon, we watched helplessly as ours headed south on a wheezing old bus. Thanks to the stumblings of but a few brief seconds, our lives had changed completely. If our tuk tuk driver hadn't stopped at that give-way sign, if the guy at the embassy hadn't looked at our photos for so long, if the bus driver hadn't decided to go against Laotian protocol by actually leaving on time, we would've made it. We would've been on our way to Vietnam instead of being left to stumble in the shadows of our parallel universe in a lopsided tuk tuk on the side of the road. Making that bus would have changed everything we ever did in our lives thereafter. I can only hope that in whatever alternate reality we found ourselves in, we're having a whale of a time.

"Well, there we go," I said as the bus wheezed down Mahosot Road. "Wave goodbye at What Could've Been."

"And say hello to What Unfortunately Is," El gasped as its exhaust fumes enveloped the tuk tuk. "Stranded in Vientiane, being farted on by a bus. This new-look destiny isn't looking so crash hot."

It really wasn't. Besides writhing in the flatulence of the incongruously on-time bus, we were also attracting unwanted attention. Our tuk tuk had stalled and, much to the vocal annoyance of the rest of the traffic, we were blocking a major entrance to the bus station.

Not that it should've mattered, considering the station was such a chaotic sprawl anyway: dozens of clapped-out buses, nodding lazily beneath the weight of travelling families and livestock, were pulled up wherever they could find a space in the dirt, while the ubiquitous tuk tuks and gaudy scooters buzzed around them like mosquitoes. A makeshift market congregated around the overloaded jalopies, with dozens of food-on-a-stick vendors hawking last-minute feeds to would-be passengers. Vehicles squeezed through whatever gap in the crowds they could find, and people were sent sprawling every time an impatient driver stepped on the gas. Where we had stalled had only become a thoroughfare rather than just another gap in the crowd because it gave otherwise bored people something to honk about.

At least they had klaxons to toot away their tedium. We, on the other hand, were hornless, hot and beginning to wilt beneath the bedlam we'd initially found so invigorating. In order to participate in the great Southeast Asian pastime of pandemonium, you need a strong shouting voice, a loud instrument (preferably not musical) and a steel will hellbent on irritating the shit out of other people while achieving for yourself a suitable gain. Usually, as much as we bitched and moaned about it, we enjoyed taking part in the game. At least it gave us the chance to do and say things that would have gotten us deported from any so-called first world nations. But the departure of the bus had left us feeling exhausted and trapped, and we couldn't even summon a feeble "fuck off" when a group of touts surrounded our bedraggled tuk tuk and tried to sell us offal. We were all chaos-ed out.

If we'd been of Pancho's ilk, we could have found rejuvenation in meditation, but despite a frightening bent towards airheadedness, we both found it almost impossible to do the required empty-your-mind thing. If Laos's dodgy "pharmacies" had been more up with the times, we could've scored ourselves some Prozac to chase away those bedlam blues. And there was nobody in the immediate vicinity who looked like they were keen on cheering us up with a few hours of sexual therapy. So we had no choice but to smother our sorrows in the time-honoured fashion employed by women around the world: binge eating.

Every woman worth her Wonderbra knows that chocolate is better than sex and that the agony of a relationship break-up/job loss/finding nothing good to watch on TV can be cured by ramming an entire tub of triple-swirl ice cream down her throat. Bad hair day? A deep-fried pizza will make it all better. Husband working suspiciously late again? Wolf down the entire contents of your fridge and let the bastard starve. Stuck in a third world traffic jam with chicken intestines being waved in your face? Get out there and get some chow into ya. It'll work wonders.

✳

After making up our minds to leave the Mahosot Road Station eating our dust while we hastened to devour things of a more edible manner, we paid off our still-stuck tuk tuk driver and lugged ourselves and our packs into a spluttering, yet mobile, songthaew, bingeward-bound. On the way, we panted in anticipation of a mammoth schnarf-up and I prayed that recent days spent devouring nothing but squid, unclassifiable market swill and pharmaceuticals hadn't shrunk my stomach. If I couldn't demolish at least two full-sized meals in one sitting, I was going to be very depressed.

I needn't have worried; once a pig, always a pig. Despite the fact that my inner swine had been slumbering for a while, it awoke with a fury the instant we pulled up in front of an outdoor café with a sign boasting "USA steaks," and it didn't think about retiring to its sty even after I'd gnawed my way through two starters, a main and dessert. I didn't really mind that my "USA steak" tasted more like Laotian horsemeat, and El only retched once when she found a random piece of variety meat in her soup, but we decided over post-gorge cigarettes that we couldn't possibly close the day's feastings on even a slightly nauseating note. We'd simply have to go somewhere else.

Like a rheumy-eyed old man lurching from bar to bar, seeking just one more cheap whiskey shot to put him out of his misery, we waddled across Vientiane for hours, trying to find salvation in satiation. We slurped up dahl and paneer cheese at one of the surprisingly numerous Indian cafés along the Mekong, vacuumed up bowls of noodles in an inner-city hole in the wall and polished off a plate of Laotian spring rolls in a sweaty corner shop. It was only when we found ourselves struggling to force down a salad in the strangely named "Just for Fun" vegetarian restaurant that we realised our quest for fulfilment had come to a satisfying end. Our guts were bursting, our heads were swimming happily in food-triggered endorphins and we'd out-eaten any other depressed females I'd ever known. Forget those lightweights who found it terribly indulgent to sneak a box of cherry chocolates in front of Ricki Lake. We were the masters of our race.

But with champion gluttony comes contentment, and with contentment comes an overwhelming lethargy. If your restaurant is some kind of foodie variation on the opium den, and comes with mattresses beneath every table, then your bliss is complete. Unfortunately, this kind of customer service was sadly lacking in Laos, leaving us with no choice but to go home and snore it off in private. All we needed was a home.

It wasn't that difficult compared to some of the accommodation problems we'd had so far. Although no tuk tuks stopped for us outside the restaurant, assuming correctly that the combined weight of our baggage and our bellies would pop their tyres, we managed to stagger a few blocks before winding up at a not-completely-trashed guesthouse. And while the lady at the desk was obviously none too taken with the explosive belchings that punctuated our requests for a bed, she nevertheless found us a room.

"Only one night," she scolded, as she led us up the stairs.

"Whatever," I said, already unbuttoning my jeans. "Burp."

The room was nondescript and grey, but it had two beds and its own toilet. For two oversized gluttons with heavy lids and an impending food hangover, it was enough. We dumped our bags and went to sit on the roof for some fresh air. Our feet dangling two storeys above the grimy Vientiane streets, we watched as two stray dogs made odd whining noises, burrowed through a pile of rubbish then ran aimlessly up and down the block.

"Not only are we now living in a parallel universe in Vietnam somewhere," El said, "but I think I've found our canine reincarnations."

"Yeah," I replied sleepily as one of the mutts began to yelp at a passer-by. "It's a great life."

We went to bed not long afterwards.

Chapter Fourteen

Savannakhet: Byword for Hell (Part II)

Veisalgia, the medical word for a hangover, comes from a Norwegian term meaning "uneasiness after debauchery," and while most people don't usually equate dahl with debauchery, believe me, there is a link. El and I awoke to find our heads throbbing and our bellies exploding. Never mind the horsemeat, the offal, the light and the healthy, it was the Indian food that came back to haunt us with a vengeance.

We could've powered a car with all the gas floating around our room, and outmoaned any porno film on the market. Our stomachs were seriously disturbed, and we weren't afraid to complain about it, through whatever orifice we saw fit. But in between the crudenesses associated with any gastronomic overindulgence, we still managed to retain a sense of excitement. We were going to Vietnam, and looseness of the bowels be damned. It was going to take a lot more than jelly belly to keep us off the bus this time.

Being late wasn't even an option. We'd passed out early the night before, thanks to the soporific consequences of excess, and after we finished fighting over the toilet, using it then using it again, it was still only 8:30 a.m. Plenty of time before the three o'clock bus . . . but not too much before the one that left at ten.

"Whaddya mean, it goes at ten?" El yelped. "What happened to three?" We'd been trying to check out before anyone got a good whiff of our unfortunate room, but the desk girl's shock announcement had us frozen in the lobby.

"Yes, the bus to Savannakhet leaves today at ten this morning," she replied in a "well, duh" tone of voice. We stared back at her blankly as she tried to clear it up, using her particular brand of logic: "It's Wednesday." Oh, Wednesday. Of course. In the same way that Thursdays across the Western world are late-night shopping and everyone goes to the movies on "tight-arse" Tuesdays, Wednesday in Southeast Asia is obviously the day set aside for timetable anarchy.

"Shit!" El barked, looking at the clock. "Quick, we've got to bolt, like now!" She threw the room key on the desk and hustled outside. "Move it," she called from the pavement.

I nodded at the girl, who was looking at us like we were a rare breed of clowns indeed, and shuffled out calmly. "El!" I grabbed her as she whistled at a fully laden tuk tuk. "We'll make it this time. We've got well over an hour."

She shook me off her arm and waved down a couple of thin boys on dinky mopeds. "I'm not willing to risk it," she said, jogging over to them. "Don't you think it's time we blew this popsicle stand?"

It was. Despite all the complaining, I'd developed a certain affinity for Vientiane—any capital city whose streets are paved in mud got a big thumbs up from me, and the locals were beaut—but it was also billed as "The Quietest Capital" in the world, despite its clamorous traffic jams, and it was getting to me. Between tucking kip into the pockets of slithering beggars, dodging bum-pinching midgets and doing irreparable damage to my ears while straining to "listen to the rice grow," there wasn't really a great deal to do. It was time to beat a hasty retreat.

El motioned me over to the bikes. "They're going to take us to the bus station," she said, nodding at the smiling lads. "I've already explained our need for speed and they reckon we'll be there in a couple of minutes."

"Brilliant," I smiled. "But, um, how the hell do we get on these things?" The scooters were smaller than your average postie bike and, from the pathetic whines coming from their engines, sounded like they were hard-pressed ferrying the tiny Laotian boys around, let alone two oafs and their backpacks.

But the boys had it all worked out. "Your bag, miss," one of them said, pointing at my oversized luggage. I looked at him in horror. It was nearly breaking my spine and I could foresee another cripple on the streets if I handed it to this 50-kilo duckling. Reading the doubt in my face, he smiled. "Please, it's okay."

Tentatively, I hitched it off my back and, with a great "ooof," lugged it over to him. With the strength of a weightlifter and infinitely more grace, he lithely tossed it onto the scooter's footrest area, leaving no place for his legs. "But where will you put your feet?" I asked. Having owned a scooter during university, I knew there wasn't anywhere else for them to go, unless you flung them over the handlebars—it's amazing what one picks up during those enlightened years of higher learning.

"No problem, I sit like this." He hopped on to the bike and, sylph-like, crossed his legs in the lotus position atop the pack. "Now, you sit." He flashed me a famous Laotian smile and patted the inch or so where I was supposed to park my girth.

"But how . . . ?"

El, who was already sitting side-saddle behind her driver, motioned to me impatiently. "Get on, for Christ's sake, and never mind the philosophy behind it all. Let's go!"

I sighed and perched myself on the rear edge of the seat, trying to hold my legs together over the exhaust pipe. The local women always looked so elegant when they rode side-saddle, but

I looked like a toad about to fall off a rock. It certainly wasn't as easy as it looked, and, my muscle control being close to nil, my leg spasmed after about two seconds and I burnt my calf on the red-hot muffler.

It's not hard to imagine the volume and intensity with which I let loose my torrent of obscenities. Exhaust pipes are made of metal, a great conductor of heat, and are not the ideal thing to rest a body part against. For a person with a pain threshold so low that she lived for two years with dreadlocks just to avoid the discomfort of brushing the knots out of her hair, the agony of the burn was excruciating. But there was nothing I could do about it—we had a bus to catch.

I tapped the driver on the shoulder and nodded grimly. With a high-pitched buzz and a quick bip of the ridiculous horn, we took off into the traffic, a convoy of drooping bums, sizzling flesh and flapping rucksacks fronted by two young boys looking like pint-sized yogis on wheels.

As ludicrous as it may have felt to us, our bizarre procession was nothing out of the ordinary to the people of Vientiane. Nobody even looked twice as we spluttered by. They, like most people in Southeast Asia, had no qualms about piling their entire families, from the four kids up to grandma and the chooks, on board their rinky-dink mopeds. People literally moved house on their mopeds, carried goats and baskets and whole market stalls on them. The entire place ran solely on the power of Nifty Fifties. Coming from Australia, a land that depends on 52-metre roadtrains to deliver food to its people, and 80-seater buses to move said chowhounds around, I felt like we'd suddenly landed in Lilliput.

But somehow, it worked. Sure, I wound up with a plate-sized blister on my calf and yeah, we met death face to face a couple of times on those slippery muddy roads, but we got there. Nobody wore helmets and our drivers kept trying to feel us up, but it was a great service. And what cab driver in Australia would drive the wrong way up a one-way street to get you to the bus on time?

*

But while we were, for once, punctual, the same couldn't be said for our bus. Panting, mud-splattered and anxious, we bolted off the bikes at Mahosot Road and straight up to the bus counter. They sold us our tickets and then let us have it: the bus was going to be nearly four hours late. It smelled like disaster. What were the chances of us being on time for a bus twice in one day? We skulked away and prepared for the worst.

In a nearby Scandinavian bakery we whiled away the hours over coffee and pastries, with our eyes alternately glued to the clock and a TV set tuned to CNN. Immersed in our own trials and tribulations, we'd completely forgotten that there was a world out there that didn't revolve around us trying to catch a bus. As I shoved the remainder of a bagel down my throat and we got up to leave, I decided that, while travelling anyway, I'd give the news a break. I liked the world revolving around me trying to catch a bus.

*

Thankfully, miraculously, my world didn't spin off its axis that day. With time to spare, we made it back to the station and, with surprisingly little fuss, clambered aboard the bus to await our departure.

Dilapidated, top-heavy and looking more like a curio than any real means of transportation, it was the doppelgänger of every other bus at the station. The windows were smeared with the remnant grime of a hundred sweaty journeys and the mismatched wheels were hubless and filthy. Any luggage was chucked by wiry porters onto the roof of the bus and moored beneath a tired-looking net. Inside, two long rows of comfortless seats groaned and creaked in weary anticipation of another torturous journey while the entire vehicle juddered as the driver tested his revs. A radio speaker above the windscreen crackled with static and the tinny squalls of a homegrown pop band, and a stick of incense burned by the steering wheel. Greyhound it wasn't, but it seemed like nothing out of the ordinary to the other passengers.

Not that they struck me as being particularly ordinary themselves. Happily squashed four-to-a-row in seats that only just coped with mine and El's combined circumferences, our fellow travellers were largely a mix of Laotian and Vietnamese men who seemed to be taking part in either an extended bender or some kind of bachelor party. With just enough room to breathe, shout and tightly cavort, the men were knocking back what appeared to be a mixture of tar and gnarly herb roots from long glass jars, mysteriously refilling them from an unseen source beneath the seats. After every prolonged gulp, they'd let loose with a wild cheer, smash their jars together and empty more of the foul-looking stuff down their throats. Riding a booze bus between inner-city strip joints was one thing, but hosting a stag on an eight-hour cross-country trek was something else entirely.

At least they were generous. As we fidgeted in the close, boiling confines of the bus and prayed for it to get a wriggle on, bloke after bloke broke free from the gnarl of revellers to offer us a sip of their esoteric swill. I have to admit I was tempted to find out what watered-down bitumen actually tasted like, but after I stuck my nose into a proffered glass of the rancid-smelling hooch, I politely turned them down. El, who was not as given as I was to investigating local tipples, merely retched in the face of anyone who volunteered their glass and by the time the bus inched out of the station, we were largely forgotten as their party launched into full swing.

Rattled, roasting and cramped, I couldn't have thought of a worse place for a drunken shindig, but to the lads, the rundown bus was a party palace. While El and I spent the first few hours of the trip smoking out the window and languishing in a silence brought on by heat exhaustion, they took turns at uproariously harassing the driver for piss stops, dancing unsteadily in the narrow aisle and breaking into bawdy song. What with their black brew, maladroit jigs and balladeering, it was like being in an Irish bar gone hideously wrong. Who were these people, the O'Xiengs?

But everyone who spends a steamy afternoon on the turps must pass out eventually, and by the time we wheeled into a village marking the halfway point of the journey, the bus hummed with acrid snoring. By that time, though, they could've been doing the charleston on the ceiling for all we cared. The monolingual bus driver had used charades to let us know that we'd be stopping in the village for something to eat and, despite our indulgent wolfing the night before and a belly stuffed full of pastries, we had become suddenly ravenous. With a haste known only to athletes and hungry gluttons sniffing out a meal, we uncricked our knotted bones and clambered over the sprawled limbs of the sleeping drunks.

The village looked less like a settlement than a golden commercial opportunity. There were no established buildings along the ditched and dusty road, but dozens of food vendors and their portable stands had created a booming, if temporary, mercantile paradise for themselves. By accident or design, it looked like every bus in Laos stopped here for a meal break, with the vendors knowing well before the driver when they would roll in. By the time our feet hit the dust, the itinerant chefs were taking their meat off the grill and their stews off the boil, all ready to serve up.

But, while there was enough food to thrice feed all the buses loitering in the village, there wasn't anything for us. Grilled chicken claws clamped between wooden sticks, fermented oxtail soup and some kind of fried eel may have been a tempting spread for your average road-weary Laotian, but I would rather have gnawed on a tree stump.

In the end, we persuaded a fish-head monger to dish us up a single bowl of plain rice, hold the brains. Wearily battling each other for the lion's share of overcooked grains of white rice made an unwelcome change from our recent oinkfests, but it was food nonetheless. With nobody on board our bus who spoke English, we had no idea if we'd be stopping again before our late-night arrival in Savannakhet, and no way of knowing if we'd be able to find somewhere to eat when we arrived. I wondered how many days of starvation it would take before I relented and opened my jaws to a plate of pig guts and lotus root, and figured on at least a calendar month.

Dusk was falling by the time we were whistled back on to the bus and, once we had stuffed ourselves back into our seats, we couldn't see anything but blurred shadows out of the smudged windows. Not that we were missing out on any awe-inspiring scenery. Since leaving Vientiane, potholes had been the only undulations we'd hit on the otherwise flat dirt roads as Laos jolted by in unremarkable scrub and the occasional flea-bitten village. Nobody stood along the road to wave us on, doubtless preferring to hang around in the lush forests that hid behind the sooty wayside scrub and, apart from the food market, we'd encountered no other people or vehicles along the way.

With nothing else to do but play highly unproductive rounds of I Spy ("Something beginning with B" . . . "Bus?" . . . "Damn!") and rub road dust from our eyes, the remainder of the trip passed like a slow dream. We only stopped a few times, when the driver screeched to a whiplash halt in the middle of some moonlit nowhere and booted out handfuls of the groaning Laotian booze artists. I presumed they were being let off at their designated drop-off points, but if they could find anything resembling civilisation in that featureless night, I'd have to reconsider my stance on drinking black ooze.

*

It was past ten o'clock when we rumbled into Savannakhet's bus terminal, but it was far from deserted. Two other buses sat beneath a row of yellow streetlights and a bunch of soldiers were lolling about outside a shadowy toilet block. At a small market in the parking lot that skirted the main depot, a surprising number of foreign backpackers were strolling around, examining tableloads of plastic necklaces and coconut-flavoured soft drinks. Apart from the annoying presence of these other farang, who were doubtless waiting for the bus to Lao Bao, we saw no reason why we shouldn't have a smooth changeover in Savannakhet. Unlike the bus station in Vientiane, this one appeared orderly and run with a sliver of professionalism, and it sat on what I guessed was the only paved tract in central Laos. We didn't foresee having any worries here.

But that's why we don't read crystal balls for a living.

*

"Wanna get our tickets?" We had been the first off the bus and were standing around shivering in the brisk night air, waiting for our packs to be thrown down.

"In a bit," El said, jumping aside as our rucksacks bombed onto the pavement. "The next bus doesn't go until midnight and I doubt it'll be such a drama. Anyway, I'm busting."

After swilling four bottles of water on the bus to keep the hunger at bay, so was I. Slinging my brick-heavy pack over one shoulder, I nodded at her and we limped lopsidedly towards the toilet block. "A piss, some food and our tickets. Ah, the simplicity of life."

"Yeah," El said, "but it better be cheap." I nodded again. Before leaving Vientiane, we'd carefully counted up what kip we had left and combined it, saving only enough for the two legs of the journey to Vietnam and a few nibbles on the way. Because kip was pretty much worthless outside Laos, there was no point in changing any more greenbacks. After buying the tickets to Savannakhet and our meagre rice lunch, we had just over twelve thousand kip left, enough for two one-way tickets to Lao Bao.

"We should be right," I said, patting the wad of stashed kip in my money pouch. "Some noodles or something should only be a couple of hundred. But first things first. Jesus," I clutched at my belly, "I'm seriously about to piss myself. Let's move it, people."

The toilet block had five cubicles, all engaged. In front of us, two Laotians hopped impatiently beneath the buzzing lampposts while El and I crossed our legs tightly and muttered under our breath. Thankfully, the locals either had very small bladders or were just in there to copy a phone number off the wall, and after only a few agonising seconds, it was our turn.

We were mid-bolt to the loo when we crashed into a wiry man in some kind of uniform. "'Scuse me, mate," I murmured, and waited for him to step aside. He didn't.

"Money," he announced with an authoritative air. "Two hundred kip for the toilet."

While it was easy to say that I would've paid a million bucks to piss in peace, there was no way I was shelling out our precious kip. Besides, nobody who'd used the bathroom before us seemed to have taken anything out of their trousers apart from the required part of their anatomy.

Bent double in the classic Bladder Bursting position, El looked up from her knees. "You've gotta be joking me."

"No kip, no toilet." The soldier or loomaster or whatever he was smiled the grin of the triumphant. "You must use it, you must pay."

"Jesus wept!" I groaned. "It's not fair. Nobody else had to pay."

"Two hundred. Each."

We had no choice, unless we wanted to let it all hang out beneath the glaring yellow lights. I doubt we could've relieved ourselves in such a fashion anyway, even if we were gutsy enough to shuck off our shorts in protest. A research experiment I'd heard of had locked twenty people in a room for an hour, filled them up with soft drink then, when they were busting, had denied them the use of the toilet. If they wanted to piss, the researchers said, they'd have to do it on the floor, in front of everyone. Not a single person could do it, preferring to clutch their groins in a frenzy of pain and social conditioning. As fully fledged members of the potty-trained culture ourselves, we could do nothing but swallow our pride and pay.

What a bargain. For two hundred kip, I not only got to relieve myself, but I got to visit the world's most revolting toilet. In the shadows cast by the yellow light outside, I squatted precariously over a raised and stained hole in the ground, balancing myself by holding the splattered walls on either side. There was no toilet paper, not even the usual bowl of water for rinsing—but there were lots of cockroaches, so I guess that made up for it. As I stood up and scraped my hands on a clean patch of wall, I decided I'd have to rethink my beliefs on pissing in public. Exposure couldn't be as bad as this.

"Well, that was worth it," El said when we met outside the block. "Let's go see what other revolting things we can spend our kip on. Maybe they'd like a couple of hundred for sitting on those benches over there. Surely they're crawling with bacteria."

"Or at least cockroaches," I said, shuddering. "I've had enough of hovering my arse above bugs looking for a home. Let's get our tickets before we run out of cash."

We hobbled past a blathering collection of scruffy farang chilling out on the waiting benches, pausing only to flinch when we heard a guitar being strummed, and found the ticket sales office. Lit by a single swaying bulb and empty but for a couple of uniformed guards and a plywood desk with a grossly fat, moustachioed man stuffed behind it, the office looked more like an interrogation room than somewhere to kick off your dream holiday. I had a strange feeling of dread. The fat guy—obesity being a rarity in Laos—had a taunting smirk on his face that was more reminiscent of an underworld boss than your average happy-go-lucky Asian. If he was some kind of don though, he hadn't enough sense to hire himself a Gucci stylist. His wobbling frame was swathed in a fluorescent Hawaiian shirt that was more likely to prompt a headache than respect. Even the guards looked more like henchmen than any joe on the beat, and were busy sizing us up in a way that made me think about cannibals.

But, as freaky as it looked, it had a sign reading "Tickets" above the door, and that's what we were there for. If those guys wanted to play Hawaii Don and the Thugs, good luck to them. We just wanted our tickets.

"Hi," El said, approaching the desk. "We need two one-way tickets for the bus to Lao Bao tonight please."

I could've sworn I saw the fat guy wink at one of the guards. "That is twelve thousand kip, please," he said in accented but clear English.

El sighed in audible relief. We'd been prepared for a shakedown, but maybe he was just some glandularly inconvenienced ticket guy. The guards were probably just hungry. "Great," she said. "Here," I handed her my money belt and she pulled out the wad of kip. "Should be twelve thousand exactly."

The man coolly regarded the pile of money then turned his eyes back to El. "And which one of you needs the ticket?"

"No," I said slowly from behind El. Maybe his English wasn't as good as it sounded. "It's only for one way. Six thousand kip each. That's for two."

He laughed hoarsely and flicked lightly at the money. "No, Miss. The tickets to Lao Bao are twelve thousand each."

Still floundering in naivety, I tried to explain. "No, see, we're not crossing the border on the bus. We're not carrying on from there. We're getting off before it. It's six thousand, it's printed in all the guides. And that's each."

"I understand," he said, looking shiftily at a smirking guard. "But you do not. Twelve thousand kip for both of you. And that's . . ." he definitely winked this time, "each."

"You thieving bastard!" El erupted, everything suddenly clear to her. "Just because there's a bunch of tourists out here tonight who don't know any better, you think you can rip us all off!"

He fingered one of his chins and struck a falsely pensive pose. "Yes, they did pay twelve thousand each. But it was no problem. I tell them the cost, they pay."

"So you're admitting to ripping us off," I cried.

"Not at all. It's the price, they pay. And you pay also, please." Behind him, one of the guards actually began to snicker. It reminded me of how my little brother would giggle when I got in trouble for something he did—the most infuriating noise in the world.

It was on. "Listen here, buddy," El snarled. "We know the real price and we're paying it."

"Twelve thousand is the real . . ."

She cut him off with an apoplectic shriek. "No! It isn't!" She banged her fists on the table and I flinched, imagining the response of the guards. But they didn't care. They were all laughing. "We only have six thousand each, that's all we bloody have. Give us the tickets!"

As if waving away a slightly annoying fly, he shrugged her off. "If you don't have the money, please go away. Maybe you try again in the morning. I think this office is now closed." Don Fatpiggio had spoken.

As he roared something of obvious amusement to the tittering guards, we backed out of the office shaking with rage. I swear I could see smoke pouring out of El's ears and I felt like my face had been stained scarlet. Corruption of my own youth was one thing, but barefaced rorting by a public official was something else entirely. Besides, even if we wanted to fund his collection of garish garb, we couldn't. We just didn't have the cash.

✳

Exhausted and pissed off, we collapsed on to the hard wooden benches that served as an outdoor waiting room. Most of the backpackers had gone to wait beside the imminently departing Lao Bao bus, and apart from a handful of suss-looking locals and an American couple huddled beneath a sleeping bag, the depot was ours to scream down. Which we did.

We ranted and raved, we took our vocabulary on a field trip of the truly obscene, but none of it seemed foul enough to sum up our dire loathing for the mercenary mongrel larding it up in the ticket office. Not only was he trying to hoodwink money we didn't have, he was obviously trying to literally freeze us out as well. Bare-shouldered and with naught but bad tempers to keep our blood boiling, we were headed for hypothermia out there.

And if the climate didn't get us, the people surely would. Someone had forgotten to tell the beady-eyed Savannakhetians who were inexplicably loitering at the bus station that smiling was supposed to be their national pastime. Grimacing with bad intent, they formed a rogue's gallery around us, instilling in me something less than a supreme confidence that I'd get through the night in one piece. It was shaping up to be one hell of a slumber party.

But maybe, just maybe, we wouldn't have to face it all on our lonesomes. The American couple was still hunkered down beneath their sleeping bag. I hoped they too had revolted against the jobbery of the evil fatman and, like us, were waiting for the morning when we could purchase a ticket for the correct fare. We could all spend the night together as revolutionaries, suffering for our cause, protecting one another from the varied treacheries of those who wished to torment us. Besides, we might even get a go under that toasty-looking sleeping bag.

No such luck. When I asked them if they planned on sticking around for the night, I was met with the sort of disdainful glare and haughty snort usually reserved by the British upper-class when asked if they wanted tinned beans on toast for breakfast. "As if," the girl said. "I can think of nothing worse than waiting around this dump all night."

"Yeah," said her boyfriend. "Have you seen the looks on these people's faces?" I said I most certainly had. "They look like they're waiting for us to fall asleep so they can eat us or something." Just what I wanted to hear—a sane person's confirmation of my most irrational fear.

"I can't see why you guys don't just pay the money," the girl, who introduced herself as Olympia, said. "It's not like it's a fortune or anything."

I was about to calmly explain that, far from being some sort of consumer rights brigade taking a stand on overpriced ticket fares, we simply did not have the cash, when El did it for me in a most un-calm word salad of scatologies and frenzied screeches. After a few moments of foaming vitriol, she began to settle down and had gotten to the less agitated stage of tutting vehemently when the sound of a nearby guitar picking out the notes of "Peace Train" sent her spiralling off again. "And as for these fucking hippies . . ." she launched, waving her arms. "Shut up!"

"That's it," Olympia spat, standing up in time with her boyfriend. "We're so outta here." As they grabbed their bags, she shot a disgusted glare at El and flashed me a look of sympathy. "Good luck," she said, casting a meaningful glance at my best friend. "You wanna get some sedatives or something for that one."

"Fuck you!" I said, surprising myself. "She's just bloody upset, so don't diss my best mate, got it?"

They got it alright. They got it and then they got out of there so fast it made my head spin. Or maybe it was just the situation that sent me suddenly giddy. It was bad: El wasn't usually quite this vitriolic; I rarely swore at people with grand names derived from Greek mythology; and I never, ever used the word "diss." It was time to get out of here before any more of my vocabulary lapsed into South Central LA.

El caught my vibe. "Right," she yelled, leaping off the bench, "that's it!" She tossed her hair back and, with the most purposeful stride I'd ever seen, stormed off in the direction of the ticket office, leaving me completely surrounded by nonplussed Laotians. Our charming display of ill-breeding and social ineptitude had not been lost on them, and they couldn't wait to see what would happen next. When it became clear that Act II would consist solely of me shivering gormlessly as the echoes of El's screams drifted out of the nearby ticket office, they decided to speed up the action with a bit of audience participation. When I curled up on the hard bench, one of them came and sat directly next to my protruding bum and stared at it. When I sighed, another one leant over and peered into my ear hole. When I did absolutely nothing for ten seconds, a man in a moustache came over and prodded my foot. And when I ran out of options and stood up, half the crowd stood up with me. It was either an ovation or a threat, and I wasn't sticking around to see if they would throw roses. Grabbing both our rucksacks, I tottered off, to the grumbles and growls of the restless peanut gallery.

But even before I stumbled through the open door of the ticket office, I could hear El's wailing demands, her choked sobs of frustration and the loud bangings on the table. I knew from experience that if El had moved on from mere anguished tirade to physical force against an inanimate object, things were getting ugly.

From the moment I appeared on the scene, they got even uglier. In a climax of drama and bad timing, everything happened at once: I started swearing; the fat guy started screaming; the bus to Lao Bao started revving; and a farang started whining, "C'maan, man, just pay the money. This driver guy's waiting and we wanna get out of here." It wasn't coincidence, it was just collision.

El and I whirled around with expressions more devilish than dervish and peered angrily outside to confront the sniveller. Through the darkness, we could just make out the lumpy silhouette of a man, backpack, duffel bag and dangling guitar, but when he stepped into the streetlight, his identity became painfully clear. Karma of all karmas, it was Pancho—the Original Pancho of Nong Khai, our arch nemesis and ultra-anathema to us two anti-hippies. Either our karmas really were buggered or the Kingdom of Thailand had booted him out on the grounds of cultural irritation. But screw it. We weren't into pre-destination. Pancho was going down, and we were getting on that bus.

In a chorus of charm and exemplary harmonising, we carolled out a resounding "Get stuffed" to the whiny figure, and turned back to face the sweating fat man behind his desk. "Look, mate," I said, "that bus is about to go. We're getting on it, so let's have those tickets."

Wiping his brow with an exhaustion that looked ripe to tumble into submission, he opened his mouth to speak but was beaten at the gate. "Just pay the guy, jeez! C'maaaaan!"

El, a.k.a. Linda Blair, swivelled her head around and let loose with the verbal equivalent of green bile. "Look, you imbecilic lentil, we don't have the money. This guy's ripping us off, so shove your guitar up your arse and be quiet, for fuck's sake." Her head pivoted back to rest in its rightful position, facing the fat guy, and she spoke with a measured degree of calm. "Can we have the tickets now? Please."

Obviously bored to tears by the entire debacle and unwilling to face the prospect of putting up with us until the morning, the fat guy relented. "Ask the bus driver," he sighed. "If he says yes, then—"

"C'mAAAAAAAAAN!"

For his mantra, Pancho had chosen a pretty poor one. But I guess our respondent "Piss off!" wasn't much better. There was certainly a communication problem between the flower people and we of the whipper-snipper philosophy. But it didn't really matter. Nasal hippie whinging or not, we were on that bus, so long as the driver agreed.

Not that we were going to give him a chance to say no. Under cover of the moonless night El ran towards the driver, for the benefit of the watching fat guy, while giving Pancho a good old-fashioned tongue lashing. Panting, she ran back into the office. "He says it's fine," she lied, throwing the sweaty, crumpled kip at the fat guy. "Can we go now?"

Emitting a huge sigh that welled from the far-off bottom of his gargantuan stomach, the fat guy waved us off and wearily signalled to the driver to take us on. After all that drama, he didn't even bother to write us out tickets or anything, which was a shame. I would've liked to have kept the stubs as tangible evidence that with a lot of harassment and a large vocabulary of abusive language, you can achieve anything.

Chapter Fifteen

The Disco Bus

When I was in my late teens, there was a "Disco Train" that ran between Cairns and Brisbane. For a slightly inflated fare, passengers could boogie away the 24-hour journey in a clackety carriage lit by a madly swinging glitterball while the sugarcane scenery hurtled past the darkened windows. But when Queensland's fascist anti-smoking, anti-fun regulations came through in the early 1990s, the "Disco Train" was derailed forever, and I bade a sad farewell to what I considered a locomotive heyday.

But here, nearly a decade later, I'd found the reincarnation of the "Disco Train." Granted, it was a bus and I wasn't lurching to the sounds of "Ring My Bell," Midori cocktail in hand, but it was disco transport none the less. As smoke-filled and uncomfortably cramped as any nightclub, the otherwise pitch-dark interior of the bus twinkled with the spin of a homemade disco ball hung above the driver's seat. Lit up by meticulously positioned spotlights, the ball sent shards of silver light careening across the tired faces of our fellow passengers and, surreally, over the day-glo Buddha statuettes superglued on to the dash. And in case the glittery flickers weren't enough to induce epilepsy, the driver had seen fit to install beat-sensitive light speakers, which flashed different beams of colour with every change of tempo.

But it was here that the disco similarities gave way to a simpler, less appealing era. Instead of cranking up the appropriate caterwauls of Gloria Gaynor or at least the Bee Gees, the speakers were emitting slow green beams of light to the lethargic tempo of "Hotel California." Not disco, but so very, very Pancho.

Clambering in through the back door, we took in all of this with fleeting doubts about our sanity before remembering that this was Laos and everything was nuts. Given everything we'd seen and done in this sliver of a country, it shouldn't have surprised us if the driver turned out to be a drag version of Tina Turner in a red-sequinned muu-muu. Not even the fact that Pancho, some more of his clones and a gaggle of Panchettes were openly lighting joints up the front was startling. In fact, the only thing that did throw us a bit was that the seats looked large enough to comfortably hold two normal-sized human beings.

"Aaaah," El gasped, collapsing into the one pair of seats still unoccupied, "comfort at last." She sprawled across the two seats with such a look of contentment that I decided I couldn't possibly rob her of the chance of a few hours of blissful relaxation before we got to Lao Bao. Besides, I didn't want to risk El making a scene at the notoriously stern Vietnamese border due to sleep deprivation. Better for me to have a highly uncomfortable bus trip than be stuck on death row in Saigon thanks to dodgy drug charges.

With a grand gesture, I told El that she could have the two seats to herself, while I would crash on the pile of backpacks that clogged the aisle. "It'll be fine," I said, when she wearily protested. "Hopefully this is Pancho's pack I'm wriggling around on. Surely he's got something breakable in there."

The idea of me squashing something of Pancho's seemed to placate her, so as she rolled herself a pillow of travel-soiled T-shirts, I adjusted myself on the bedraggled pile of rucksacks. Apart from a vague musty smell and the intolerable thought of the hippies' crusty laundry fuming beneath me, I was actually very comfortable. It was somewhat akin to lying on a hundred cushions in the tent of a sheikh, without the sheikh. And who wants some arrogant male chauvinist around when you're chilling out?

But to ensure our sense of luxury didn't wear thin after the bus started rolling, we decided to pop a few tabs of Valium. El doubtless needed them after her night of violent denunciations, while I wasn't 100 per cent convinced that my harem illusion would last when we got into serious pothole territory. Anyway, the Pancho Brigade was busy discussing the "rumour" they'd heard about being able to get Valium without prescription in Southeast Asia, and it gave me a pathetic secret thrill to know we had beaten them to it. For such stereotypical travellers, they weren't very on the ball.

Just after 1 a.m., the bus finally revved its farewell to Savannakhet and we tiredly raised two fingers in our now-standard salute before collapsing back on to our makeshift cots. It had been a long and hectic day, but now I was buggered and well on my way to getting smugly stoned. With the disco ball swaying hypnotically and six hours of heavily medicated sleep awaiting me, I couldn't think of any reason why the rest of the trip wouldn't be bliss.

*

I forgot my bladder.

That blasted, infernal, mongrelised piece of equipment that so often has to step in and make life a misery. If it isn't costing you two hundred kip, it's making you look like a pervert by forcing you to sit on your foot and jiggle. Unlike other body parts that can be controlled or at least appeased, the bladder is an insistent beast which isn't afraid to use humiliation as a means of getting its host to cater to its every whim. But what about when it decides to play funny buggers?

After a couple of hours of uninterrupted snoring on my bed of bags, I was jolted to the floor as the bus skidded to a halt. Groggily grasping at the feet of other reclining passengers, I pulled myself up and realised I was busting. Thankfully, the reason I'd nearly been concussed was that we were pulling up for a piss stop and I, along with nearly everyone else on board, descended the steps into the thick, silent night.

I never expected there to be an actual toilet, but I also never expected I'd get stage fright. While everyone else, male, female or otherwise, was unabashedly squatting and spraying away, I slunk away to the back of the bus. I believe wholeheartedly in freedom of expression, but I didn't think that my urinating in front of dozens of other people was going to make much of an artistic statement. Besides, I had enough of a problem going in a walled-off public toilet with people around, let alone letting it all hang out in a free-for-all on the side of the road. But even when I got into position in my secluded, invisible spot, I froze. My bladder was throbbing in anticipation of release and I was twitching in strange places but, no matter what, I couldn't do it. I was completely stuck.

All the begging and cajoling in the world wouldn't make me piss and even after I pressed a fist into my guts to speed things along, I was still high and dry. I closed my eyes, plugged my ears, even imagined I was in a delicately appointed porcelain heaven behind a heavy locked door, but I simply could not wee. I even adopted Pancho's "C'maaaan" mantra, but nothing worked.

Except the starting of the bus engine. Like some cruel tormentor, my bladder finally looked as if it were about to give in, but my mind had other ideas. If I stayed and pissed, it told me, the bus would leave without me, abandoning me to a lost life of outdoor urination in this nowhere wilderness. Immediate physical gratification was tempting, but I dreamt of a life outside the Laotian scrub so, with a sobbing moan, I slunk back on board.

The next two hours were misery incarnate. With Valium no match for the overwhelming strength of an engorged vesica, I was bolt awake and sorely aware of every single crater our suspensionless bus ploughed into, every hairpin bend it careened around. Perched up on my unsteady bed, I sat on my foot, then, with a display of balance that had to be seen to be believed, sat on both my feet. During one mercilessly short stretch of straight, ditchless road, I even managed to get a hand in there. I cried my eyes out and muttered curses at Pancho, who was sleeping happily back in his seat after successfully relieving himself in the full glare of the bus's headlights. At one stage I caught myself moaning loudly enough to stir a smacked-out El from her sleep and, at another, I squatted in the back doorsill, ready to let loose and damn the consequences. But of course, I couldn't do it. When I got back home, I told myself, I was going to have a word to my mother about all this social conditioning.

And just when it felt like my teeth were going to float away, the unthinkable happened. The police saved my life.

For some reason, they had formed a roadblock on what didn't really constitute a road, at 4 a.m., and were hellbent on searching our bus. Were I not about to explode, I would've been content to make myself invisible and guard my bag from anything being planted in it, but not this time. As far as I was concerned, they could've dropped fourteen kilos of hash right into my daypack and rubbed coke smudges under my nostrils so long as I could get outside and piss.

The instant the two policemen boarded the bus I leapt off the backpacks and, after tripping over various feet in the aisle, pushed roughly past them with one hand clutching my crotch. With their incomprehensible cries ringing in my ears, I dashed around to the back of the bus, half-expecting them to give chase or, at the very least, display a bit of pseudo-military prowess by firing their guns at me, but nothing happened. What with my frenzied groping, they probably figured I was just another sexual reprobate and, from what I'd seen, this didn't seem to be much of a crime in Southeast Asia.

Oh ye gods, the relief. Even if I were a sexual reprobate, the orgasmic satisfaction couldn't have gotten greater than this. It felt like I'd evacuated the entire contents of my body onto that dusty patch behind the bus and I was a gorgeously light empty vessel once more. When I climbed back on board, with the lazy grin of post-piss climax riding on my face, I felt like a new woman.

*

And when I finally climbed off the bus, two hours later, I really was.

I'd started the journey as a stock-standard Australian woman, maybe a little worse for wear but basically a presentable specimen of humanus ontheroadus. But when we pulled up, a mere few feet from Vietnam, I caught a glimpse of myself in the bus mirror and realised with horror that I'd morphed into an anthropoid. My hair was dreadlocked, my clothes were caked in filth and my teeth crunched down on dirt. And my sleepy monosyllabic grunts didn't do much to dispel the theory that I'd taken a trip to the *Planet of the Apes* sometime during the night.

Thankfully, I wasn't alone in my new position as crusty primate. El, who has the whitest skin I've ever seen on a living person and makes a valiant effort to rinse out her clothes in guesthouse sinks, was almost as filthy as I was. As I gazed around the bus, searching for answers, I noticed that the Pancho Population up the front had remained true to their feral selves but hadn't taken that final leap into the simian zone. As I wondered aloud, with no small degree of paranoia, if they'd decided to crust us up in our sleep as revenge for the Savannakhet Station brouhaha, El shook her head and pointed to the back door flapping jawlessly next to us. In the eye-smarting light of dawn, I could see that it held on to the remainder of the bus by just two loose hinges. No seals, no firm frame, no anything to prevent four hundred tonnes of road dirt making its ticketless way on board the disco express and doing the boogie-woogie all over our heads. I shuddered, remembering how I'd nearly leant against it during my late-night delirium of bladder bustage, and for the second time in both that night and my life, thanked God for the police. I'd rather be a Neanderthal freak than roadkill any day.

But as morbidly satisfying as it would have been, there was no time to reflect on my could-have-been demise. We could see Vietnam, and the bus driver was shouting something at us which I took to mean "You wanted to walk, now get the hell off and walk."

We got the hell off.

*

From where we stood, shivering in the early-morning glare, Vietnam was a bare plot of dirt and a couple of badly built huts, just visible through the exhaust fumes of the spluttering bus. It didn't look quite as I'd hoped, but then again, neither did we.

"Here," El said, rummaging in her daypack for a tissue. "You look like Tarzan with a hangover. They'll never let you into the country like that."

I was about to protest, but she was too quick. For someone who claims to never want kids, El has the Mum's Method of Face Cleaning down pat. A bit of spit on a grotty old tissue, the firm hand on the shoulder to prevent any escape attempts and an intolerable smear of stale saliva across the moosh.

"Bugger off, wouldja?" I cried, waving my arms. "This is mega-dirt we're dealing with here. It'll take a lot more than your slobber to get it off. Look—" I pointed to an incredibly dirty man hunchbacking his way from the border crossing, "—you think his mum never tried the old spit-on-a-tissue trick?"

Like a slow dream, the tiny Vietnamese man hobbled silently towards us, an overbearing basket on his back and what looked to be a wicker lampshade on his head. When we came face to face, he bared his black teeth at us. I wasn't sure if he was challenging us to some sort of grime showdown or displaying a disturbing interest in eating us.

It turned out to be neither. The old man had obviously been reading too many "Practice Random Acts of Kindness" bumper stickers, for, as decrepit and hungry as he looked, he reached into his basket and handed me what appeared to be half a corncob before limping mysteriously away again. I was about to call out my thanks, but then I took a look at the lump in my hand.

Chicken claws on a stick, fine. Fish brain soup, dandy. But honestly, this fascination that certain Southeast Asians seem to have with pushing the boundaries of culinary experimentation has to have a limit somewhere. I hate to sound like a whopping big ingrate, but where I come from, handing an innocent stranger a cornhusk stuffed with rotting grey stuff and writhing parasites is more akin to an insult than anything the Welcome Wagon drops off.

"Good morning, Vietnam," I muttered, passing El the hors d'oeuvre from hell. "Nothing like a balanced breakfast to get your strength up for border crossing."

El took one look at the bundle of filth, retched loudly and chucked it towards the bus. "If we need that to help us through, then we're more doomed than I'd ever imagined," she said, wiping her hands on her dusty shorts. "C'mon, let's go see what trouble we can find this time."

*

Incredibly, amazingly, there was none to be found. While it had somehow become a reflexive habit of ours to create scandal and melodrama in the most innocuous of situations, we breezed through what could have been the biggest fiasco of the whole trip with no worries at all. While our fellow Disco Bus passengers were wearily turning out their every possession beneath the withering gaze of the guards, we merely flashed our passports and kept on walking. No barked orders to empty our bags, no suspicion as to why we had taken a sudden slide down the evolutionary ladder, no nothing. With zero pomp and a disturbing lack of ceremony (a drum roll would've been nice), we walked into Vietnam.

Chapter Sixteen

The Wannabe Bootlegger Blues

Bent beneath our heavy packs and beginning to perspire as dawn's chill gave way to the heat of the day, we staggered into what appeared to be the commercial heart of Lao Bao.

Granted, this consisted of a sole outlet, a lean-to whose commodities seemed to be limited to Coca-Cola and piles of dirt but, unless we're talking Niagara Falls, what do you expect from a border town? Champagne and spa baths?

We had no need for any more dirt, somehow having acquired even more of the stuff on our long trudge to town, but the Coke was a blessing–even warm, even at two US dollars a can. Not only had the sudden blast of the sun extracted whatever liquid El hadn't spat on to a tissue and I hadn't smoked out of my system, but our throats were hoarse from doing the standard battle with the locals along the way.

Somehow, the grapevine had extended its tendrils from the border all the way into the tiny settlement with incredible alacrity, and before we'd even finished jinxing ourselves with a conversation about how lucky we were to get into the country hassle-free, the crowds had started to throng. Dodgy moneychangers chanting "kip for dong, dollars for dong" crawled out from behind the rocks and trees that dotted the wayside. Pillion motorcycle passengers hooted at us and lasciviously poked their fingers through their open fists in the international gesture of childish obscenity. Kids appeared from out of thin air to throw pebbles at us and a few deadbeats strolled by for a good gawking. All this at 6:30 a.m. on a Tuesday morning. Obviously, a rousing game of Make the Foreigners Scream was higher in the popularity stakes than say, sleeping in or callisthenics when it came to early-morning activities in Lao Bao.

By the time we came out of the shop, the crowd had dispersed, perhaps not willing to risk the wrath of the storekeeper who harboured hopes of selling us some dirt, and with them went our hopes of thumbing a ride out of Lao Bao.

"Jesus!" El spluttered through her instantly flat can of Coke. "How the hell are we going to get out of here?"

"Yeah," I said, scanning the now completely empty street. "Even better, where are we going when and if we do manage to get out?"

"Um."

It was a good question, and one we'd never really considered in our haste to get out of Laos. All we knew was that we wanted to go to Vietnam, which wasn't the most detailed travel itinerary in the world. I'd seen *Platoon* and I knew all the words to "All Along the Watchtower," but that didn't help us much. And nor did our travel guides, which we'd decided to use only in times of emergency—the kind where you run out of toilet paper. But unless we got out of Lao Bao, Vietnam would forever consist of one freshly paved road, a few sickos on motorbikes and a shop selling dirt.

It was my turn for the purposeful stride. Slamming my sticky can down on a nearby mound of merchandise, I marched outside just in time to spot a mammoth old truck careening down the road towards the town. Perfect, I thought, taking in its knocked-about blue body, its load of ridiculously large boulders and its huge cabin, empty but for a lone driver. It's used to the roads, is obviously going somewhere, and has plenty of room for us. With an elated grin, I stuck out my thumb.

Two seconds later, I replaced it with my middle finger. Instead of pulling up calmly, and graciously offering us a lift, the driver had stuck his head out the window and given me an unsolicited look at his tongue. It was quite long, granted, but could it drive me a hundred kilometres out of town? I doubted it.

I had pretty much the same luck with the next three trucks. All of them were lugging the same cargo of stones to some unknown, obviously rockless destination and every driver saw fit to waggle varying parts of their anatomy in my direction. It was beginning to look like we'd wandered into the Udon Thani of Vietnam.

Glancing around for a doppelgänger Pizza Hut in which to make jackasses of ourselves, my eye caught another blue truck. Only this time, it was parked on the side of the road and, unless the driver was a cretin of the highest order, he wasn't about to risk the consequences of flashing me without being able to make a quick getaway. Whether he liked it or not, this guy was our new chauffeur.

I called out to El, who was still in the shop slurping down another insanely overpriced can of warm syrup, and jogged over to the driver, who was engaged in what seemed to be an articulate debate with his back tyre. "Hi," I panted. "Speak English?"

Submitting a closing argument to the tyre, the man looked up and squinted. I tried again, affecting the annoying volume and slowness that no doubt irks non-English speakers the globe over: "Um. Speak! English!"

The man shrugged at his tyre in a brotherly display of affectionate confusion and answered me in Vietnamese, giving me the vague feeling that, no, he didn't Speak! English! It was time for Plan B—charades.

Charades is an easy game to play when you're pissed and your crowd all understands the mimes for "Uh . . . movie?" and "Small word! Small word!" They're even easy in a foreign country when you're wanting a drink or attempting to find the toilet. But when you're trying to explain to a rock-carting truck driver in the border-wilds of Vietnam that you and your mate are looking for a free ride to God Knows Where because one of the villagers gave you a handful of rotting vegetable matter and some kids threw rocks at you and really you'd better leave soon because your insane redheaded friend just called a moneychanger a mongrel swine, well, things get a little more difficult.

✳

But I'm here to tell you that it can be done. Ten minutes later, whether thanks to my latent Marcel Marceau talents or because, as an ex-boyfriend once told me, I sure know how to wear a guy down, we had our lift. We had no idea where our driver was going and he most likely thought we were chronically disturbed individuals, but there we were, throwing our backpacks onto the pile of rocks and clambering into the front cabin like a bunch of old mates going on a road trip together. Although none of my old mates keep a burning coil of incense or a beer can filled with toothpaste on the dash.

And, I'm almost sorry to say, none of my friends smuggle whiskey either. If they did, I doubt I would have been tempted to come on this trip in the first place. I would've been content for them to teach me the provocative arts of bootlegging so I could start up my own business. I'd have an adventurous life of my own, instead of travelling around the world pestering people who already did. Like this bloke.

What a guy—stone carrier by day, contrabandist by, uh, day. I could only dream of what he got up to by night, and, in my dreams, it was rather exciting indeed. Actually it's kind of pathetic how fringe participation in illicit activities carries me off on a cloud of quixotic romance. Maybe I need to stop watching gangster movies and take up embroidery instead.

But anyway.

As our driver had pointed out when we enthusiastically hopped into his giant cab, our seat was a false cover for the cache of booze nestled in a hollow beneath it. And this was no mere moonshine either. Squirreled away with only a thin layer of padding to protect it from the considerable squashing power of our arses, the stash was comprised of dozens of crisply packaged bottles of Johnny Walker, J&B, Jim Beam and Cutty Sark, all awaiting delivery. God only knew where he got this stuff, but it was definitely primo gear, far better than the junk I bathed my liver in back at home. None of this Old Crow shit for the good village folk of central Vietnam.

Finger raised to his lips in the universal "Shut the hell up" gesture, our man patted the seat back down and slid over to the driver's side. In this case, that happened to be on the left-hand side of the vehicle, and this was neither common nor a rarity. In our weeks in Southeast Asia, we'd noticed that people had a tendency to take whatever they could get and then drive the shit out of it. We'd already come across American army jeeps, Russian hunks of junk, a Polish Skoda (ibid: Hunk of Junk) and some jumped-up contraption with centre-wheel drive. To lessen the inevitable confusion that came with steering wheels planted all over the shop, they simplified things by driving flat out down the centre of the road.

∗

Our driver had given us each a thin pillow for the journey and, with El nuzzling into hers against my shoulder and mine planted between my other arm and the window, I felt both a sleepy-eyed comfort and a wide-awake zap of exhilaration. We were doing it! We were going somewhere, wherever the hell that might have been, and we were doing it in style. What better than to careen our way into a brand-new place in a gigantic blue Smurfmobile with a bunch of rocks and what probably constituted a capital offence tucked neatly under our bums? It had all the hallmarks of a package tour in the making.

"El?" I nudged her. "Is this brilliant or what? Our first hour in Vietnam and we're aiding and abetting a crime." Like I said, it's sad what turns me on.

"Mmmm," she groaned sleepily into my shoulder. "Brilliant. Can I abet in my sleep?"

I considered that for a second. "Sure. Asleep or not, we'll both be in trouble if he gets caught for this."

"Try not to sound so impressed by that idea, Gangsta Girl. Anyway, what the hell? We avoid customs so we don't get arrested and now we're practically begging for it?"

"This is different." I wasn't sure how, but it was. "It is," I asserted.

She grunted something else but it was lost between her dribble and the pillow, and within five seconds, she was sound asleep.

Trying not to buck her slumped head off my shoulder, I stretched my neck over her and tried to engage in a spot of hitchhiker/driver conversation. You know, the usual stuff: How long have you been bootlegging for? Where are you going with all those rocks? Why do you keep toothpaste in a beer can? But to no avail. Between keeping an eye on the road, looking down with an unsettling level of interest at El's thighs and peering suspiciously into the surrounding scrub, he just gawked uncomprehendingly at me as I rabbited on. I got the hint and shut my trap.

✳

With nobody to annoy, I took out my camera and hung out the window, watching Vietnam roll past. Astonishingly, the paved road hadn't given way to gravel or dirt after we'd gotten ten kilometres out of Lao Bao, as it did on the Laotian side of the border, and we tottered along just as smoothly as any oversized truck and its cargo could. Bordered on both sides by featureless green plains, there was nothing much of interest to me or my camera until we came across a forty-strong group of high-school students cycling to class.

At first I couldn't believe that these rosy-cheeked and orderly individuals were actually schoolchildren. For a start, they were all riding in a straight line, three to a row, with no wise guy pulling tricks on his BMX for the girls or pedalling off into the bush to wag it. None of the bigger kids were thumping the littlies, nobody was smoking fags and there was not a single shirt untucked from their pristine pyjama-like uniforms. All of this without some teacher on their arse, brandishing the threat of detention like a whip. That was weird enough, considering the school I'd gone to, but the freakiest thing of all was this: they were carrying flags. Every sixth person or so was flying a Vietnamese flag, in all its red-and-yellow socialist glory. And as far as I knew, it wasn't even a holiday. If you'd tried to get my class to do that, those flags would've ended up as boob tubes, togas or a neat place to hide your weed.

I hung out the window, snapping off shots like a woman possessed. To me, they looked like an animated version of one of those brightly painted, old-fashioned communist propaganda posters of comrades living it large beneath the hammer and sickle. To them, I probably looked like a crusty round-eye devil stealing their souls with a product of capitalist evil, but if so, they showed no sign of fear. A couple of the kids smiled gently in my vague direction, and not even one of them pumped their arm to the driver in the familiar "Honk that rig, big boy!" move so well-practised back at home. This was no ordinary adolescent excursion; it was the Stepford Schoolkids.

No sooner had they disappeared neatly from view than I found myself shooting off frames as we hooned past an old tank mounted on a slab of bright pink cement. Pink? Either the local historical preservation society was run, as it is everywhere, by old ladies who favour florals and pastels, or this was a proud display of the nation's Red leanings. But really, pink?

As the scenery gave way to the beginnings of lush jungle, I was suddenly possessed with history fever. Surely we were in the midst of a former battleground, rolling atop the graves of terrified soldiers, bouncing along beside a million tragedies and braveries of decades gone by? Spontaneity and living in the moment be damned, I wanted to know where we were and where we were going. But I wasn't getting any answers.

Frustrated, I leaned back inside the cab and lit a cigarette. I'd always imagined that when I got back home, I'd be able to join in on the conversations of some of the Vietnam vets that I'd met at the local RSL, but where was this kind of gig going to get me? "Yeah, I've been to Nam myself." "How fascinating, young lady. Where'd you go?" "I dunno, but there was a tank and a pink thing." There were no shouted beers in that kind of chat.

Sulking, I threw my cigarette out the window, aiming for and missing a white-painted stump on the side of the road. But what I lacked in aiming prowess, I more than made up for in my keen powers of observation. Something told me—perhaps the large red writing emblazoned on it—that this was no mere stump. I squinted at it, trying to find my place in the world, and gasped. "Khe Sanh," it read, "5 km."

*

Khe Sanh! Geographically, it didn't do much for me, but I was a good Australian pub-goer and I knew Khe Sanh like the back of my hand. Well, I knew the lyrics to "Khe Sanh" like the back of my hand. And which true-blue Aussie over the age of eighteen didn't? "Khe Sanh," Jimmy Barnes's bittersweet tribute to the Vietnam War, was our anthem, the one thing that we could depend on in this zany, madcap world. If you played the pub jukebox, went to see a cover band or, God forbid, got into a bit of post-rugger karaoke, Cold Chisel and "Khe Sanh" would be there. Jimbo would forever be leaving his heart to the sappers, having Vietnam cold turkey, telling us it was something only vets could understand. The bit about hitting some Hong Kong mattress all night long had always thrown me a bit, but who the hell cared? Thanks to "Khe Sanh," I wasn't floating around in some nameless nether region any more. I could find myself on a map—and just wait till I next got to a karaoke machine . . .

Khe Sanh turned out to be our first stop along the smuggling trail. Unlike in my imagination, it wasn't marked by a huge placard reading "Jimmy Barnes Sung About Here" and there were no Aussie-themed pubs in the near vicinity either. The only way I actually knew we'd arrived in Khe Sanh was because I'd kept an eye on the truck's speedometer, counting off the clicks—and maybe because there was another white stump, which obviously served as Vietnam's uniform road signage, reading "Khe Sanh." Keen powers of observation will get you everywhere.

I nudged El frantically and poked her in the ribs. "Hey, oi, get up. You'll never guess where we are."

Her head rolled off my shoulder and she groaned the groan of the Interrupted Sleeper, the inarticulate equivalent of "Piss off." But I knew she'd freak if she missed this. El could be a classy chick when she wasn't running around swearing at everyone, but she was as given to belting out a bit of Jimbo with the Friday-night crowd as anyone.

"No El, check it out, listen." I fastened my lips to her ear and started crooning the familiar chorus of "Khe Sanh." Just as I was about to shatter her cochlea with the heartfelt climax, she finally started writhing.

"Christalmighty," she muttered, pushing herself up into sitting position. "I'll get up, just don't torture me first thing in the morning."

Dismissing her attack on my vocal artistry, I excitedly told her where we were. "Smack bang in the middle of Oz's greatest rock song!" I finished with more than a touch of hyperbole. I flushed, suddenly feeling like a yobbo tour guide taking my peers on a trip of the truly hick. Where next, Slim's Town and Country pub?

But my pangs of ignominy vanished immediately. El was sitting up now, peering frantically around and repeating "Rock on!" under her breath, and I was also entranced. Whether or not anyone had written a nostalgic hit song about the place, Khe Sanh was still a name to remember. It was beautiful.

Surrounded by overgrown hills, Khe Sanh passed in a slow procession of palm and banana trees, scrubby huts and patches of the deepest red volcanic soil. I found out later that not only had this once been a prosperous area and home to a number of coffee plantations, but it had also been one of the Vietnam War's most infamous battlegrounds. For someone too young to have been in the war, old Barnesy sure did his research.

It was also, apparently, home to a great devotee of Johnny Walker Red Label. As we marvelled at the riotous greenery, singing under our breath, the driver veered suddenly off the road onto a dirt track, bumping past some crazy chickens and a few naked kids squatting in the earth, before pulling up at a small hut.

"Uh!" he grunted at us, waving us down into the dirt from our seats. So this was it—the great smuggle was under way. My mind instantly ran riot with images of Hemingway's rum-runners in *To Have and Have Not*, Al Capone and other crazy gangster shit. I wondered if there was any sort of Asian equivalent, but all I could think of was *Monkey Magic*. And I couldn't quite recall the last time Monkey and the gang sped off on their cloud with a dozen magnums of hard liquor.

But no matter. It was happening now. With three boxed bottles of Scotch retrieved from their hiding spot, the driver jumped down from the cab and started walking towards a hut, with us on his tail. I wasn't going to miss this for anything. Only wild horses could have dragged me away from checking out this little encounter.

Wild horses or a disapproving tut, perhaps. The moment the driver realised we were prowling around behind him, he scolded us with that universally infuriating noise and shoo-ed us back to the truck, watching unwaveringly until he was sure we were going to stay put. "Yes, Dad," I muttered as we sat back down. "Harumph."

I could harumph as much as I liked, but we weren't going anywhere. No crazy gangster shit for us. The instant our driver had disappeared into the hut, a mind-blowingly old woman smoking a long-stemmed pipe had doddered out and fixed us with an iron gaze. Harry Morgan and Al Capone wouldn't have stood for it, but we were petrified by this amazingly well-preserved woman and her pipe. If she could survive for a hundred years out here, smoking Godknewwhat, I didn't even want to think about what she could do to us corn-fed weaklings if we so much as made a move. We were stuck in the truck with the Wannabe Bootlegger Blues.

∗

It was, unfortunately, a pattern that repeated itself throughout the journey. Drive, smoke, silence, until without warning we'd turn off down a rutted track to some flea-bitten old hut. We'd learnt in Khe Sanh to stay in the truck, but the driver had nonetheless sent various guards out to keep an eye on us while he did his deals:

someone's big brother with no teeth but an impressive machete; a couple more old ladies and their pipes; even a tiny child who had nothing more threatening at hand than a dried old palm leaf. This kind of intimidation wasn't doing our egos much good at all.

On and on we drove, past stumps reading Ca Lu, Cam Lo, Con Thien, and we never caught a glimpse of anything that even slightly resembled a real town. As time dragged on, we began to worry that we'd reached the end of the line. In muted discussions, El and I agreed that we would refuse to get out unless we were in an actual town. What with being terrified of small children and wilted shrubbery, we weren't quite sure how we'd make our refusal stick, but we'd figure that out when the time came.

Thankfully, we didn't have to. Sometime around noon, we rolled into what struck us, after the best part of two days of seeing naught but darkened bus stations, dirt retailers and shantytowns, as a major metropolis. An intersection of busily beeping streets was thronged with dozens of motorbikes, rickshaws and more blue trucks, all going whichever way they damn well pleased, and a lively-looking market was squashed beneath two ruined buildings. It was certainly no Bangkok, but it was hectic, noisy and stunk like a fishmongers. As far as we were concerned, these had become the hallmarks of big-time civilisation.

"Ug," or something much like it, said our driver, waving us out of the cab for the umpteenth time that day. But something told me, perhaps the lack of flea-bitten huts filled with peasant alcoholics with high-class tastes, that this was no delivery site. This was it. The end of the line.

"And away we go!" El said, shoving me out the door. "Off into the great wild wonder."

"Wonder alright," I called from the street. "I bloody wonder where we are." Looking studiously at our surrounds didn't help; it was a town, that was for sure. But which one? There were no stumps to read, and the shopfront signage was taken up with words like Huong, Trong and Dong. We had reached the rockless, rhyming city.

"Ug," the driver snapped again, and I blinked out of my reverie. He was quite right to be ugging us along. Not only had he been coerced into lugging us—two people who could well have been deranged maniacs or even police informers—on a long and busy journey, but now we were refusing to get our bags and piss off.

"Okay!" I held up a finger. "One second!" I turned to El, who was looking anxiously at our bags, which had become gigantic mounds of mud perched atop the trailer of rocks. "Get ready to catch, I'm going up."

I may be one of the most uncoordinated people to ever stumble across the face of the earth, but when it comes to climbing, well, I know rocks. Probably, as some ungracious people would say, because my head is full of them. But never mind that. Thanks to my scrabbling prowess, I was up that pile of boulders before most people would have finished strapping on their hiking boots. And if I seem like I'm bragging, it's because I am. After getting laughed out of every Phys. Ed. class I'd ever tripped over a shoelace into, I think I have a right to boast if I can manage one physical activity without killing myself.

"Bombs away!" I called, launching El's rucksack on to the busy street below, where it landed with a massive poof of dust.

"Hey!" El coughed. "You trying to kill us down here?"

Us? Getting a firm grip on a teetering rock, I leaned over the edge of the trailer and saw that a crowd had gathered. Oh, of course, us. And why wouldn't there be an audience? Two people getting their bags off a truck was quite the action-packed event. I took it there was no television reception in this area.

I volleyed my bag off the side and clambered down to retrieve it. "Thanks, mate," I called to the driver, who looked like he was going to have palpitations soon if he didn't get away from the goggle-eyed crowd surrounding his smuggle-mobile. "Cheers!" we chorused and, with a brief wave, he was gone. We were all alone. Not counting the twenty or so other people around us, that was.

"So," I said, hitching on my filthy pack. "Where the hell are we?"

El, who was being slowly circled by a midget eyeing her hair, looked at me in vague annoyance. "Like I know," she said. "Maybe it's time we pulled out those two-bit guides to see if they can help."

They couldn't. As far as we could work out, we were somewhere on the central coast, somewhere perhaps along the vast 200-kilometre stretch between Dong Hoi in the north and Hue in the south.

"Well that was useful," I muttered, as El threw her book into the gutter with a litany of curses that sent the crowd into fits of giggles. "Go and pick it up, for chrissakes." I wasn't in the mood for a comedy routine.

But that was just too bad for me. Everything we did seemed to amuse the gathered mob senseless. El picking up the *Lonely Planet* was obviously akin to some kind of vaudeville. My lighting a cigarette was a real knee-slapper. And when the two of us tried to have a conversation, people were actually belly laughing. I would've hated to have seen what won the prize pack on Vietnam's Funniest Home Videos.

"Right," El grumbled, "enough's enough." She held her *Lonely Planet* under the nose of a chortling merrymaker and pointed to the map. "Where are we?" she asked.

In the true spirit of audience participation, people clamoured to be a part of the action, and within seconds, about twenty people were guffawing over the *Lonely Planet*. I couldn't blame them really; it was a sketchy map. But surely they could still find themselves on it.

No chance. These people either had no idea where they lived, or the information had been deemed classified. But wherever we were, we didn't want to stay there. If we were the most amusing act around and these people didn't have enough civic pride to tell us the name of their hometown, then we were outta there.

"C'mon, El," I said, "let's just keep walking before they give us our own sitcom." She nodded and shut the book, much to the dismay of the hooting crowd, and we began to push our way out into nowhere.

✳

I'd never thought much of people who went through life sporting the mullet cut. The old "short in the front, long in the back" or "Sho-Lo" 'do had never done much for me except provide comic relief during rodeos or illegal drag-car events, and even then my amusement was tinged with the slight repulsion any sane person feels when watching Billy Ray Cyrus videos. I certainly never expected any dealings with a proud mulleteer to extend beyond the local auto mechanics. But I never expected the police to save me from drowning in my own urine on a Disco Bus either, so it should probably have come as no real surprise when a man sporting the old Achy-Breaky-Big-Mistakey materialised to deliver us from obscurity on the nameless streets of Vietnam.

"Hey, lady!" he called. "Lady!"

Sweat-streaked and by now almost indescribably grubby, at first it didn't occur to El and me that anyone shouting the word "lady" could be referring to us, and we kept on schlepping our way towards Anywhere. But after a few more insistent calls, it dawned on us that we were hearing the first English we'd clapped ears on in days and we whirled around to face the linguist.

Oh lord, what a mullet. Slouched "Greased Lightning"-style on a souped-up Honda Dream was our first look at a Vietnamese

199

mid-life crisis. Aged about forty, not only did this guy have what some mullet connoisseurs like to call "The Chop-n-Flow" but he also enjoyed the added glory of having had it permed. And what's a mullet without a gold chain? I looked around for a matching Shazza riding pillion, but she must've stayed home to stonewash her jeans.

"Lady," he oozed, in his best I'm-Recapturing-My-Youth voice. "You need help?"

El and I looked at each other, and it took about one second flat to decide that yes we did. Had we been anywhere else on earth, his offer would have been rejoined with a quick "No, but I know someone who does." This was no time to get smart, though. Permed neckwarmer or no, this guy was our saviour.

"We're lost," I said, stating the blatantly obvious.

El threw me a glance and took up the case. "We don't know where we are, we don't want to be here and we have no dong to get out."

Mulletman chewed this over with a suitably cool, thinking face. Running a hand through the explosion of curls sitting on his neck, he filled us in. "This town is Dong Ha. This is what they call the 'DMZ.'"

Sighing with the joy of finally being somewhere, I reached for my guidebook and riffled the pages before coming up with Dong Ha. As I suspected–nothing to see here, folks, keep on moving. But the DMZ was another matter entirely. The acronym stood for "Demilitarised Zone" and, with mixed emotions, I discovered that for the past four hours we'd been rollicking through the sites of some of the most brutal fighting of the Vietnam War. Previously the no-man's-land dividing the French-run south and the Communist north of the country, the DMZ had become a casualty itself, a bleak and battered region still littered with live mortar rounds and landmines. Sounded like everything I wanted in a holiday destination.

"Right," El said, turning back to Mulletman. "Great, the DMZ. We want to get out of here. Like, now." I nodded along with her. I was given to picking up shiny rubbish, and it would be difficult for me to tell whether I was scoring myself a free bauble or a trip to the amputee's ward.

"Where do you want to go?" Mulletman asked. "Hue?"

"That's it," I said. "Away." He may have had the most abominable hairstyle ever forced upon mankind, but he was no dummy.

Unfortunately I was. Hue, while it was pronounced like a breathy version of "Away," was actually a fairly large city about seventy kilometres south of Dong Ha. After getting that cleared up, with a red face I scurried back to the book to look it up. Hue. Not in the DMZ, plenty of culture, architecture, not in the DMZ. Sounded great.

"Fantastic," I said. "Hue it is."

"Now," Mulletman said, narrowing his eyes. "You need dong and a bus. If you give me some dong, I will help you." I curled up my lip, then almost immediately brought it back down again. Big deal, I thought. Bit of dong to keep those Soul Glo curls in action. Either that or we walk the streets forever, waiting to run into our one-legged destinies. "Okay, lady?" he finished.

"Fine," we said. He patted what was left of the seat behind him on the Dream and beckoned to El. "You, pretty lady. Come with me to get dong. You," he motioned coolly towards me, "wait at the bus station. It's there." He held out his hand towards a distant clutter of buses and market stalls. "Easy," he smiled.

And incredibly, it was. El had thrown me a look of amused repulsion as she hopped, rucksack and all, on to the back of the Dream, but we both knew she'd be fine. No guy worth his midlife crisis was about to go blowing his chances at looking like hot shit with a babe on the back of his bike by taking her down a secluded alley and mauling her to death. As for me, what was a bit more trudging going to hurt? By this stage, trudge was my middle name.

✳

It was nearly an hour later when El and Mulletman found me, curled up between my backpack and a mound of unsavoury sludge at the bus station. Overcome by weariness and the overpowering stench of ancient chickens and dried fish, I'd passed out the instant I sat down, not caring that piles of unsavoury sludge were hardly the equivalent of a down-stuffed doona. When your best mate's off doing trophy-chick duty in the middle of a war zone and mangy chooks are doing their best to make you throw up, sleep is the only escape.

It's the waking-up bit that's difficult. As El dug her boot softly into my snoring side, I peeled open my eyes and nearly gagged. "What the hell?" I cried, smacking my flailing arm into the middle of the sludge. "Shit!"

"I certainly hope not," El replied, extending her hand. "C'mon, derro, if you can tear yourself away from your luxurious sleeping quarters, there's a bus out of here in ten minutes."

I smirked and pulled myself up, trying to ignore Mulletman's undisguised look of disgust at my condition. "Didja get everything?"

El nodded and patted her money pouch. "All set. Dong in hand and we get tickets on board."

I flung a stray piece of slime off my hand to the ground. "And you took care of . . . ?" I asked El, tilting my head towards the now completely revolted Mulletman.

"Yeah," El sighed. "All seventy thousand dong's worth."

If I'd nearly gagged before, I was certainly retching with that little admission. "Seventy thousand! Where'd he take you, bloody Mars? That's enough to keep him and his unfortunate family in hair scarves for generations!"

"Relax," El muttered. "Seventy thousand dong is five bucks. It's nothing." I wiped my forehead in relief, no doubt leaving a trail of ooze on my already stain-cluttered head. "Actually," she continued, "you'll be pleased to hear that we're millionaires. Dong-wise, that is."

This was good news indeed, whatever the currency. One second before, I'd been some white trash scumbag dossing down in sludge piles, and now here I was, a millionaire. I had a sudden urge to smoke a cigar and snap my fingers at people.

But fat-catting would have to wait. With no private jets in the vicinity, even us millionaires had to endure the rigours of public transport, and the bus to Hue would wait for no-one, plutocrat or otherwise. Besides, it would be healthy for me to get down with the common people. I'd been one myself, once.

*

By the time we found our seats, we were no longer millionaires. The one-way tickets had cost us nearly fifty thousand dong each and before we'd boarded, I'd palmed off another few thou to a crippled child wearing nothing but dirt. Philanthropy is the in-thing for us fat cats.

So we were down some dong, but, as those who have never been millionaires like to say, we were richer for the experience. The bus, which was more like a van than anything Greyhound would put its name to, looked like the runty cousin of the truck which had brought us from Lao Bao: blue, battered and with incense burning on the dash. But where the truck had provided us with ample space to stretch out, the bus gave me that old sardine feeling again. And the only thing stashed under my arse was hardwood and rogue springs.

About a billion people had somehow crammed their way into the fifteen-seater, all of them yabbering away at lightning speed. If you thought those clicking guys in *The Gods Must Be Crazy* sounded pretty wild in full discourse, just wait until you're squashed in a rolling coffin surrounded by a zillion Vietnamese folks all going off at once. The language has sounds and tones I'd never thought it would be possible to make with the human larynx, and while I realised that it was my duty as an ambassador of goodwill to try and learn at least one phrase of Vietnamese, there was no way I was going to be able to do it unless I sprouted a second tongue. Hopefully they'd take my silence as a compliment. At least I wouldn't be mangling their language to death.

So the bus was thrashed; it was crowded to the point that our filthy laps had become a makeshift couch for the otherwise seatless; and it sounded like the world's biggest human beatbox. But after El's mentally scarring experience with Mulletman and my sleeping with the chooks, it would've taken a lot more than that to keep us from dozing off. I, for one, could now officially sleep anywhere, anytime. And I did, all the way to Hue. Travel may be fatal to prejudice and intolerance, but boy does it nail insomnia.

Chapter Seventeen

Hue Crazy: A Night at the Apocalypse

It took three hours to travel the seventy-odd kilometres to Hue, and when we finally disembarked, sleepy-eyed and in the most wretched physical condition of our lives, we weren't quite sure that we had left Dong Ha. With Eau de Chicken in the air and countless piles of unsavoury sludge everywhere, the bus station was the carbon copy of the one we'd supposedly paid fifty thousand dong for the pleasure of leaving.

"Oh God, no," I cried, hitching on my pack for the umpteenth time that day. "This is déjà vu of the worst possible kind."

"Kinda," El said. "But before you get tempted to kip on down with the ooze, let's get out of here."

"Sure," I replied grumpily. "Walk around aimlessly like last time? Fantastic."

"Snap out of it. They do have public transport in Vietnam, you know."

"Mullets on Honda Dreams? Fine for you maybe, but last time I got stuck with trudging."

I was wallowing in self-pity, which made a change from wallowing in sludge, and as much as I love a good funk,

205

my petulance was annoying me, not to mention El, to tears. Thankfully, she snapped me out of it. "Look, freak. Over there. Cyclos!"

I followed her gaze to a virtual army of the weirdest-looking pushbikes I'd ever seen, and felt my spirits rise immeasurably. These cyclo things may have looked like the lovechild of a high-rise wheelchair and an alarmingly shoddy pram, but they were our ticket off the trudging path for a while. The drivers, who pedalled the cyclos from a long seat behind the passenger cradle, were even scruffier than we were and pretty suss-looking, but none of them had even the slightest hint of a mullet. For that alone, I would shower them with my hard-earned dong.

Not that they seemed overly keen to take it. Unlike in Nong Khai, where we were nearly chewed alive by the rabid throng of tuk tuk drivers, these cyclo guys couldn't really have cared less whether we walked or went with them. I suppose I can't really blame them for their disinterest; if I had to pedal a bunch of oversized foreigners around on a spindly bike for a measly handful of almost useless cash, I wouldn't be foaming in anticipation either. But by that stage, I was just not interested in anyone else's lethargy. After over thirty hours of buses, trucks, vans and lunatics, my own raging torpor took top priority. If I didn't get a dink to a real bed soon, my already thrashed body was going to give up completely, and it wasn't going to be a pretty sight.

"'Scuse me," I said, tapping a seemingly unconscious cyclo driver. He responded with a slow blink, a good sign. At least a vital sign. "Can you take us somewhere?" He didn't blink this time and I looked to El for help.

"The Mimosa Guesthouse," she said, nose buried deep in my copy of *Let's Go*. "On Le Loi alleyway?"

This time he blinked, and went as far as to nod in our general direction. "Great," I muttered, my nonchalant croak no true indication of the true joy I felt. A ride, oh yes. A guesthouse, oh orgasm. Even the fact that we nearly flattened the tyres of the cyclo when we both wedged into the tiny passenger box couldn't diminish my joy; I simply went and tapped the other drivers until I found one not obviously in the throes of rigor mortis and hopped in with him. Badly pronouncing my destination, I waved to El, nodded to the driver and we set off in convoy.

People go to New Zealand for bungy jumping, the Swiss Alps for avalanche chasing and Canada for white-water rafting, but the one extreme sport that doesn't get its fair share of coverage is cyclo racing in Hue. With speed, danger and the probable ending of life in a very messy manner, it has what every adrenaline junky craves. Despite the fact that, by that point, I was less craving adrenaline than a bed with white sheets, I can't say I didn't get off on the thrill.

Trapped in a small silver box reminiscent of a Tilt-a-Whirl enclosure without the safety chain, I was hurtled through the anarchic streets of Hue with complete disregard to any hopes of longevity I may have harboured. While the driver was perched high enough to be able to see over the haphazard sprawl of oncoming vehicles, I was hunkered about wheel-high to the hundreds of spluttering scooters that threatened my lifespan with every rev. And by the looks of things, El's chances of hitting middle age seemed about as slim as mine. Her previously comatose driver had morphed into Peter Brock the minute he'd pedalled into the main street, and was hellbent on beating my ride to the Mimosa, even if it meant going on one wheel to do so. Once I saw El nearly get tipped out, but I was too busy hanging on for my own dear life to do anything about it. Besides, if she fell out, we'd beat them to the guesthouse and win the coveted prize. Okay, there was no coveted prize, but cyclo racing was still in its developmental stages. One day, when it was an Olympic sport, I could reminisce about my victory back in the early days.

It was a tie.

*

We didn't plan on staying very long in Hue, despite its wealth of cultural and historical attractions. Or maybe because of its wealth of cultural and historical attractions. El only had about another week's worth of travelling before she had to get back and yell at kids in Japanese, and she wanted to see Saigon and at least venture briefly into Cambodia. As for me, blissfully unemployed with all the time in the world, I was more interested in pursuing my original philosophy of travel: if I could see it in a book, then I didn't have to see it in real life. Granted, that was a rather blanket philosophy and obviously didn't apply to things like photogenic pubs and village pharmacies selling hard-to-get prescription drugs over the counter. But, as disgraceful as it may sound, I simply wasn't interested in things like ancient citadels or royal tombs. Citadels, in my extensive experience, were usually empty forts full of tourists and Disney-like re-enactments, and royal tombs were just holes full of royal dead people I'd never heard of. Besides, I was liable to disgrace myself and invite the ghostly wrath of some unpronounceable monarch. I had enough on my plate without being haunted because I tripped over someone's headstone. Nup, I was more interested in scruffing around local markets, retching at what passed as food in these far-flung places and pestering the natives in out-of-the-way bars. Besides, what made for better travel tales to tell the poor sods stuck back at home: a non-eventful, but politically and culturally correct, day of staring at incense-lit graves or a rambunctious, totally wrong, night on the piss with amusingly named local studs?

Wasn't that tough a question.

After shakily paying off our panting cyclo drivers and scrubbing ourselves to sparkling point in the Mimosa Guesthouse's freezing shower, El and I had decided to delay the bliss of going to sleep by taking a brief walk around Hue. With twilight descending on the city, it was too late (damn!) to start scarpering around any ancient, meaningless monuments by that stage, but we figured it'd be nice to get even more tired before allowing ourselves the luxury of sleep. Besides, it would be a unique experience to know just where we were for once. Who knew when that would happen again?

Le Loi, the street after which our hotel's alleyway was named, was the Hue version of Khao San Road. Running parallel to the Perfume River—a misnomer if there ever was one—Le Loi ran for an eternity in either direction and was busting with souvenir shops, guesthouses, tattoo parlours and cafés emblazoned with the legend: "As Recommended by Lonely Planet." At least we knew where not to eat. But unlike Khao San, there seemed to be at least a shred of original character left along Le Loi; nobody tried dragging us into their gimcrack shops and there were even a few locals who weren't touting anything. But it was backpackerish enough for El and me, and after tripping over someone's Birkenstocks and shuddering at a hairy group of farang strutting around in crisp new "Ancient City of Hue—It's Hue Cool!" T-shirts, we beat a hasty retreat down a sidestreet. Anti-social, yes; looking for trouble, no. We'd seen the usual result when we loitered for too long around those of the facial hair and chunky sandals persuasion, and we figured we'd save our obscenities and bad tempers for someone who really deserved it. After all, we were bound to run into Pancho again.

We kept on walking until we reached a virtual farang-free zone, a crossroads of local grocery shops and darkened cafés marked only by signs containing lots of Xs and words that rhymed with "ong." We were lost, but it didn't matter. There was always some cyclotic or another trailing us around if we needed Mach-3 style transport back to the Mimosa.

"You ready to go back?" El asked me. We were walking deeper and deeper into X and ong territory and streetlights were becoming a rarity.

"Kind of," I replied. "What I'd really like is a beer." It was almost true. I didn't feel like I'd "really like" a beer, I was craving one with all my soul. Ever since we'd passed through Khe Sanh and I'd been reminded of things like Sunday Sessions and five-dollar jugs and bad cover bands, my body had been sending out sporadic signals decrying the lack of booze it had been receiving. But what with smuggling, sleeping in filth and trying not to be decapitated by nifty fifties, I'd been ignoring its anguished cries for help. This time though, I was all ears.

El, so often the voice of teetotalling reason, surprised me. "Sure," she said. "I could go for a cold one right about now. Find that bar and I'll shout ya."

I wasn't about to argue. I wasn't about to say anything, as a matter of fact. One mistimed peep from me and El could've woken up to the very un-El-like things she was saying and hopped a cyclo back to the guesthouse for a very sober sleep. For the sake of beer, I could shut up for a few minutes.

As it turned out, the need for beer even meant I could go back on everything I thought I believed in. After about ten minutes of searching silently for anything resembling a pub, I clapped eyes on what had to be the most obvious backpacker dive I'd ever come across. Lit in tacky, Hawaii-style neon with outdoor blackboards advertising the trendy Western alcho-pop specials of the day, this place looked like a giant beacon to the Red Bull singlet set. And its name didn't give me much hope for any intimate chit-chat with the locals either: Apocalypse Now. Under normal circumstances, I would've thrown out a disparaging comment and kept walking until we got to something a little less reminiscent of napalm and Martin Sheen. But these were not normal circumstances; I hadn't had a beer in four days, and El had never promised a shout.

I led her to the door.

*

Totally bare of any Hollywood souvenirs or movie memorabilia, Apocalypse Now was nonetheless a fitting moniker. What with the bar's non-existent lighting, smoke-filled interior and the howls of torture supposedly representing Western music coming from the stereo, I could have easily been led to believe that the end of the world was nigh. If not here already. As we peered through the gloom, we made out the crude squiggles of chalked-in graffiti sprawled across the black slate walls: "Pants!", "Newcastle Utd Roolz!", "Fuck the IRA!" My God, I thought. Bring on the apocalypse, it's a Pommy bar. Beer or no beer, I was ready to walk out stone-cold sober the instant anyone started singing Chumbawumba.

But it was our lucky night. The walls may have been cluttered with scrawled declarations of Jem's love for Squidge and badly drawn cartoon bulldogs, but there wasn't a soap-dodger in sight. Actually, there wasn't anyone in sight, apart from a shady-looking bartender and a couple of his cronies idling pointlessly over a ball-less pool table.

"Charming establishment," El huffed sarcastically from the doorway.

"It sells beer," I said hopefully. I pointed to a chalked-in ledge above the pool table. "See what it says? 'Don't be lazy.' C'mon, we'd better not be slack. Go and get us a beer, hey?"

El didn't budge. "'Don't be lazy'? What's that supposed to mean? And who," she squinted through the darkness, "is Mama Hanh? See, that's what it says under it, and her name's written all over the place."

I thought about it and shrugged. "Probably some trashy Brit chick carried away with oriental delusions of herself. C'mon, grab some beers and we can make up Vietnamese names for ourselves too." Anything for a beer.

She finally got the hint and after leaving me fidgeting alone in the gloom for a couple of minutes, she returned with two gigantic stubbies. "Check this out," she said excitedly. "Two beers for twenty thousand dong. That's just over a buck. At this rate, we could get smashed on ten dollars."

After a tentative sip, this struck me as a great idea. The beer, a local brand called Huda, was smooth and tasty, and I could easily have sunk a few hundred grand on it. But despite her enthusiasm, I doubted El would go the distance. She was bound to remember that she wasn't a drinker soon enough.

I became an avid fan of amnesia that night. Three hours and six mega-stubbies later and El was still under the delusion that she was born to swill. "Two more, Mama Farang?" she slurred.

"Too right, Mama Ham." I threw some dong at her and she chucked it back.

"My shout, 'member?" She crashed into our table and started lurching to the bar.

"Get some chalk while you're up there," I called. "Don't be lazy!"

"Don't be lazy, don't be lazy," I heard her sing as she wove her way up to the bar. There's nothing like a blossoming drunkard to make any evening entertaining.

Somehow, she managed to get both beers and chalk back to the table. And she bought a little something extra as well.

"This is Fool," she announced, slapping a devastatingly handsome Vietnamese boy on the back. "Sittdown, Fool!"

I gazed at the amazing specimen which had been placed before me. With wavy, thick black hair, a slight but well-built physique and almost Eurasian features, he was the most attractive thing I'd seen in weeks. Beer goggles or not, this was something I could stand waking up next to. But Fool? "As in 'on the hill'?" I asked.

"Guess so," El shrugged, taking a hearty swill of ale. She peeked at him over the bottle. "Fool, huh?"

With a gorgeous grin, he swept us both with his dark eyes and corrected her with some unpronounceable word that sprung from that second larynx he must have been toting around. Right then. Fool it was.

"And who's yer mate?" I nodded to a second beautiful, if not quite so dishy, man hovering nervously around our table.

"This is Hung," Fool said.

It had to happen. "As in 'well'?" we chorused before breaking into a spasm of giggles to rival any pre-teen titterfest. I accurately guessed that travel hadn't done much for our maturity levels.

We composed ourselves as much as was possible, hoping they weren't well versed in crude English axioms, and introduced ourselves. The boys had a bit of a guffaw at our names too, but whether that was for revenge or because our names actually translated as "Idiot" and "Fat," I'll never know. Besides, after the laugh-in at Dong Ha, we were used to our new roles as impromptu comedians. It was all we could do to avoid being kidnapped by circus clown scouts.

We did the usual limited-vocab traveller/local chat thing for a while. They waxed lyrical, or as lyrical as their moderate English skills would allow, on the delights of their hometown and we tried to politely limit our adjectives in bland recountings of our adventures so far. But after about fifteen minutes of using words like "very nice," "oh wow" and the occasional resort to charades, their English gave out completely and we were left staring at each other. This can get rather tedious after a while, no matter how attractive the object of your blank stare, and after a few minutes of studying a small scar on Hung's nose, I gave up and went to draw on the walls.

Thankfully, graffiti was an encouraged method of decorating the otherwise bleak walls of Apocalypse Now. By the time I'd completed my masterpiece, a five-foot rendition of a deranged cyclo driver chasing a lovestruck chicken, I had the management cheering me on and bringing me free beers. As I strutted back to our table, covered in chalk dust but triumphant, I was proud to see the atmosphere had changed, with El and the boys chatting animatedly away. Amazing how a little artistic flair can spice up the conversation.

Or not. As I proudly pointed to my chef-d'oeuvre and announced its completion, they gawked at me and it, only now registering that I'd even left the table. Nothing like a good old-fashioned ego whuppin' to round off the night. And to make it worse, they were discussing my chief rival in the graffiti stakes, Mama Hanh. I'd had to erase her name and her "Don't be lazy" catchphrase from the slab of wall I'd annexed for my drawing, but it was still scrawled all over the place and it was driving me berserk. As a dyed-in-the-wool Leo, I was quite firm in my belief that if anyone's name and personal motto was going to hog the limelight, it would be mine.

"So who is this woman, anyway?" I huffed. "And what's with this 'Don't be lazy' shit? I don't see her in here pumping anyone into an aerobics frenzy."

El, who was by now the drunkest I'd ever seen her, tilted off her stool and grabbed Fool's arm. "Aerobics!" she hooted. "Ya hear that, Fool, ya big fool?" Fool just sat there, a grin plastered on to his lovely face, looking much as his moniker suggested. Language gaps can be a blessing sometimes.

"'S not aerobics anyway," El said, turning on the drunken I'm-serious-here tone. "She just wants to getcha stoned."

Oh, of course. This was getting me nowhere, and with Fool still simpering like one and Hung resting on his signature laurels, I had no choice but to wade through El's opaque ramblings to get the full story.

From what I could gather, Mama Hanh was a mythical hero of the backpacking set. A deranged woman of indeterminate age, she supposedly ran boat tours from the seaside town of Nha Trang to the surrounding islands. But these were no average tours, and Mama Hanh was no average deranged woman of indeterminate age. There were plenty of both to go around in Vietnam, apparently.

What made her and her tours so different was simple. Instead of serenely anchoring her boat in the lagoons off Nha Trang and encouraging her charges to dabble in a bit of snorkelling and a picnic lunch, Mama Hanh turned on the biggest floating party this side of, well, anywhere. Would-be suntanners and on-deck loungers were booted into the water with lifejackets and bottles of wine and forced to join in aquatic skulling competitions against her well-pickled self. And to keep things interesting, she had an underling who floated around with handfuls of pre-rolled joints, doling them out generously to whoever drifted his way. It was every backpacker's dream. It was everyone under the age of forty-five's dream. It was too good to be true.

"And y'know what she means by being lazy?" El asked. "Lazy is when you don't get stoned or totally pissed. If you don't get fucked up, you get in trouble." Now I knew this whole thing was bullshit. Not even in Amsterdam would they punish you for not being off your dial.

"Sure, El," I said, casting a knowing look towards Fool and Hung. "It's crap, hey."

"No crap," Hung said. "It's true. Mama Hanh is crazy woman."

El, who'd morphed into a bit of one herself, gave him a thumbs-up sign. "Let's go tomorrow," she slurred. "Don't be lazy." She grinned the grin of the impendingly ill and passed out on the table.

*

Not surprisingly, we didn't go anywhere the next day. Or night. While I suffered through a fairly average hangover, El writhed in a severe case of delirium tremens, leaving her hot, rumpled bed only for sporadic lurches to the loo. Even if she hadn't been in the throes of nausea and suspected alcohol poisoning, there was no way we were going out into the streets, risking a possible run-in with Fool and Hung. After El had passed out, the three of us had been forced to drag her into a loitering cyclo and, as I later, perhaps cruelly, informed her, she'd drooled heavily over Fool's helping hand. He hadn't really minded all that much, but as far as El was concerned, we were to remain invisible until we left town. Public salivating wasn't her thing.

When we woke at noon the following day, I was claustrophobic and El was cured. Yet despite a regained appetite and the disappearance of her violent shakes, she remained adamant about leaving the room. "I drooled on him," was all she could say as I clawed at the walls. I'd hate to have seen her response if she'd actually puked on his shoes. I would still be holed up in that room in Hue.

"Fine," I said, clutching at my belly and watching the world pass, Fool-less and Hung-less, out our window. "So we stay in here forever because you slobbered on some guy named Fool outside a seedy bar. That's the most unlikely excuse for a hermetic lifestyle I've ever heard."

"Who said anything about being a hermit? I just want to leave this town, that's all."

"And go to?"

She looked at me slyly and lit a cigarette. "What do you think, Mama Clam?"

I thought for a beat and then it hit me. She was obviously still delirious. "You think Mama Hanh and her scoob-at-sea tour actually exists? Like she's a real-life version of *The Beach* or something? Get back into bed," I said, shaking my head. "You're still deranged."

She grabbed the *Let's Go* and riffled the pages. "Oh yeah?" she cried triumphantly, opening to a page marked "Nha Trang." "Boat tours, blah, blah. Floating bar, blah blah, 'mould was cast by the infamous Mama Hanh.' See! Scoob-at-sea really does exist."

"Gimme that." I whipped the book from her hands and read for myself. Oh, well, ahem. Okay, so she wasn't delirious. Not completely, anyway. But by all accounts, Nha Trang was still an overnight train ride to the south of Hue. "So you're telling me that you wanna go all that way for one measly afternoon of all the dope you can smoke and piss you can swill while floating around in a tropical lagoon?"

We looked at each other for a minute and dissolved into laughter. Well, duh.

Chapter Eighteen

Don't be Lazy

The train ride to Nha Trang turned out to be the least complicated overland journey I've ever undertaken, either in Southeast Asia or in other, supposedly more developed countries. I've been left stranded at Berlin's Zoo Station in the usually über-efficient Germany. Yelled off a bus by a normally obsequious London Transport worker. Half-molested by an ordinarily stolid Czech cab driver. So it came as quite the surprise to chug halfway across a country renowned for its transport traumas, experiencing nothing more dramatic than sinking a few quiet beers with the kitchen staff. No on-board coups, no accidental running over of landmines, no waking up with fourteen people asleep on my lap. There wasn't even a Train Nazi in sight. The force was with us.

We were Luke and Leia for the rest of the day. The train had pulled into bright, bustling Nha Trang at 11 a.m. and, after a restful sleep in a gently rocking bunk, we felt ready to conquer the world. Nothing could go wrong, and in the first rebuttal of Sod's Law that I'd ever experienced, nothing did. Our moto drivers from the station into town were courteous and honest. We found a lovely, cheap hotel, with no cockroaches or hidden snares to make up the "pain" bit of the "pleasure and" maxim. We even managed to find a café flogging authentic cuisine that actually filled our stomachs instead of turning them. And Nha Trang itself was a beautiful city, with colourful buildings and ruffled beach huts skirting the clear turquoise South China Sea. Had it been situated almost anywhere else but Vietnam, Nha Trang would have sported at least one Club Med, its white beaches littered with sunburnt, paunched old Frenchmen in bad G-strings. With the country poised to usurp Thailand as the region's Next Big Thing, it's probably only a matter of time before Nha Trang falls victim to this double curse of wedding-cake buildings and fat guys in string. But for now, it was content to loll languorous and unassuming, like a pretty girl who's not yet become swollen-headed with a million declarations of her beauty.

We spent the day strolling along the six-kilometre beachfront, acting for once like completely average tourists. Kicking coconuts and posing for pictures beneath the palm trees, we looked just like any normal geeks on their tropical fantasy holiday. What with Mama Hanh and her various mindwarps awaiting us tomorrow, normal was exactly what we were going for. Who knew when we'd see it again?

✳

"Follow please, crazy people. You crazy, I very crazy."

There were about thirty of us waiting at the boat launch, and crazy was the last word I'd have used to describe a bunch of people with puffy morning heads and sleep in their eyes. We looked about as manic as a bunch of sloths. Then again, maybe we were all suffering a collective lunacy. Who else but the clinically mad would drag themselves out of bed at 7 a.m. to kick off a day with the sole intention of making ourselves as sick as possible by the end of it?

But if we were bordering on certifiable, then Mama Hanh was, by her own admission, completely bonkers. While the crowd of twentysomething travellers was intent on cramming a lifetime of debaucheries into the one boat ride, Mama H had done this every single day for the last twenty years. And from what we'd overheard while waiting to board, she was no slacker, daily challenging the "crazy people" to keep up with her as she sparked joint after joint and poured countless bottles of wine down her gob. For Mama Hanh, running a Booze 'n' Scoob Cruise was not a spectator sport.

Standing no higher than five feet off the ground with a toned, if leathery, body clad in innocuous shorts and white T-shirt, the "infamous" Mama certainly didn't look like a notorious mistress of mayhem. She looked about as disreputable as a peanut-butter sandwich. But when she opened her mouth, everything changed. Her voice was grating and shrill, but so were a million other people's. Piss off your own mother enough and you'll know what I mean. It was what she did with that squawk that, depending on your sense of obscenity, either elevated her to the status of innovative linguist or damned her to an eternity in hell.

"You, fucka, move it on my boat!" she cawed at nobody in particular, waving the bumbling herds on to a creaking wooden junk. "Go and I fuck you up." She'd obviously gotten her hospitality degree at a very liberal university.

Stunned, excited and with the natural twinge of bewilderment that comes with being called a "fucka" by your gracious host, we all clambered on board, plopping down on the ubiquitous kiddie chairs and anywhere there was room between massive open eskies of beer. El and I annexed a shady spot beneath a rotten-looking awning and sparked up our breakfast fags, eyeballing our giggling peers and muttering the odd exclamation on our surrounds. If memory serves, I believe "bloody freakshow" was our most popular turn of phrase that morning.

But any conversation, either between El and I or our more sociable crew of English, Australian and the odd North American backpackers, was made impossible the instant Mama Hanh switched on her megaphone. In much the same way as her name dominated the slate walls of Apocalypse Now, her voice drowned out everything else in her presence. Even the circling seagulls swooped down for a listen.

"Hey, crazy people!" she screeched. "I say, hey, CRAZY PEOPLE!"

"Uh, hey," murmured the crowd, obviously confused as to whether they were on a leaking old boat or in the audience at a Monsters of Rock stadium tour.

"I say, HEY!"

"HEY!" chorused the crowd with slightly more enthusiasm. El and I looked at each other, both thinking the same thing: uh-oh. If Mama Hanh was trying to get us in the part-aaay mode with a bit of group bonding, she was out of luck when it came to us two. Insta-Camaraderie wasn't our thing. As far as I knew, we didn't have to forge lifetime bonds with a bunch of strangers just to get wasted. And getting wasted was the point, wasn't it?

Evidently so. "Hey, crazy people, I am Mama Hanh. Today, I take you to beautiful place. And I fuck you up." Pause for gasps. "That's right, I fuck you up. You no fuck up, I sorry." Pause for giggles. "I work hard every day to fuck you up, and you work too. Work at getting fuck up. Don't be lazy."

And there it was. I'd spent my entire life being told by respectable figures of authority to stop being such a layabout and had never listened to a word of it. Now, thanks to the exhortations of a diminutive madwoman, I was going to mend my indolent ways. I was going to work really hard. Now pass that bottle.

As we began drifting out of the small harbour, Mama Hanh continued to fill us in on what awaited us. Snorkelling, stops at a few islands, a seafood feast. Yeah, yeah. "But the best is party," she yelped. "I give you free fuck-up party in the water. Wine, free. Smoking, free. Fuck up, free.

"Now you meet Chris," she squalled into the crackly megaphone, pointing at a thin, bronzed English boy in his mid-twenties who was slouched at the front of the boat, rolling an army of joints. "Chris is crazy like Mama Hanh. You want smoking, you see him." Chris glanced up briefly from his handiwork and smiled victoriously to the crowd, who gawped back at him with a mixture of adoration and seething jealousy. I wondered what kind of TE Score you needed to get a job as a professional spliff roller, and mentally damned my high-school guidance counsellor. She'd never bothered filling me in on this particular career opportunity.

"You wanna breakfast, I have cold beer," Mama continued. Good to hear she was looking after our nutritional needs. "Is good breakfast."

She was either very persuasive or our peers were hardcore pisspots, for El and I were nearly trampled in the stampede to the eskies. There was never a question of getting El to bang down a beer for brekkie, and as much as I liked to consider myself a first-class dipsomaniac, I knew I was beaten on the lush front by our cruisemates. It wasn't even eight in the morning and the idea of stomaching food, let alone quaffing warm ale, made me retch. When it came to early-morning repasts, it was nicotine, tar and carbon monoxide or nothing at all.

"I just hope Mama Hanh doesn't see us," El muttered, taking a swill of the very un-beerlike water she'd brought along. "We'll get in trouble."

I felt my head swim into a strange vortex. In trouble for not getting pissed. If the world ran by Mama Hanh's rules, I'd be a model citizen.

"I'm going to have a drink in a couple of hours," I said, justifying my lamely sober existence. "Aren't you?"

"Course. But till then, let's keep a low profile, in case she finds us and makes us walk the plank or something."

"Or pours a six-pack down our illicitly sober throats."

But Mama Hanh was too busy cavorting with the more dedicated boozehounds to worry about the antisocial abstainers dorking it up over water and Indonesian smokes. While we hunkered down like the original wallflowers, she was holding court before a rapt group of admirers, each of them keen to earn her praise as one of the true "crazy people." They shotgunned beers, blew smoke in each other's mouths and came up with some admittedly creative variations of the word "fuck," but there was no way in hell any of us mortals were ever going to reach Mama Hanh's status of "very crazy." Reeling off dirty jokes in her trademark broken English, she cracked a new beer every thirty seconds and steadfastly refused to share either of the two joints she was smoking. "You wanna smoking, you see Chris. These are mine," she cackled. "Don't be lazy!" Sharing and caring weren't her big points, but she made a fine motivational speaker.

By the time the junk anchored in the crystal waters off a dazzlingly perfect deserted island, nearly everybody was rat-arsed. Everybody, that was, except El, me and Mama Hanh. She'd downed a couple of six packs and inhaled about a plantation's worth of grass, but she seemed completely normal. Or at least as normal as a cruise host who called one of her guests "Dickhead fuckboy" could be, anyway.

"Okay, crazy people," she barked into her megaphone. "We here at island now. Now we have fuck-you-up party in water. I bring the bar and you get in the water." She paused and looked around. "Now!"

The Svengali had spoken and, within seconds, the lagoon was a-splash with the bodies of dozens of flailing drunkards. "C'mon!" she cried, pushing the more timid off the bow of the ark. "Go to the best bar in Vietnam! Go! Go!"

We went, we went. Mama Hanh, finally noticing our beer-less state, had pegged a couple of cans at us before unceremoniously shoving us overboard. "You're lazy! Lazy!" she yelled to us as we slunk, as much as slinking was possible in two fathoms of seawater, over towards the frolicking group.

Despite our public branding as bone-idle layabouts and the fact that everybody else was going out of their way to avoid us and our possibly communicable un-coolness, we couldn't have been happier. We swam and swilled through swells of clear blue and green water, marvelling at the verdant backdrop of the perfect little island, feeling on top of the world. Nothing could bring me down, not our rapidly diminishing social status, not even the stray lifebuoy Mama Hanh tossed over the side of the boat, thunking me on the head. It was an idyllic morning, and, as it tends to do, beer made it even better.

Not so the wine. "Hey, crazy fuckas," Mama Hanh called. "Here comes the bar." With a gigantic splash, a massive floating crate was shoved into the water and, hardly raising a bubble, she jumped in after it. "A bottle for everyone," she gurgled, tugging the bar towards us.

Like seagulls to a discarded chip, the crazy fuckas descended on the buoyant bar, squabbling over unmarked bottles of wine. "Okay, enough for everyone!", Mama cried above the din. "And you compete with me to drink the fastest. All of you." Suddenly, she was bobbing beside El and me. "This means you, fuckas."

El, who couldn't swill a shot of sambuca without coming up for air, pleaded cirrhosis of the liver, but I'd had enough. Lazy, eh? I'd once downed a pint of Guinness in nine seconds and was occasional boat-race champion at university. Besides, I was Australian and I had the luck of Bob Hawke on my side. If he could manage to hold the world's record in yard-glass skulling, surely I could do my country proud in a measly vino-downing comp with a woman half my size. "Gimme that," I said, swiping a bottle from Mama Hanh. "You're going down."

She didn't go down, but if I'd eaten any breakfast that day, I bet it would've come up. That shit wasn't wine, it was swine. It was the rankest, most repugnant and overtly offensive crap I'd ever purposefully poured down my throat, and that's coming from someone who's tried every cask in the Stanley line. But my pride was at stake and I had no choice but to keep on guzzling. And guzzling. And.

"Hey! I win, crazy fucka!" I tore the bottle away from my lips in disbelief and squinted at Mama Hanh. Bobbing serenely beside me, she held her empty bottle up in triumph and glared disdainfully at mine, still a quarter full. "I win," she said, without a slur to be heard. "But you one crazy fucka!"

As she swam away, already screaming for another challenger, I felt the world slide sideways. I was suddenly, irrevocably smashed off my dial and I felt my gorge a-risin'. But it didn't matter. I was now officially a crazy fucka. I've never been so proud.

✳

And I've never been so wrecked. El had taken the wine off me after it looked like I was going to keep trying to swallow it, but once we'd hauled ourselves back on the boat, I'd launched myself immediately at the eskie, grabbing an armful of beers to keep us going. By the time we'd replenished our supply about four times, we'd anchored at yet another island, which looked to my glazed eyes like the identical twin of the first one we'd stopped at. But such trifles didn't bother me, or anyone else on board, by then. All anyone seemed to care about was getting their fiendish hands on some more grog and keeping their joints from going out. With a clarity known only to the mega-hammered, I found that I could see the deep philosophical truth in Mama's "Don't be lazy" edict.

After hours of swilling and smoking, we were dependant on our supply of illicit substances to keep us going. To stop would mean to pass out. And how lazy was that?

The rest of the trip was just a haze. There were a couple more islands somewhere along the line, and more skulling contests, all of which I lost dismally. I distinctly remember El throwing a prawn at me during an on-board seafood munchfest, just before I fell off the boat and had to be retrieved. And I faintly recall seeing Chris, floating in a lifebuoy and handing out joints by the dozen, just before El and I accidentally dive-bombed him and ruined his fistful of merchandise. Thankfully, my memory shut down for good right about then. A lynching wouldn't make for the most joyous of holiday memories.

*

When we woke early the next morning, disorientated and sporting the macdaddy of all hangovers, we decided it probably wouldn't be in our best interests to stick around Nha Trang. While we partially remembered the douse-the-dope scandal and had a vague inkling that the aftermath hadn't been too pretty, we had no idea what had happened after that. We were both alive, for a start, so that ruled out any possibility that we'd been forcibly drowned in revenge, and a quick once-over revealed no rope marks around our necks, proving there'd been no attempts to hang us for treasonous behaviour. But we doubted we'd be very welcome additions to the Mama Hanh Reunion Party that was supposed to be taking place that evening at the Nha Trang Sailing Club, and I suspected I'd been stripped of my illustrious "crazy fucka" title. Nha Trang was no place for a couple of plain old fuckas.

We decided on Saigon. It was close enough, reportedly just an inexpensive flight south from Nha Trang and was obviously a must-see stop on any traveller to Vietnam's agenda. Why this was, exactly, we weren't too sure. All we knew was that its real name was Ho Chi Minh City and that some stuff had happened there during the war. Oh, and it was big. It wasn't much to go on, but we'd travelled on far less during our twenty days in Southeast Asia so far. Besides, it was just another city, and all cities, essentially, were just the same. Lots of people, lots of noise and a bit more crime than you'd find in your average hill-tribe village. A city's a city, right?

Chapter Nineteen

Jinxing the Hosts and Other Dinnertime Faux Pas

Wrong. By the time we found ourselves in an airport cab late that afternoon, screeching and crashing our way through the astonishingly frenetic streets of Saigon, I realised I'd morphed from a fucka, to crazy fucka, back to fucka and straight into the realms of dumb fucka in less than twenty-four hours. Saigon, as I'd arrogantly assumed in my ignorance, was not just another city. It was an über-city, a mega-metropolis, a massive seething ant farm of humanity with a good dose of inhumanity thrown in to boot. Lots of people? Try four million of them, all squashed together at an average of twenty-two thousand per square kilometre. Lots of noise?

"What?" El and I screamed above the cacophony of the traffic to the cab driver for the eighth time that minute.

"I said, look out for your bags! Saigon has the most pickpockets in the world!"

And that took care of a bit more crime.

A city's a city indeed. Outside the taxi window, what appeared to be every single one of the four million people living in Saigon were diligently going out of their way to bust my adage. I've seen some pretty wild stuff in cities like New York, London, Sydney and Berlin, but never have I seen a fully suited businessman scurrying along the crowded pavement, holding a gigantic, still-writhing fish above his head. Or seventeen children piled on to one bicycle. Or a girl, dressed head to toe in the purest of white silk pyjamas, ride through a mud puddle and emerge immaculate. There was not an inch of pavement on which someone wasn't busy doing something completely bizarre. Mama Hanh would have liked Saigon. There was nobody lazy around here and these were the craziest fuckas I'd ever seen.

"Where you going again?" cried the cab driver.

"To the asylum," I muttered, goggling out the window as a teenage girl plucked a legless man off the kerb and dragged him inside a shop door. "Did you see that?"

El looked up from her book and grunted. She was still edgy and ill from the previous day's carousals, and was in no mood to watch pavement abductions of amputees. Gave her a headache, I think.

"Read this out to him, would you?" she asked, passing me the *Let's Go* and pointing to a highlighted entry. "If I have to scream one more time my brain's going to collapse."

It took a few attempts, but I finally mauled the pronunciation of the Ngoc-Hue Guesthouse to a decipherable level. Nodding at me in the rear-view mirror, the driver swung a right down a blessedly quiet street. "Ngoc-Hue," he said, "very nice garden on the rooftop."

"Great," I said, grateful to be able to stop screaming for once. I didn't give a stuff about any garden, but I was more than stoked that we'd chosen to stay on what may have been the only street in Saigon that didn't foster industrial deafness.

"Here we are." We hopped out and grabbed our bags from the boot. As El paid the driver, I lurched into the middle of the traffic-free street and breathed a sigh of contentment. We were supposedly smack bang in the middle of Saigon's famously profligate District One, the wild and crazy place for foreigners and locals alike, but from where I stood, the place was more akin to an Asian Sesame Street. A gaggle of kids played ball further down the street, while chattering women swept the pavement around gorgeously rumpled old men slouched atop plastic boxes and fanning themselves languidly in the late-afternoon heat. With an ingenuity familiar to those without cable TV, a couple of enterprising middle-aged men had established an outdoor barber shop along the bend of the street. With the ubiquitous coils of incense burning at their feet, the men had set up a handful of battered chairs and hung broken mirrors on the side of a vacant building, offering haircuts and shaves to the more hirsute passers-by. Everyone seemed to know everyone else, and there was a breezily intimate feel to the place.

A small hand tugging at my backpack brought me out of my reverie and I jumped in surprise. The taxi driver's warnings about pickpockets were fresh in my mind and I was determined not become a statistic.

Instead, I became an Oop.

"Lady, hey lady," cried the small boy attached to the tugging hand. "You Oop?" Puzzled, I stared down at him and over to El, who was busy waving goodbye to the departing cab.

"Am I what?"

"Oop, Oop!" The kid had let go of my hand and was happily prancing around me like I was some kind of maypole. We may have left the clamour and din behind, I thought, but the weirdness was city-wide.

"I dunno," I said, getting dizzy trying to keep an eye on the whirling kid. I didn't really feel like an Oop. Whatever the hell that was. "What's an Oop?"

"Oop! You know, Oop." He stopped twirling and cleared his throat. "Oop is 'G'day mate'!"

Jesus wept. An Oop was an Australian. Stick an "s" on the end, and you've got the most appropriate name for an ill-conceived race of convicts and misbegotten mongrels that I've ever heard. "Yeah, we're Oop," I said, sparking off another round of joyful whirling on the boy's part. It looked like we were in an Oop-Friendly Zone.

"You want stay at Ngoc-Hue?" asked the boy, coming to a panting stop at my feet. "Is my family guesthouse."

"Um," I said, trapped between practicality and distrust. Maybe all this mind-reading was part of the pickpocket's trade.

"You come!" He grabbed my hand and, as I called out to El to follow us, started dragging me down an alleyway. "Oop, you like my place," he said in a sing-song voice. "Is nice garden on the rooftop."

Any misgivings I may have had vanished the instant we turned into the alley. Crowded with guesthouse signs and dozens of Vietnamese people selling trinkets and drinks from tiny stalls, it was obviously no den of thieves. Not counting the bandit who was trying to palm off bottles of Fanta for thirty thousand dong, that was.

The alley veered off to the right and, with a happy yelp, the boy pushed open a heavy door. "Ngoc-Hue," he cried. "You like?"

What was not to like about a place that looked and felt like my grandmother's house? Granted it was about thirty times larger than Granny's besser-block cottage, and her place had a noticeable dearth of neon-lit Confucius shrines lying around, but the essence was the same. Comfortable. Clean. Gaudy velour rugs on the wall. It was a family operation and it felt like it. It was perfect.

Overcome by the happy familiarity of it all, we collapsed beneath our packs on to a well-loved couch while the boy's mother ("Call me Mama") came over and checked us in. As she printed our names neatly in a guest register, she filled us in on what the Ngoc-Hue had to offer, almost none of which we could use. El and I were of the opinion that exercise puts the "hell" in "healthy," so we wouldn't be renting any pushbikes. We usually suffered from hypersomnia when it came to getting up before 9 a.m., so the free breakfast was no good to us either. But they left their doors unlocked until 3 a.m., allowing for us who "make party" to get to bed without scaling the walls, and the fact that there were hardly any other guests came as a relief. I'd expected a truckload of Oops to come rollicking down the stairs. "And best is garden," she said, pocketing our dong in a tatty apron. "Nice garden on the rooftop."

*

Unless the much-lauded garden came with two supremely comfortable beds and indoor plumbing, I highly doubt it could have out-ranked our room as "best." Not since we'd arrived in Southeast Asia had we come across so much luxury; not only did we have a toilet that flushed, but we got tepid water to boot. After weeks of shivering beneath dribbling showers or bathing in tiny sinks, the feeling of washing in a spray of water that was approximately the same temperature of warm saliva was pure indulgence.

Clean-scrubbed and glowing, El and I were collapsed drowsily on our beds and dreamily contemplating not moving for the rest of our lives when someone knocked on our door.

"If that's some kind of room service, then I know I've died and gone to heaven," El murmured.

"Only if they have beer will it be heaven," I corrected. What a disgrace. Only one day since the ultimate piss-up and already craving grog. "Otherwise, I'd safely say we're stuck in purgatory."

It turned out, in the long run, to be a knock from hell. Not that you could tell by looking at the clean-cut young man who stood in the doorway that he was a harbinger of doom. But I can safely say that, after what happened next, El and I are now assured of two first-class tickets across the River Styx.

He had come, he said, to invite us along to a special feast the family was putting on in the living room. There would be many different types of Vietnamese food, he assured us, and we would try many family specialities.

El and I love food more than life itself sometimes, but we love lying around doing bugger all even more. After a millisecond of indecision, we politely declined the offer. There was lounging to be done.

"No, you must come," insisted the man. "All the guests are come. Is very important. Is the Feast of the Ancestors."

When it came to reasons just why we should not abandon our beds, this came as a double whammy. Other guests and a solemn occasion. We weren't too crash hot at dealing with either. "Uh, I don't feel so good," I muttered weakly. Surely the ancestors would forgive an invalid?

Maybe they would, but our man here wasn't having a bar of it. "You must come," he said, backing out into the hallway. "Five minutes."

$*$

Dressing in haste for the Feast of the Ancestors is an unusual fashion dilemma that doesn't get many write-ups in *Cosmopolitan*, but El and I managed to put together a couple of outfits with stylish aplomb. After turning out our backpacks and throwing everything we owned across the room, we opted for the "slob-casual" look. Not too clean, not too showy. Just a lot of dirt stains and ill-fitting trousers. With the ancestors most likely having spent their lives toiling the land and scarpering about in baggy pyjamas, we figured they'd appreciate our efforts. Besides, it had been a long time since we'd seen a washing machine.

Not so the Ngoc-Hue family. As we made our grand entrance into the living room, now chock-a-block with tables, chairs and countless photos of expressionless long-dead people, we shuddered to see dozens of spiffed-up Vietnamese people taking their places for the big nosh-up. Even the guests, two Japanese couples and a broad honky taking up an entire couch, looked as if they'd managed to find some respectable clothes not battered by the ravages of travel. I hoped the ancestors, whose spirits were apparently present for the banquet, weren't the snobby kind. There's nothing more annoying than a trendy ghost.

But just as we were about to flee back to our room, pleading the sudden onset of bubonic plague or something, we were grabbed by a hearty-looking Vietnamese fellow who was obviously the patriarch of the Ngoc-Hue family. "Sit! Sit!" he boomed, not looking even slightly put-out by our uniform of stains and patches. "Special place for you!"

Either this family really did have a thing for those of the Oop persuasion or we looked ridiculous enough to be considered an amusing centrepiece, because we were steered to two seats right in the middle of the room. Flanked by half a dozen prim-faced living Vietnamese and their expired Kodak counterparts, we were the only farang at the table bar the big European who had lugged himself off the couch to squeeze into one of the tiny chairs provided. Considering our knowledge of Vietnamese extended only as far as the word "Oop," and goofy smiles cannot a conversation make, we turned to him to break the ice.

"Fred," he said, stretching his hand across the table to shake ours. Somehow, it figured. To my mind, the name Fred immediately conjures images of basset hounds and, while this Fred didn't seem to be of the canine variety, he wasn't too far off. With droopy eyes, a slightly jowly face and a woebegone look about him, our Fred came about as close to Hush Puppy as humanly possible without drooling on the table or doing rude things to my leg.

We introduced ourselves and launched into the usual traveller spiel: Where you from? Where ya been? Watcha doin? Ever notice you look like a basset hound? Looking hungrily in the direction of the bustling kitchen, he answered us with an apathy bordering on the comatose. He was Dutch, which explained his mishmash accent, and this was the first stop on his Asian junket. The hound thing didn't get a mention. "I've been here for seven months," he finished, looking dolefully at his empty plate.

"Seven months!" El exclaimed. "That's a pretty thorough look at Vietnam, isn't it?"

Fred shook his head. "Seven months here, I mean."

"In Saigon?" I asked with a hint of reverence. Anyone who could spend over half a year in this screwball town had to be hardcore. Forget all the pitstop Panchos with their "been there, done that, bought the spiritual-looking T-shirt" mentality, forget the package-tour geeks who thought they knew a place after looking at it out of the window of an air-conditioned bus and forget us, with our blithering and blundering through God knew where; Fred was so down with Saigon he was practically a local.

"Yeah, Saigon," he sighed. "But really only here, as in here." He pointed to the floor. "I just live here in the Ngoc-Hue."

"But surely you've seen a lot of the city," I said.

"Not really."

"You working?" El asked.

"Nope."

"Oh I get it," I said. "You're here learning Vietnamese."

"Nuh. Don't speak a word."

El and I exchanged muddled glances. "So what do you do here?" we chorused.

"Nothing," Fred said. "But I do like to hang out on the roof. There's a . . ."

"Don't tell me," I sighed. "A lovely garden."

✳

With our conversation brought to a halt with the verbal equivalent of a slap to the head with a dead fish, we three farang sat in an uneasy silence while the Vietnamese chattered merrily away. Either the gloomy-looking ancestors had yet to make an appearance or they weren't as doleful as their portraits would have us believe. As we shifted uncomfortably in our chairs, I found myself staring at the grim pictures and wondered just why it was that every old-time photographer ensured his subject looked as much like a miserable stunned mullet as possible. Every one of the ancestors, from the ancient grandfathers with their long Ho Chi Minh beards to the unfortunates struck down in their infancy, appeared to be on the verge of hurling themselves off the nearest cliff. OK, times were tough in the days before Prozac, but surely these people could find something to smile about? Or maybe, I thought, these mournful poses were part of a cunning, long-term plan. Any future progeny would surely feel compelled by guilt to hold a feast day for venerable-looking, woeful old sods, while those who'd left behind jazzy pictures of themselves, say, playing beach volleyball, wouldn't get even a prawn peeled on their behalf. They were clever buggers, these ancestors.

"Come and git it!" or the Vietnamese equivalent thereof, came the cry from the kitchen, and we turned around to face the most elaborate mobile smorgasbord we'd ever clapped eyes on. Dozens of women were approaching the tables bearing bowls, plates, platters and trays of what to us was a completely anonymous array of apparently edible treats. There was some green stuff, some orange stuff and some jellied stuff, not to mention some egg-impersonating stuff and some stuff I wished was impersonating a snake but actually was. All of this stuff, plus rice, gallons of homemade dipping sauces and more unidentifiable creations, landed on our table and as I stared stupidly at my chopsticks, the hoe-in began in earnest. No solemn prayers, no holding up of dishes to the looming ancestors, no lighting of incense, just a lip-smacking free-for-all.

Dish after dish of dubious delicacies was passed around, and at the risk of offending someone, I plucked a little something off each one, placing it timorously into my bowl of rice. In the end, my bowl overflowed with scaly meat, something reminiscent of rubber and all sorts of crunchy things that scared the wits out of me. I actually enjoy trying new food, but when there's a risk of losing a tooth in a hard piece of meat that may or may not be the remnants of Poochie, I tend to get a little worried.

Fear is not an easy emotion to suppress, and El, who was used to shovelling strange things into her face after three years in Japan, nudged me in the side. "Go ahead and just eat it," she muttered through a mouthful of something. "They'll take offence if you don't eat it all."

Whether "they" meant our hosts or our unseen guests of honour, I wasn't too sure. But I wasn't going to risk the ire of either, so I turned to the tried-and-true cure-all for scary meals. Sauce, and lots of it.

I scanned the table for an appropriate liquid to drown my dinner in and immediately spotted a bowl of a spicy-looking sauce. Saved, I thought, and stuck my chopsticks into my rice before reaching for it.

"Aah," I said, pouring lashings of the eye-smarting sauce over my jumble of otherwise inedibles. There's nothing like chilli to turn an unpalatable meal into a real treat.

And there's nothing like cultural ineptitude to turn a simple gesture into a catastrophe. As I returned the nearly empty sauce bowl to its place, I looked up to find everyone at our table and the one next to it staring at me with ill-concealed venom in their eyes. The conversation, which had been pelting along at an ever-louder pace, had suddenly dwindled away to a few murmurs and the sound of chewing was deafening. I'd done it now—I'd bogarted the sauce.

"Pick up your chopsticks," Fred hissed across the table. "Hurry up!" I looked back at him in confusion and down at my chopsticks, which were sticking up from my bowl like antennae.

"Take them out!"

"What do they have to do with sauce?" I asked, trying to block out the glares of everyone but Fred.

"Sauce?" He shook his head urgently. "Screw the sauce and take out your fucking sticks!"

"That's fine language to use in front of the ancestors," I muttered, plucking the chopsticks out from my bowl. "Happy?"

I wouldn't say anyone in the near vicinity was actually ecstatic but at least they weren't giving me the evil eye any more. I glanced at El, who just sighed and looked at the ceiling, and back over to Fred. "What was that all about?"

He shovelled a lump of gristle into his gob and leaned over the table. "Sticking your chopsticks in a bowl like that is a classic death sign, you idiot! Now you've gone and jinxed the whole family."

And there I was thinking that hogging all the sauce was a social blunder. But wiping out an entire family line with one flick of the chopsticks? Now that really was gauche. Being an "Oop" never seemed so appropriate.

"Sorry," I mumbled, not so much to Fred, who had, after all, called me an idiot, but to my now-doomed hosts. I just hoped they wouldn't start keeling over while I was still at the table. It was hard enough trying to stomach this stuff without people carking it all over the place.

With no response from the accursed crowd, I decided the best I could do to get back in their good books, and those of the ancestors who must've been none too thrilled when I inadvertently cast a hex on their progeny, was to eat everything on my plate. No being picky, no "leaving a little something for Mr. Manners," just full-scale schnarfing.

The plan was going swimmingly until I put it into action. Picking up a mangle of meat and rice in my maledictory chopsticks, fine. Putting it into my mouth, no worries. But when my tastebuds got a hold of the nuclear chilli coating the lot, things went a little bit awry, if you can call frenzied choking followed by the pelting of one of the infernal chopsticks across the room in a spasm of agony, "a little bit awry." I doubt the Ngoc-Hue crew would've.

The table talk screeched to a halt once again, and everyone was staring at me in disbelief. Only this time, instead of the sound of chewing filling the gigantic room, it was my heaves and retches echoing off the walls. It was a none-too-pretty sound, and it didn't feel all that great either—imagine gargling with Ajax and you should get the idea. This wasn't sauce; it was a radioactive leak.

"Gak!" I choked, grasping at my throat o' fire. "Drink!" While everyone else seemed to momentarily forget their English, Mama, bless her, hustled over and plunked a cold beer in front of me.

"Slow, slow," she soothed, "eat slow."

I slurped at the beer and nodded gratefully up at her with red-rimmed eyes, drool making its way out of my mouth and my upper lip brimming with snot. If there was ever a more pathetic example of an Oop Abroad, I was willing to bet these folks had never seen it. Come to think of it, nor had I.

After a few moments, with my throat now merely burning over warm coals and my face wiped of all extraneous fluids, people went back to their food, bent slightly lower in their chairs to avoid any other wayward chopsticks. The conversation picked up a tad, but now, it seemed a more gentle, reverent type of talk. It was as if they had suddenly recalled that this was meant to be a serious occasion, and everyone chose the moment to become simultaneously solemn.

Unfortunately, it was also the moment El and I chose to become hysterical. Throughout my ordeals by chopsticks, she'd remained fairly aloof, interjecting only to pat me on the back or mutter condolences. But now, with everyone else concentrating on chewing respectfully and occasionally glancing up at the ancestor shrines, she somehow lost it. I don't know if it was a delayed response to my rampant idiocy or just one of those horrid moments when everything is hilarious that shouldn't be, but suddenly, El was giggling so hard that she started to cry.

She looked at her food bowl and found it uproarious. Ditto the stern photos on the wall. And when she looked at me, she let loose with a howl I'd previously heard her use only during premiere screenings of Jim Carrey flicks. Things were getting out of control.

"El," I whispered. "Shut up! Everyone's looking and we're gonna get lynched."

"I know," she gasped, rubbing her hand over her face. "It's just . . ."

I never found out what it just was because, in a flash, my mouth was quivering and my eyes were running. If yawning is contagious, then cracking up in totally inappropriate situations is as infectious as the plague. I completely lost it.

For the next five minutes, we tried desperately to get ourselves under control. We bit our lips, pinched ourselves, hid behind napkins and pleaded with each other to shut up, but to no avail. Even the increasingly murderous glares from our tablemates served merely to fuel another side-splitting dose of belly laughter. It was only a matter of time before the spectres of the ascendants made themselves visible and really kicked our butts.

"My God," I choked, trying to stifle a guffaw at the sight of a strangely amusing bottle of soy sauce. "Run!"

We bolted. Sobbing with laughter and bawling useless apologies, we crashed out of our chairs and stampeded past the astonished onlookers. On the verge of vomiting, we ran up the stairs, past our second-floor room, and kept going until we suddenly found ourselves gasping for breath beneath the glittering night sky. Beyond pots of daisies and chrysanthemums, beyond a dribbling fountain and a hand-carved bench, the lights of Saigon danced before our watering eyes.

It really was a lovely rooftop garden.

Chapter Twenty

Please Don't Do Anything Weird

In the old days, Japanese people used to atone for their shameful doings by committing harakiri. Other, less self-disembowelling-inclined folk deal with personal disgrace by writing songs or indulgent poetry. Many people get a grip on their guilt simply by making amends for whatever ignominious acts they have committed through apologies or good deeds. All of these methods of redress are bold, noble and, with the exception of pushing a sword through your guts, wise. But for those of us looking for a totally painless solution to facing up to our awful actions, there is but one option: don't.

No show of remorse, no begging for forgiveness. As they say in the most unapologetic city in the world, New York, fuhgged-abboutit. So when it came time for El and me to choose between a nasty double suicide attempt most likely not covered by travel insurance, penning mournful lyrics, a brave apology to the Ngoc-Hue clan or slinking out of the building before anyone noticed us, there was one option that stood out like a beacon. We beat it.

Anyone who saw us sneak surreptitiously out of the building the next morning could have been forgiven for thinking we'd just committed a horrific crime, and with no evidence that my death spell hadn't come to fruition, we may well have done. It wasn't that we didn't feel agonisingly horrible about the havoc we'd wreaked on the family's feast. On the contrary; if someone had handed me a samurai sword at that moment, I actually would've have gone the big lean. Well, at least pricked my thumb on its tip. But we were so terrified of getting thrown out of the guesthouse or worse—like being invited to another dinner—that we simply couldn't go up and say sorry.

"We'll apologise tonight," I said as we bolted down the alleyway. "Maybe they won't be so angry then."

El nodded and cast a glance behind us. "Maybe if they realise they're all still alive, they'll forgive you."

I grabbed her arm and pulled her to a stop. "Me? Forgive me? What about you? You're the one who nearly pissed herself at what was practically a funeral dinner."

"So did you, remember? And at least I didn't go chucking my chopsticks all over the room like a maniac."

"Fine," I harrumphed. "I'm a freak. But you're still coming with me to say sorry too."

"Sure. Just do me a favour, you Ooping lunatic. Stop cursing the natives."

Head bent over a cigarette, I was about to reply when she interrupted me. "Hey, look at that bastard!" So much for not cursing the natives.

Swinging my head around, I found the latest target of El's trademark vitriol: an old, wrinkled man tugging an arthritic, toilworn monkey on a chain. As I gawped in horror, the man grinned at us and yanked the chain, giving the long-suffering monkey the appearance of a dancing marionette. I'm scared shitless of puppets as it is, thanks to the evil clown from *Poltergeist*, but this was worse than a horror flick. It was out-and-out cruelty.

"You like? You like?" asked the man, limping towards us, oblivious to our disgust. He barked something to the monkey and jerked the chain again, sending the beast into a grotesque line-dancing routine. "Dancing!" The man cried in glee. "Dong for monkey?" He pulled the monkey's ear, and it scampered up to us, its hand outstretched. Whoever had told this guy that foreigners would be entertained by an abused animal tripping the light fantastic was sorely mistaken. It was the most pathetic thing I'd ever seen.

As I bit my lip, holding back a well of tears, El launched into the old man. "Do you know how cruel that is?" she shrieked. "That's a living creature you're tugging around there! You think that monkey likes dancing?" The man, who didn't catch a word of it except "dancing" grinned and pulled the chain again.

"Dancing, yes! Dong?"

As the monkey painstakingly began its piteous routine again, I watched as El's eyes narrowed into angry slits. Oh no, I thought. She's going to go, aptly enough, ape. While there are many reasons why people first turn to crime—dysfunctional family background, poverty, addiction—I was damned if rescuing a wretched primate from a life of bootscootin' was going to make the list. What with the previous night's debacle still weighing heavily on our minds, we certainly didn't need a kidnapped monkey to add to our woes.

"Elissa!" I barked, clasping her shoulder. "Step away from the monkey before you do something idiotic." As far-fetched as it may have seemed, I could actually visualise El shanghaiing the poor thing. Despite her occasionally crude mouth and usual cynicism, she had rare moments of dangerous idealism. "Away!"

She shook me off and tossed her head. "I'm not going to steal the damn thing," she spat, reading my mind. "I just think it's sick." Casting a stony glance at the old man, still jerking the beast by the chain, she began to walk off, then stopped and spun back around.

"I'd like to sic every animal rights group in the world on your arse," she snapped, pointing her finger at the uncomprehending handler. "Monkeys don't like dancing—and they like country and western dancing even less!" I would've liked to have seen the footnote for that particular gem of information. "This isn't a bleeding circus, you wanker!"

∗

While El was correct in assuming the alleyway was indeed no circus, the same couldn't be said for De Tham. The main tourist drag in downtown Saigon, De Tham was a carnival of debauchery and excess. Despite being but a two-minute stroll away from the guesthouse, arriving on De Tham was like landing on another world, one in which a dancing monkey would probably go completely unnoticed.

The shop-lined streets were crammed to bursting point with freaks of every persuasion; touts selling everything from ivory opium pipes to hammocks raced between outdoor café tables of wide-eyed farang, each vendor trying to out-do the other in eye-catching garb and ear-aching volume, while prostitutes—male, female and otherwise—cavorted before neon-blinking shopfronts, winking lasciviously at all passers-by. Bare-chested men dotted with perfectly round red scars (the garish reminders of hot-glass cupping sessions purported to bring good health) strode purposefully though the human traffic, while rabbles of dogs, which made the line-dancing monkey's mange look downy, trotted almost invisibly along the slimy gutters. Tiny boys dressed, for some obscure reason, in white suits and red bow ties, thronged the more crowded backpacker haunts, selling packs of Wrigley's Spearmint that had surely been in storage since the Vietnam War, while their less fortunate counterparts limped painfully up and down the pavement, begging mournfully. And on the street itself, an unmoving block of clanging noodle vendors, mopeds and rustbuckets spluttered in exhaust fumes, waiting to get a wriggle on. De Tham was alive, electric and deranged with seething variety and mayhem, and it wasn't even nine o'clock in the morning.

Pushing our way tentatively past pink "host bars," tailors and cramped art-reproduction sweatshops, in which dozens of young men painstakingly copied famous works, we goggled at the early-morning pulse of De Tham. Although the sun was already high in the sky, it seemed like all the passions that were usually reserved for nighttime knew no lunar boundaries in District One. Clinging to our daypacks, we watched as a Vietnamese woman trapped in the traffic was relieved of her handbag by a fast-moving man and his even faster strap razor, and were nearly bowled over by a French sailor hastily escorting two hookers of questionable X-chromosome status to a pay-by-the-hour hotel. It seemed the one concession De Tham was making to the time of day was the "American Brekfest" menu plastered to the wall in the Sinh Café.

"Hungry?" I asked superfluously. Having stomached nothing of substance since Nha Trang, my belly felt like a shrivelled balloon. Even El, who'd managed to put away a fair amount of giblets and godknows before turning into a hyena at the Feast of the Ancestors, looked pallid and malnourished.

"Can you not see my drool? My God," she slobbered, peering at the faded menu. "'Bluberie pencake.' If that's what I think it is, bring it on."

A few moments later, we joined the throbbing masses at a plastic table outside, smacking our chops over plates of pencakes, sosajes and tost. Typos had never tasted so good.

"So what shall we do?" El asked, lighting up a couple of smokes once we'd completed the demolition. "Going back to the hotel is out. Maybe we should just hoon around and see where we end up."

I shuddered at the thought. Given our less-than-auspicious start in Saigon, I felt like just sitting still at the café for the rest of the day and avoiding any more dramas. If we hung around De Tham, we'd most likely end up pickpocketed, roped into buying dodgy "local-style" gowns at one of the badgering tailor shops or spending all our money on gum and hammocks. And if we went wandering, who knew the horrors that awaited us? I'd read that one of the nearby districts was infamous for its daily pet market, a bazaar that specialised in cuddly pups and kittens, not to mention snakes and live fish. Unfortunately, Spot and Snuggles were flogged as additions to the dinner menu rather than the family unit and, after the monkey debacle, I could just imagine the scene if we happened upon that particular venture. I had the feeling the locals wouldn't appreciate the sabotaging of their edible zoo.

I was just about to open my mouth and suggest anchoring ourselves down with some more kofee when a speaker above our heads shrieked to life. "People going on Temple and Tunnel Tour please go to bus now. Bus is leaving please," it crackled. "Go to bus." A handful of honkies stood up from the surrounding tables and looked around in a bewildered daze, trying to distinguish their bus among the three parked outside the café.

"This way, please," a rather distinguished Vietnamese man proclaimed, ushering his small herd towards the middle bus. "Step aboard." He cast his eyes over the remaining farang slouched at the Sinh Café tables. "Anyone else? There is still room on the Temple and Tunnels Tour."

Given our aversion to group anything, it should come as no surprise that El and I are avowed opponents to organised tours. As far as we're concerned, group excursions turn otherwise normal individuals into a collectively retarded clot of helpless fumblers who, for the duration of their junket, hand over their free will to some hyper jerk with an overworked script. Living in the aggressively marketed tourist town of Cairns, I'd seen too many fully grown adults being herded around like the proverbial bovids.

But then again, I thought, maybe a day of acting like a docile idiot instead of a trouble-seeking missile of an idiot would do us no harm. We could spend the day tucked up in a bus, far removed from performing primates and the temptations of the crazy city, lulled into harmless vacuity. Besides, we might actually see something really neat.

I shrugged in a vaguely positive way at El and called the guide to our table. "Where's your tour going?" I asked.

"Ah!" he cried. "This is the best tour in southern Vietnam. We go first to the most strange temple you can ever imagine, the Cao Dai Holy See, and we watch a very crazy ceremony with these odd people. Then we move on to the Cu Chi Tunnels, which was the underground home to the Viet Cong in the war. You can even crawl through a tunnel yourself!"

Being completely ignorant when it came to anything to do with Vietnam, or the rest of Southeast Asia for that matter, I had no idea what he was talking about. All I could gather between all the Cao Dais and Cu Chis was that we'd get to barge in on some cult freaks before rolling around in the dirt. If nothing else, it beat fending off other tour touts for the rest of the day.

"El?"

She shrugged and squashed out her half-smoked cigarette, surely a sign in the affirmative. "Why not?"

*

Why not indeed. Even if the sights turned out to be duds, we would get to spend a few hours drowning in the luxury of an air-conditioned bus with seats so plush they nearly swallowed us. After three weeks of caning our tailbones on wooden planks and seats so small our arses felt as if they had been sharpened to points, this was our little way of saying "thank you" to our butts.

But as we sank deeper into the seats, groaning with the extravagance of it all, our tour-mates looked singularly uncomfortable. Apart from El and myself, everyone else on the bus was either an American war vet or the wife of one, and the ex-servicemen looked about as pleased to be back in Nam as they must have been to be here the first time around. Speaking as someone who has never had to endure the horrors of war, this kind of Return to Hell trip always baffles me. From what I've heard, wars are not especially nice places to find yourself in, what with all those bad haircuts and people shooting at you in different languages, and I can't imagine why someone who managed to get out of one alive would come back for a second look. I've heard some vets describe the return to the battlefields as some sort of catharsis, but surely they'd be happier making the arduous journey to a condo at Fort Lauderdale instead?

"Hello everybody!"

I tore my eyes away from an overweight old soldier in matching Hawaiian shirt and shorts and looked up to the source of the sound, at the front of the bus. Standing karaoke-style with a bright red microphone was the guide I'd talked to at the café, steadying himself as the bus pulled away from the kerb. He cast his eyes over the awkward crowd and I could almost hear his mind clicking over from Wild and Crazy Guy mode to a Watch Your Arse respectful manner. Unless he wanted to deal with a dozen angry vets caught up in a communal flashback, there'd be no offhand Yank jokes on this bus.

"Welcome to the Temple and Tunnels Tour. My name is –" he made some kind of tuneful gulping noise, "but you can call me Gary. As we begin our journey today I would like to tell you a bit about what we're going to see." I looked at El and nodded in relief. We still had no real idea where we were going.

"As we are going to see the Cao Dai Holy See first, I'll tell you a bit about that," Gary said in nearly faultless English. "Some of you may, er, know about the Cu Chi Tunnels and we'll get to them later." I had a feeling that extolling the virtues of the guerrilla hideouts to a group of malcontent US veterans was going to be no easy task for old Gazza. "So now, let me try to explain a little about this confusing religion, native to Vietnam."

Quantum physics is confusing. So is trying to figure out what the fuck Michael Jackson is doing to his face. But these things are child's play when you compare them to the perplexing enigma that is Caodaism, without a doubt the biggest collection of bizarros, apart from rodeo groupies, ever to stalk this planet.

According to the Gazmeister, Caodaism was founded in 1919 by a public servant named Ngo Minh Chieu, who spent his days off communicating with the dead. As you do. Apparently, Ngo managed to transcend the usual conversational rabble of common ghosts and workaday spirits, because he soon started receiving personal dispatches from the Cao Dai, which was another catchy nickname for God. The Cao Dai gave Ngo a blueprint for the ideal religion, one that would ultimately free its followers from the endless human recycling bin of reincarnation and lead them straight to heaven. The concept seemed fair enough, but either the Cao Dai was having a bit of a lark when he laid down the actual guidelines or poor old Ngo got things hopelessly muddled, because what transpired was very weird indeed.

By the time Caodaism was released on an unsuspecting public, it looked more like a jumble sale than any cohesive belief system. Incorporating bits and pieces from such seemingly irreconcilable faiths as Christianity, Islam, Buddhism, paganism, Confucianism and Hinduism, its overriding doctrine seemed to be "variety is the spice of life." And no-one was excluded from its holy ranks: Jesus was named a saint, as were Confucius and Victor Hugo, the latter also being given the added distinction of Chief Spirit in charge of Foreign Missionary Works. And while they weren't listed as saints, Lenin, Will Shakespeare and Louis Pasteur, to name but a few, got in on the gig as well, regularly contacting Caodai mediums with news from the other side. I began to wonder how Shakespeare's ego coped with old Vic bagging a saint's seat ahead of his infinitely more popular self, but when Gary told us that the Bard had clammed up since his last visitation in the mid-1930s, I figured it hadn't gone down too well. You would have thought professional jealousy would be taken care of by the time you hit nirvana, but that's writers for you.

Caodai followers, of which there were about two million, gave up a lot to be among such esteemed and varied company. Priests were celibate, while the rank and file adhered to a strict code including vegetarianism, sparse living and enforced communication with spirits. They were also big into conversion, and I pitied the person who answered their door to find a Caodai believer standing there wanting "just a minute of your time." These people were serious evangelists, and I almost couldn't blame them for their impassioned proselytising. If I couldn't eat cheeseburgers or have a comfy bed, then I'd be taking everyone else down with me too.

As we neared the village of Long Hoa, home to the Cao Dai Holy See or great temple, Gary reeled off some of the rules and etiquette surrounding the building but, by that stage, our minds had lit up the "No Vacancy" sign. Between trying to imagine Louis Pasteur hobnobbing with the Confucius set and wondering if Jesus managed to stifle the urge to say "told ya so" every time he passed the fervently atheistic Lenin, there was simply no more room at the inn for absorbing temple protocol. We'd figure it out when we got there.

✳

The Holy See was, as Gary had promised, "the most strange temple" we had ever clapped eyes on. Painted bright yellow with splashes of turquoise, the two-storey pagoda was adorned with 3D images of psychedelic saints, dragons and pineapples. Flanked by adjoining towers that would have looked more at home on a Mexican wedding cake, and cluttered with bright, woodblock eyes representing the all-seeing Cao Dai, the temple somehow managed to be both imposing and cartoon-cute at the same time. There was even a day-glo mural of three of the Caodai saints: Sun Yat-Sen, an unpronounceable Vietnamese poet and old Mr. Hugo himself, signing an airbrushed copy of the "Third Alliance Between God and Man," the central tenet of Caodaism. Very groovy indeed. If Elvis had formed his own church, I imagine it would have looked very much like this one. The Holy See was definitely the Graceland of religion.

"Look, hon," called out one of the vet wives, pointing at one of the large eyes on the temple walls, "they copied that eye thing off our dollar bill."

"Those bastards!" cried her husband, a red-faced man in a clean, starched war correspondent's vest, proving, if proof were actually needed, that he was no roving reporter. "That's sacrilege." He spun around, his face rapidly turning to deeper crimson. "Hon," soothed his wife, patting his tattooed arm. "You told me yourself, these people are savages. They don't know any better."

It was going to be a long tour.

"Okay, everybody!" Gary called, clapping his hands together, oblivious to the grumblings of some of the vets. "The ceremony is about to start, so if you remember everything I told you about the polite way to do things going in and inside the Holy See, we'll get started."

El and I looked at each other anxiously. Polite way? Do things? What things? Gary had already disappeared, leaving us loitering in a crowd of fellow day-trippers who were bickering among themselves as to whether or not they should go inside.

"That's the Eye of God they've got hanging up all over the place," Correspondent Vest said. "The American Eye of God, not of some bullshit Cong God! I ain't settin" foot in that place."

"You got it, RJ," piped up the wife of another vet in a Deep South accent. She obviously had the hots for Correspondent Vest in a weird, right-wing sort of way, and she was sticking by her man, even if he wasn't actually hers. Yet. "I'm proud of our God. He put His eye on our money, not their church. I'm stayin' right here, in my protest as a 'mercan citizen."

As some of the other wives nodded along, El began to snicker. "Crazy, hey?" I muttered.

"You don't get it," she spluttered. "A merkin is a pubic wig."

I looked over at the woman and clapped my hand over an explosive snort. "You're a merkin, hey?" I called to her.

"Damn straight," she said. "And proud of it."

"Good to see." El and I dissolved into idiotic giggles before pulling ourselves together under the confused gaze of the vets. With our mandatory cheap laugh for the day out of the way, it was down to business. Seeing that the Merkin Crew were still undecided whether they were going to desecrate the holy greenback by going inside or not, we turned to the experts.

"Look, over there," I said, nodding my head towards an old man with Fu Manchu whiskers lingering near a side door to the temple. Swathed in a sunshine-coloured robe and sporting a tall paper hat emblazoned with the controversial eye, he certainly looked like someone who might know what he was doing. And if he wasn't a Caodaist, then this guy had serious wardrobe issues.

"Do whatever he does." I nudged El over towards the door and we stood surreptitiously behind the old man. Although I'm the least religious person on earth and, after falling asleep during the local production of Les Miserables, would be the last to revere

Victor Hugo as anything but a prattling old bore, I felt somehow blasphemous tailing this wizened old man as he prepared to worship. But he didn't seem to care, let alone notice us looming inquisitively over his tiny shoulder, so we decided to go with it. When he took off his shoes, so did we. When he bent in what was either a reverent bow or an arthritic stoop, we shrugged and did it too. When he stepped slowly through the doorway, we had no qualms about following him. But when he turned around, saw us and stifled a scream, we decided we better not go there. Where his old-man eyes had been glazed with piousness and love for the big CD, they now watered with fear and alarm. Something told me this wasn't a response to the sudden realisation that he was wearing a rather gaudy frock.

"!!!" he whispered furiously, "!!!" Linguistics be damned, I can tell when someone's pissed off with me. He shook his head in horror and shoved us back out the door before closing it silently, but with great fury, in our faces.

It was bad enough that we'd been kicked out of the temple, but for the entire Travelling Xenophobes League, Confederate Chapter, to catch us at it was truly shithouse. As we stood there, less shoes and clues, they gawked at us with solemn pity, no doubt of the belief that "those savages" were up to their dirty tricks again. But it was when Gary reared his head from whatever rock he'd had it stuck under for the last fifteen minutes that our humiliation became complete.

"What the hell were you doing?" he raged. "Was that you following that man in that door?" We hung our heads and grunted. "That man was a priest! You can't go near him!" So we figured. "And that's the men's door. Don't you remember what I said on the bus? Women go in on the left side of the temple!" He sighed despondently, and I hoped the Caodaists weren't a revengeful lot. If Gary got the sack for this, our karmas would be well and truly stuffed.

"Sorry," we chorused. We really were, and I was especially remorseful. If I kept sentencing entire families to an early demise, desecrating sacred sites and getting people sacked, I was on my way to becoming a local antichrist. Or anti–Hugo. Whatever. I was sorry.

"Fine," Gary said, running a trembling hand through his hair. "Go in the left door, around the other side. And once you're in, please don't do anything weird."

*

Even if we'd tied our bras around our heads and started lighting farts while yodelling "The Macarena," there was no way we could even begin to seem weird next to these people. From where we were standing, in a viewing tower, they held the monopoly on weird.

To the strains of a choir, some of whom were singing while others played what appeared to be the world's skinniest banjos, hundreds of Caodaists filed into the gigantic temple. Those dressed in white robes, who I assumed to be the rank and file of the organisation, plunked themselves neatly down on the mosaic floor, while the pooh-bahs marched along in blue, yellow and red vestments, their eyes fixed on the strange altar before them.

Framed by a blue satin curtain, the altar looked less like a sacristy and more like the boudoir of an extremely eccentric old woman: beneath the stoned gaze of the omnipresent eye, heavy wooden tables supported bizarre fake flower arrangements and copper urns; ornate red-and-gold lounge suites faced pink statues of one-eyed flamingoes; and, from where I was squinting, what looked like an engraved turtle was balancing a delicate china teapot on its back. It was the Sesame Street of the altar world.

Not that it didn't fit in with its surroundings or anything. The entire temple interior looked like it had been designed by someone with an unlimited supply of Blue Meanies at their disposal.

Concrete snakes coiled around pink pillars, unfeasibly large sculpted roses posed as window frames and, on dozens of rainbow cloth lanterns, little embroidered saints threw tapestry horseshoes. In keeping with the faith's "nirvana express" philosophy, the ceiling of the Holy See was painted like a heavenly zenith, resplendent with ethereal clouds and blue skies, while ornately carved spiral staircases wound around lollipop poles, stopping midway between the floor and the roof. I gathered that this was in keeping with their "we're completely bonkers" philosophy.

Sticking admirably to their theme, the Caodaists spent about an hour doing lots of things that made no sense to me, or anyone else who didn't find flamingo likenesses to be part of the grand scheme. While the plebs in white remained cross-legged on the floor, occasionally gesticulating before some fluorescent deity or another, the priests wandered aimlessly for a while, stopping to pour cups of tea off the turtle's back and bowing at random staircases. Every now and again, the brightly coloured druids would break into a synchronised kneel-kowtow-moan routine which seemed to send the white-robed throng into fits of ecstasy. If a Vietnamese recording studio ever wanted to get a boy band together, I knew where they should start recruiting. These fellas really had the moves.

Thanks to the overriding outlandishness of the ceremony and our fear of being spotted by the priest we'd menaced earlier, El and I managed to keep our mouths shut until Gary quietly summoned us out to the bus. Sneaking a last glance at the choir, who had substituted their anorexic banjos for what looked like musical hash pipes, we crept out into the sunshine completely baffled by what we'd seen. Although nobody had tried to initiate group sex with minors or implored us to drink purple Kool Aid, it certainly seemed cultish enough. And while no ghosts of minor historical or literary figures had been floating through the rafters, there was definitely something spooky about the whole thing. As we'd found out, Caodaism had definite rules, but somehow everything seemed tinged with anarchy. And I'd grown up thinking my Catholic school was the epitome of weirdness.

"What did you think?" asked a visibly relieved Gary as we clambered on to the bus.

"Very strange," I said. "It's like they're after the one thing, but are going about it in a million different ways all at once."

"Ah," shrugged Gary. "This is true Vietnam."

Chapter Twenty-one

Subterranean Hoedown

As we bumped along the sixty-odd kilometres between Long Hoa and the Cu Chi Tunnel complex, the general mood of the bus grew increasingly dour. The majority of the vet entourage had refused to go inside the Holy See, as one of the wives whispered to us "because I heard they have them black arts or sump'n in there," and they were refusing to look at either El or me–which, as you can imagine, disturbed us greatly. But as the roadside jungle grew thicker and white stumps reading "Cu Chi" counted off the clicks to our destination, their indignation gave way to an almost palpable fear. Many of the vets had been to the tunnels long before they'd become some sort of macabre tourist attraction, and some of them had even lost their mates there. But they were paying in dong this time, not in lives, and goddamned if they weren't going in and facing their past like men. We, on the other hand, were going in like ignoramuses. Apart from the short spiel Gaz had given as we'd pulled out of the Holy See parking lot, informing us that the tunnels were a 200-kilometre stretch of underground passageways built by Viet Cong guerrillas in the war, we didn't know diddly. I just wanted to crawl around in the mud.

"There is an information video when we arrive," Gary said when we pestered him for more details. "It's better to watch it than for me to tell you." He glanced around the bus with a tweak of nervousness. "Yes, it is better."

"Old Gaz has gone a bit schizy," El muttered as he turned his back on his charges and began blathering in rapid Vietnamese with the bus driver. "Surely he's taken a bunch of disgruntled vets out here before and they haven't flashbacked on him the minute he mentioned the words 'Cu Chi.'"

"Maybe it's just a really good video," I said in one of my rare fits of optimism. "I'm sure everything'll be fine."

As they tend to do, these bouts of occasional optimism result in nothing more than a reason to remain a diehard pessimist. Drifting along to my little mantra of "I'm sure everything'll be fine" in the bus, I had no idea of the nightmare that awaited us in Cu Chi. Of course, there was nothing I could have done to stop it, but if I'd remained true to my inherent cynicism, at least I wouldn't have been so surprised by it. From now on, my glass is half-empty and staying that way.

*

By the time we got to the tunnel complex and were seated in an open-air humpy, the supposed pre-tour briefing centre, our curiosities were aflame. Our surroundings looked innocent enough, just another scrubby jungle landscape dotted with fading signs in Vietnamese, but something about the place had sent just about everyone into a full-scale panic. Our supposedly seasoned tour guide, who'd grown increasingly jittery as we neared Cu Chi, had scampered off into the bush the instant the bus doors had opened, while many of the vets looked as if they were hovering somewhere between pulling out imaginary grenades and partaking in a mass barf-o-rama. Only Correspondent Vest looked like he wasn't on the verge of losing it, probably because he was too busy sending death vibes at our hosts, two tiny women in matching long black pyjamas.

"Welcome to Cu Chi," one of the women said. "Before you go to the tunnels, we have a movie for you to watch which explains what happened here during the war. Enjoy it, please." She nodded to her counterpart and they hurried outside.

The television flickered and instantly, the sounds of combat filled the hut. On a screen tinged with the green gloom of age, grainy B52s pelted dense forests with bombs, blurred peasants went berserk as they scrambled madly for cover and diminutive Viet Cong in the ubiquitous black pjs assembled dodgy-looking rifles. "The Tunnels at Cu Chi," a heavily accented narrator squealed. "The true story."

As the soundtrack of gunfire and high-pitched shrieks gave way to something akin to the theme from Bambi, images of idyllic village life filled the screen. "Cu Chi, the land of many gardens," said the narrator. "Peaceful all year round under shady trees." As Bambi continued la-la-ing away, monochrome children frolicked and the grown-ups did peasanty stuff, smiling toothlessly all the while. Teeth or no teeth, it did look kind of nice. I wanted a shady tree.

"But then," intoned the narrator, "everything changed." Right on cue, so did the music. Bye-bye Bambi, hello Wagnerian melodrama. "Mercilessly, the American bombers ruthlessly decided to kill this gentle piece of countryside."

El and I glanced at each other, a mixture of anxiety and amusement in our eyes. For propaganda, this was hilariously blatant stuff. I wondered if the vets could see the humour in it.

Obviously not. "Gentle?" Correspondent Vest cried from the back of the room, "Gentle, my arse! What is this shit?"

Immune to the heckling, the narrator droned on. "Like a crazy bunch of devils, they fired into women and children." A blue baseball cap emblazoned with "PROUD VET" flew at the screen, bouncing harmlessly off it as the war played on.

"Bastards!"

"Bullshit we did!"

"My buddy died down there, you arsehole!"

It was like going to a midnight showing of *The Rocky Horror Picture Show*, except everybody was screaming along to the words, rather than singing. Thank God there were no fishnets in evidence.

". . . insane Yankee devils . . ."

A few of the wives were trying to calm down their husbands with pointed reminders of blood pressure and the dire consequences of ruptured arteries, but to no avail. Even the vets who had previously steered clear of any aggro were swearing loudly, while guys like Correspondent Vest were actually on their feet, ready to charge the TV screen.

"Elvis has left the building," El muttered as the guy in the Hawaiian print combo cried out for revenge. "Maybe we should too. These people are nuts."

I took another look at the screen, where dozens of Viet Cong were slithering through underground passages about as wide as my head, and shuddered. "I dunno what's worse," I said, as one of the vets started furiously karate-chopping the air. "Being stuck in here with the *Apocalypse Now* extras or going down one of those wormholes."

"Let me help you with that decision," El said, tilting her head towards a stocky guy in fatigues who was staring blankly at his lighter flame while his wife sobbed quietly in the seat next to him.

"Well, that does it for me." I threw on my daypack and we hustled outside as the two hosts, oblivious to the entire debacle, scuffled in. With pathological curiosity, we listened at the door as the women switched off the set to the hooting abuse of the crowd.

"We hope you liked the movie," one of them said. "Before you see the tunnels, maybe some of you would like to try our firing range where you can shoot a real AK-47."

Now that's bad timing.

✳

With our entire group having stampeded out of the hut looking for a bit of pump action, we milled aimlessly around a tatty gift shop until an embarrassed Gary poked his head from around the corner. "Oh," he exclaimed, "you're still here."

We'd forgiven Gaz his disappearance now we realised that he would probably have ended up replacing Jane Fonda as Public Enemy Number One had he stuck around, and we smiled gently at him. "Don't worry, mate," I said, "we understand."

A half-grimace, half-smile flitted across his face and he absent-mindedly smoothed his hair back. He'd wind up bald if this kept up. "So, uh. How was it?" he asked timidly.

"Well," El said. "No points for guessing why you took off so fast."

Gary cleared his throat and tugged at his earlobe. When it came to nervous tics, he was racking them up faster than you could say involuntary spasm. "That movie is too old, too much bullshit. I keep telling the people here, 'Change it! We're all friends now,' but they keep playing it." He plucked at the hem of his shorts, and I stifled the urge to shove his hands in his pockets. "Was it really that bad?"

El took out a pack of cigarettes and offered them round. "Let me put it this way," she said. "I wouldn't be going down to that firing range if I were you."

Shaking his head mournfully, Gary accepted a fag and exhaled loudly. "I've never had a group like this one, ever in all my years."

El and I read each other's minds with a quick glance. Bloody typical.

"Most of the Americans come back looking for what they call 'closure,' and are very nice people. They like us and we like them," he continued. "The war's over." A rifle clap and a shout sounding vaguely like "Gook!" floated through the afternoon air. "Or," he sighed, "maybe not."

We all stared blankly at our feet for a moment, smoking in uncomfortable silence. It was times like this that I wished my life was a movie. At least then we could have had "Give Peace a Chance" piped in through the forest or something.

"Anyway," Gazza said, putting on a resolute face. "I am your guide and you are here to look at the tunnels. We'll go and find you another group." We nodded gratefully and followed him over to another hut, this one crammed with people who seemed less inclined to know the recipe for a Molotov cocktail.

Or any cocktail at all. These people were the most cornfed and all-out wholesome group of honkies I'd come across since my days listening to eight-track tapes of The Partridge Family Christmas. Overweight women in elastic-waisted pedal pushers clutched at the hands of towheaded children, while the men stood together in polyester clumps looking politely impressed. While a handful of the blokes were possible Vietnam vet contenders, the majority of them looked like they'd be more familiar with the Battle of the Somme than the fall of Saigon. God only knew what they were all doing hanging around on what our new guide, a short man in fatigues, was calling "one of the most bombed and bloody grounds in the world."

"Maybe this is part of some Fire and Brimstone tour," El whispered as the guide shunted us into yet another hut. "Give them Bible Belters a peek at hell."

One of the women spun around at us, a small cross glinting at her neck. "Ssssh!" she commanded. "We're tryin' ta lissen."

Not that there was anything to hear that couldn't be seen. And what could be seen made me want to shut my eyes until I got back to Australia. The hut was evidently some kind of torture museum, boasting a galaxy of horrors that made *The Texas Chainsaw Massacre* look like an episode of *Little House on the Prairie*. The walls were daubed with graphic murals showing cartoon US soldiers keeling over in pools of crusting red paint, and the "exhibits" consisted of dozens of nifty gizmos employed by the Viet Cong spelunkers to make their enemy's lives, or what remained of them anyway, complete hell. Spiked ankle traps, homemade spears and bombs clogged the shelves, while inside a display case, sharpened spikes lurked beneath innocuous piles of jungle vegetation. Who knew how many soldier kebabs they'd gotten out of that one. But all of that was child's play compared to what I impulsively dubbed "The Ultimate Push-Up." According to an information leaflet on the wall, a captured soldier would be tied spread-eagle over a freshly-planted plot of bamboo. He'd be left there for weeks, months even, unable to move as slowly but surely the bamboo grew, pushing relentlessly through his body until he became nothing more than an ill-hung tree ornament. Until that moment, I'd always thought of bamboo as a good-guy plant: pandas ate it, Gilligan and the crew built rafts out of it and it made for good backdrops in Kung Fu movies. But I knew then that I'd never look at a stir-fry in the same way again.

"Come now," the guide called to our increasingly nauseated group. "Time for the tunnels." With a strange combination of fear and relief, I grabbed El and we pushed our way to the head of the crowd. I was the most claustrophobic person I knew, but burying myself in a tiny, underground tunnel had to be better than this archive of agony.

$*$

On the short walk to the tunnels, our guide (who also called himself Gary) expanded on what we had already learnt about their history. While the cornfed gang, who had spent most of their time in the museum crossing themselves, may have been well briefed, El's and my collective knowledge equalled nil. What with the vets drowning out nearly every word of the introductory video and our being preoccupied with retching at the more revolting murals in the museum, all we knew was that the tunnels were underground. And we could have figured out that much with the use of a dictionary.

But Gary II rectified that. Without resorting to phrases like "crazed demons raining hell from the skies" or demonstrating torture techniques, he got his information across in a manner that avoided mass outbreaks of fury or queasiness. Which is more than I can say for most teachers these days.

By his account, the tunnels were first constructed as a place for the impoverished peasant insurgents, the Viet Minh, to hide from and fight against their original enemy, the French. But it wasn't until the 1960s, with the uprising of the communist Viet Cong against the South Vietnamese government and later the Yanks, that the tunnels reached their highest point. Or, to be literal, their lowest. Dug to depths ranging from a few feet to several storeys underground, the tunnel system ran from Saigon to the Cambodian border, which would have made for a bloody long crawl, not to mention some really dirty knees. Apart from using the sprawling yet gaspingly narrow network as an infuriatingly clever base from which to attack and a damn good place to hide minuscule hospitals, kitchens and weapons factories, hundreds of guerrillas actually lived down there for months at a time. But they had plenty more tricks up their dirt-caked sleeves. When US troops sent sniffer dogs into the tunnels, the Viet Cong used American-made soap to throw them off the scent. And when the Yanks replaced the hounds with slender grunts specially trained as "tunnel rats," the communists used their superior slithering skills to wage deadly surprise strikes in the subsurface gloom.

"And there were other attack spots besides the tunnels," Gaz II said, steering us into a forest clearing. "Does anyone here see a good place for a sniper to hide?" I looked around. Tree, too obvious. Behind a nearby rock? Sure, if you're three inches tall. But as far as I could tell, the guerrillas weren't Smurfs.

"Sure," El announced with a toss of the head. "Right there." She pointed to what was, in hindsight, a conspicuous mound of leaves by my feet. "Well, duh," she muttered as Gary II looked at her in amazement.

"Uh, very good," he said, with a flummoxed look on his face. Booting me out of the way, he burrowed his hand into the pasty pile of compost and whipped off a hidden lid about the size of a besser block. He swept his hand through the air in the universal gesture of voila: "Secret shooting hole."

We peered down into it. As far as we could see, the narrow pit went straight down about two feet, leaving no visible room for a sniper to crouch once inside. Maybe they really were Smurfs.

"Any volunteers to go into the hole?" Grumbling like an empty stomach, the cornfeds muttered a collective "Heck, no," while El and I stood there wordlessly. I doubted my big toe would've fitted in there.

"Well, it's up to me then," Gary II shrugged. In one liquid motion, he slid into the hole and all but disappeared but for his grinning head and arms which stuck out like a jack-in-the-box. "See? Like you say," he looked up at El and me, "no worries."

Smiling cheesily for the whirring cameras which had simultaneously made their way out of a multitude of Sears carry cases, Gary II made sure everyone got a good glimpse of him down there. After all, it was only fair—from down there, he got a damned good glimpse up everyone else's shorts.

"Now, see how they hid!" he cried, folding himself down into the pit while dragging the covering lid over his head. Everyone dutifully oooh-ed and aah-ed, genuinely impressed. If we'd kicked a few of the leaves over the top of him, Gary II would have been well and truly camouflaged. I shuddered involuntarily at the thought of American patrols stalking the jungle, and tried to put myself in their shoes. How would I feel, stuck in this alien place with no one to watch my arse, knowing that at any time, a tiny mass of Viet Cong fury could leap out from nowhere?

Two seconds later, I got a pretty good idea. "Yaaaahhhh!" Gary II shouted, leaping back out of the hole, sending the lid, not to mention me, flying.

"Fuck's sake!" I cried, sucked in by the drama of my roleplaying. "Holy shit!"

El rolled her eyes and a number of the mums slapped their hands over their kids' ears while glaring at me disdainfully. "Sorry," I muttered sheepishly, "I got a bit carried away." This was precisely why I'd never played Dungeons and Dragons.

"Okay," Gary II said, brushing clumps of mud and vegetation off his knees. "Now you see it's safe, who wants to try it next?"

There was a brief millisecond of total silence before the kids went completely apeshit, rushing the pit and crying "Mememememe!" The screaming of children has always driven me into a frenzy of irritation, but I was actually relieved to see that these brats hadn't had their natural rambunctiousness shushed and prayer-meetinged out of them by their holier-than-thou parents.

However, that didn't mean they were going to get to act on said impulses. "No way, no how," one of the dads said, grabbing the arm of an excessively freckly sprog. "Over my dead body," whined the mother of a particularly wriggly girl. Judging by the look in her daughter's eye, I guessed that if she had anything to do with it, that time wouldn't be long in coming.

"Oh, for crying out loud," I sighed. "I'll do it." I felt the eyes of the group burn into my six-foot frame. "What?"

"Hello," El murmured. "You're the least likely dirt-pit guerrilla I've ever seen. For a start, you're over three feet tall."

"So? I can stand in there and flop out over the sides easily enough."

"Charming image. Anyway, whatever happened to your claustrophobia?"

"It's not like my head's going to be under there. I'm not scared of standing in a hole." I handed her my camera and winked at the jealous kids fidgeting under the iron grasp of their parents. "Stand back."

As I circled the pit, looking for the least muddy place to kneel and so begin my descent, Gary II sidled up to me. "You know, miss, these people were ah, very tiny."

"Like you said, Gary," I crouched to my knees and dipped a foot in the hole. "No worries."

*

And there were none. Not for the first minute anyway, as I stuffed myself into the pit inch by inch, until my feet hit the damp earth at its base. It was a tight fit, but I'd worn snugger jeans. "Hooray!" I called, waving at the highly unimpressed crowd. Unlike with Gary II's expedition into the hole, only El was taking my picture when I pulled what I believed to be insurgent rebel faces and held the lid above my head. Apart from the vague discomfort that comes with the sensation of having a million earthworms crawling up your unreachable legs, there were still no worries on the horizon.

"Alright everybody, we go to the tunnels now," Gary II said, gesturing down at me. "Come out, please."

"Sure thing," I grinned. "Give us a hand, hey?" He and El each grabbed one of my filthy wrists and tugged until I felt my legs drag upwards against the earthen walls. "You've got me," I cried. "Keep pulling!" The clouds of worry rumbled ominously.

From the moment I supposedly hit puberty until the instant I poured myself into that hole, I'd had the body type of a surfboard. Training bras were de rigueur and I had no curves to speak of, not counting the outward swell of my developing beer belly. But just as I was about to be yanked back to the surface, wouldn't you know it, I became a woman.

"Ugh!" El gasped, dropping my hand to the earth as my feet hit the bottom of the pit again. "I think you're stuck."

"Try again." El, when not battling it out with the misguided monkey-keepers of the world, was about as strong as Monty Burns. "Just pull harder, bloody hell."

An impulse to slam the lid on my head and leave me to the worms flashed across El's face, but she simply sighed and picked up my hand again. "I told you," she muttered. "Bloody secret shooting hole."

"Just pull, for fuck's sake." By this stage, I couldn't have cared less about the sanctity of the ears of innocent children. I just wanted out of that hole. The Aussie motto of "No worries" had somehow backflipped into an Arabic curse, "May you be stuck in a pit with a million worries."

"Pull, fuck ya!"

But it was no use. El and Gary II wrenched, dragged, tugged and jerked, but the only part of me willing to come out lay above my belly button. Suddenly, inexplicably, I had sprouted childbearing hips.

"Shit!" I yelled as they dropped me into the hole again. "You're ripping my arms off!" It wasn't the most grateful of comments to be making to two people trying to rescue you from an eternity as a garden ornament, but I couldn't help it. Pain and humiliation are not conducive to polite turns of phrase.

El and Gary II sighed and wearily picked up my hands again

before two of the beefier granddads from the wholesome brigade stepped in. "You guys take a breather," one of them said. "We'll flush 'er outta there in no time." Flush? Great. Instead of being just a fat lard stuck in a hole, I now felt like a tampon lodged in the septic system.

"Hold yer arms up there, missy," said the second grandpa, a rugged Southerner. As I did, he wrapped his strapping arms around my chest and squeezed me tightly. In a Mills & Boon novel, this sentence would have led to romance of the most saccharine sort. But here, all I got was bruises.

Oh, and freedom. With one loudly strained "Heave!", which did my ego immeasurable damage, the two old guys yanked me and my hips out of the shaft, dropping me like a flailing fish on the damp ground. "Gotcha!" the rugged one said, winking as he strode proudly back to his wife.

Swollen and stained, I lay exhausted in the mud while the group hastened away to the tunnels. The majority of them were too disgusted to even look in my direction. Us tampons sure had it tough.

*

"The tunnels we will go in have been widened so that Western tourists can crawl through them," Gary II said, as we gathered around the entrance to a dark cavern. "Nobody could fit into the real ones." He glanced over to where I was half-hiding behind El in all my fat, dirt-smeared glory. "Maybe not even many modern Vietnamese," he added in what I guessed was a means of softening my humiliation. It didn't work.

"Now please follow me and we will see what it was like to be a real Cu Chi guerrilla." He hopped into the ditch and crouched by a dusty staircase hand-carved out of the hard earth. "Let me warn you, there is no light under here and it is very narrow. Anyone who is pregnant or scared of the dark should not go in." I looked at El with trepidation, and she offered a half-smile in return. She hadn't been thrilled with my escapades in the pit, but we were used to each other's public indiscretions by now, and she was back to playing the loyal friend.

"You'll be right," she whispered. "Listen."

". . . gets scared or feels panic, they can come out at any of the exits we have made every fifty feet along. Or for the brave," Gary II chuckled, "you can go the entire way."

"Fat chance," I croaked, my earlier enthusiasm about "playing in the dirt" having completely vanished. Reading historical novels, dressing up in costumes and using your imagination were all perfectly legitimate means of getting a grasp on the past, but slithering around in unlit subterranean passages was going a bit far. "What next," I mumbled to El, "giving us all grenades and going for it, Charlie-style?"

A large woman in a badly screenprinted "Clogging 85" T-shirt stepped between El and me with a none-too-pleased look on her face. "Would you two please shut yer pie-holes? If you're too scared to go in, fine. But us folks wanna hear what's going on."

That did it. If some hick with a penchant for clog dancing and screamingly downhome colloquialisms could go in there, then so could I. No hayseed was going to beat me at the adventure game.

But she did, alas, beat me into the tunnels, and by the time I found myself on all fours, enveloped in dust and gloom, the moon of her arse blocked whatever line of vision I may have otherwise had.

"Jesus," I grumbled back to El, who was no doubt getting a similar view of my upwardly mobile hindquarters. "I'll bet the Viet Cong never had to put up with this."

"Hang back a sec," El said. "We'll give ourselves some space. Nobody's behind me."

I paused, letting the slow-crawling conga line shuffle a few feet away from us, and took stock of my surrounds. Fixating on the arse of a fifty-year-old woman had been eerie enough, but as we crouched almost alone in the dark, I was seized by the unnaturalness of the tunnels. Although they'd been widened for us mammoth honkies, I still felt as if I was being swallowed by a constricting oesophagus. Dirt was getting into my lungs, my nose, my mouth and, as my gritty eyes adjusted to the gloom, I realised there was nothing else to see. Just dirt and darkness, swallowing me up. Oh Jesus.

"Uh, El," I said, trying in vain to turn my head around. "I feel sort of sick." It was a remark in the running for Understatement of the Year. What I actually felt was my gorge rising, along with a wave of anxiety and indescribable revulsion. I wanted to scream at the top of my clogged-up lungs, but I knew that to do so would open the flood gates of panic. And then I, like so many tunnel rats had done before me, would drown down here.

"It's okay, it really is," she replied from somewhere in the shadows. "I'm not that keen on it either, but just keep going. The first exit is around here somewhere."

Buoyed by the idea of busting out into the afternoon sunlight, I lurched forward at top crawl speed. Which, unless you're an infant heading towards a dangerous flight of stairs, is not very fast at all. But at least I was moving. Straight for the exit, yes sir. Straight for . . .

"Ow!" the Clogger cried, as I slammed straight into her bum. "Watch it!"

"Mummmph," I mumbled, trying to dislodge my head. "Is this line moving or what?"

"Someone's having a panic attack," she grunted back to me. "I think it's one of the old guys. He's refusing to move."

"Oh, lordy." I passed the news back to El, who responded with a resigned sigh. "Can we back-pedal outta here?" I called back.

"Don't be stupid. Just wait a sec and we'll be moving again, I swear." I usually don't hold with unsubstantiated promises, but it was all I had to cling to if I didn't want to lose it big-time.

We waited a "sec" and nothing happened, apart from an increase in my discomfort. The air was damp from communal exhaling and my chest was heavy with fear and breathed-in dirt. Apart from an imminent panic attack of my own, I was possessed with admiration for the determined guerrilla fighters who lived and died down here, sometimes without ever coming up for air. I doubted I, or any of my Western peers trapped in the tunnels, had enough love for our respective countries to willingly bury ourselves alive in the name of freedom. In the name of a few million bucks, perhaps, but even that was a bit iffy. It'd have to be totally tax-free.

"We're moving!" came the cry from somewhere in the distant dim.

"Thank the lord," I cried. "Go, lady, move it!" I stifled the urge to slap her on the khyber and waited for an intolerable five seconds until we actually began worming our way forward again.

Oh, the ineffable relief. Until you've been trapped several feet underground with an obese clogging fanatic's arse stifling your air supply, you can't possibly know hell. And it wasn't until I clambered out of that tunnel, squinting in the relatively bright late-afternoon sunlight with forest air filling my lungs, that I truly knew joy. Sex has nothing on oxygen and burnt corneas, I tell you.

"Ye gods," I said, as we attempted in vain to brush off the dirt which had taken up permanent residence in our clothes. "That was the most horrific thing ever."

"Yeah, and you think you've got it bad. Check that out." El tilted her head towards an old man, presumably the one who'd lost it down there, clawing at his throat and panting, while some rock ape of a child tugged at his trousers, screaming, "Can we go again

Gramps, huh? Can we? Can we, huh?" If this kept up, there was going to be some very justified violence going down soon.

"Take my uterus, please," I mumbled. "Bloody kids. Quick El, let's get the hell out of here before I boot that brat myself."

El, whose arm was raised in the classic backhander position, nodded. "Now I remember why we don't go on group tours. Jesus," she looked at the increasingly hyper child with disgust, "I can't take any more. Run now, or I'm going to freak out."

We ran. Past re-creations of guerrilla hospitals and kitchens, past terrifyingly lifelike mannequins decked out in Viet Cong camo gear and cut-out weapons, past mysterious mounds of debris, we pushed our aching, unfit bodies as fast as they could go. When we got to a café-cum-souvenir shop, we slowed to a winded canter, but picked up the pace again when we saw that their main attraction was a black bear pacing in a cage about the size of a large lunchbox. No grappling with the shop manager would have set that bear free, we realised as we jogged mournfully by, and it was too late anyway. The bear was frothing at the mouth and rolling its eyes, obviously quite insane from its years spent trapped in the inhumane pen. Whether this was supposed to be a metaphorical statement on the tunnels and war or just a diversion for the kids, we'd never know. Giving tourists a timely reminder of man's brutality to fellow man was one thing, but a pointless display of man's cruelty to animals was quite another. We kept running with burning tears in our eyes.

"There you are!" Gary cried, as we collapsed breathlessly in the parking lot. "Everyone's waiting. We're just about to head back to Saigon."

"The . . . bear . . ." we puffed. "Wrong . . ."

"I know," Gary said as he pushed us gently towards the bus. "I keep telling them, but . . ."

Chapter Twenty-two

Dumb Luck and Other Staples of Survival

The bus ride back was uneventful, at least as far as we knew. Traumatised by the pit, the tunnels and the bear, and quite unwilling to listen to the vets bragging about their pseudo-slaughter on the target range, we utilised our newfound talent for sleeping anywhere, anytime by passing out straightaway. Apparently, we were supposed to have stopped somewhere for a bite to eat along the long journey home, but nobody bothered to wake us up, and by the time we pulled up outside the Sinh Café, we were starving.

Over squid chilli noodles and glasses of 333 Beer, or "Ba-ba-ba" as the locals called it, El and I wearily went over our day. It had all been too much, too ridiculous, too much of a head-fuck and all we wanted to do was pass out in our room.

"If we still have a room, that is," El reminded me through a mouthful of chewy squid. "Our stuff could well be on the pavement by now."

I glanced around at the hordes of touts and street vendors swarming down De Tham. The twilight had brought them out in even greater numbers and they were pestering anyone brave enough to sit outside with "special price for you" deals on everything from mantle clocks to garden tools. But nobody was flogging anything even remotely resembling our dirty laundry or shucked-out backpacks.

"Our stuff's still there," I told El, "or it'd be all over this joint by now."

"Hope so. We still have to apologise, and the sooner the better. Otherwise who knows where we'll find a place to stay tonight."

As it turned out, we hardly had to do a thing. When we crept into Ngoc-Hue about fifteen minutes later, the only soul around was Mama, and she accepted our clumsy apology with a breezy wave of the hand. "Is okay," she said. "Nobody is upset." Which I took to mean, no-one is dead. We sighed gratefully and took her hands, desperately hoping that this wasn't another damning gesture.

"Go to your room and sleep," she said, shooshing us jovially up the stairs. "Believe me, it is, how you say? No worries, mate!"

With images of tampons and muddy shafts reeling through my exhausted mind, I shuddered and slowly climbed the stairs to bed. I was beginning to believe my national motto carried the curse of the devil.

$$*$$

Although Mama had assured us that we were back in the good books at the Ngoc-Hue, the next morning we decided not to push our luck by sticking around for too long. While the Vietnamese contingent may have welcomed us Oops back into the fold, Fred seemed to harbour a deep grudge against us. Maybe he'd been hanging out for the chopstick curse of death to take hold, so he could spend the rest of his life yukking it up on the roof, rent-free. Or maybe he didn't want any other farang muscling in on his turf. Or perhaps he just thought we were a couple of twerps that he disliked on principle. But whatever it was, he didn't have to worry about us for much longer. We were gone.

We'd also realised with a shock that El only had three more days left until she had to be back in the classroom, and she was intent on getting a Cambodia stamp in her passport. With no such obligations back home, I decided to stay in Southeast Asia until I ran out of funds, patience or sanity. And I figured Cambodia would be as good a place as any to see which gave out first.

After frantically consulting our guidebooks, we decided to ignore every shred of advice they offered about "booking two days in advance" and "confirmation" by aiming to hop the first plane out that afternoon. Doing things by the *Lonely Planet* letter only seemed to lead us to places like Udon Thani and Savannakhet.

"Why you go?" Mama asked as we handed in our keys. "You stay, please!" We turned around to smirk at Fred, who was glowering at us from his annexed couch.

"Sorry, Mama," I said. "El here has to get back to Japan soon."

Mama fixed El with a clever eye. "You no Japanese," she said, stating the blatantly obvious. "Red hair, is no Japanese."

The little boy who had met us an eternity ago at the kerbside popped up next to his mother, and pointed at El accusingly. "You're Oop! Remember, Oop!" This was turning into a real family affair.

"I live in Japan," El explained. "Teacher."

"No Japanese," Mama asserted. "Oop."

"Yes, I know but—oh, forget it. Yes," El said, leaning down to face the boy. "I'm Oop." Satisfied, the boy went whirling off out the front door and Mama accepted our keys.

"You go Oop today?"

"Nup," I said, hitching on my pack. "Cambodia."

Mama seemed alarmed. "Kampuchea!" she breathed. "Bad place. Bad men there." This coming from a woman who had spent her entire life surrounded by war, famine, pickpockets and, more recently, by fat bludgers named Fred.

"It's okay," I reassured her. "I have a friend in Cambodia. He'll take care of us." I tried explaining to Mama in my simplest lingo that Wazza was a big-shot businessman, a farang no less, who would be protecting us from the "bad men," but she didn't budge. In her eyes, we were walking straight towards our doom.

"Speaking of your Wazza," El interrupted, "have you spoken to him since you left Australia?"

Mama looked curiously at me and I shot El a glare. "Sure," I proclaimed loudly for Mama's benefit. "All the time." Under the pretence of picking up an invisible something that had fallen near El's feet, I mumbled sotto voce out of the corner of my mouth, "Not a word." Well, how could I? I could barely use chopsticks, let alone a public phone.

"Anyway," I said brightly, straightening myself up. "We'd better go. Supposedly our plane leaves in less than two hours."

"Yeah, and we'd better not miss it. Waz is meeting us at the airport." She smirked sardonically at me and I grimaced. Bloody smart-arse.

Mama would not hear of us calling a taxi when she had an incalculable number of kids, grandkids and assorted relatives with motorcycles in the vicinity. While we waited for them on the kerb, El gave me an earful: "Why didn't you ring him? Or at least email?" I shrugged. Trademark laziness, I supposed. "We need your mate Wazza. What the hell do we know about Cambodia?"

"What have we known about anywhere we've gone? Besides, uh, he's not really my mate. I only met him once and that was when I barged in on him and some bimbo at the pub."

She rolled her eyes to the grey Saigon sky before fixing them back on me. "Fine," she huffed. "So what do we do when we get to Phnom Penh?"

I lit a cigarette and exhaled in astonishment. "Whaddya mean? We do the same as we've done everywhere else. Cambodia's not that bad, I'm sure."

"I guess not," she snorted. "How bad could it be in a country whose greatest tourism draw is a place called the Killing Fields? Where, when a kid out playing screams 'mine!' he's not talking about the ball coming at him? Sounds rather idyllic, if you ask me."

"Yeah, but . . ."

"And, while you're at it," she filched my cigarette and took a draw, "put away that useless guidebook. It's about time you got out your stolen copy of The World's Most Dangerous Places. I think you'll find Cambodia gets a mention."

I stole my fag back. "Fine, already. I get your point. I'll call Wazza when we get there."

We stood in aggravated silence for the next few minutes, waiting impatiently for our rides. The crazy thing was, I knew El wasn't really pissed off at me because I hadn't gotten in touch with some old bastard I hardly even knew, and I wasn't really upset by her sarcasm. All of our glares and snipes and argumentative one-upmanship were sprouting from the fact that, within a couple of days, El would be sent packing back to Japan, leaving me to the mercy of my bumbling, solo self. I didn't want her to go and she didn't want to leave, so we were letting each other know we cared in the most human way: brawling.

I was just about to launch into a purposefully irritating spiel on whether Phnom Penh should be pronounced "Puh-nom Penh" or "Nom Penh" when, thankfully, two young blokes pulled up on their mopeds. "Transport to airport?" We nodded wordlessly and lumbered on to the backs of the bikes, tilting and groaning beneath the weight of our gear. My driver, a squat guy in his mid-twenties, looked at our determined frowns and patted my leg. "Smile," he said. "It makes life lighter."

And I thought Panchoism was a Western phenomenon.

*

We were given two seats on the next flight to Phnom Penh the moment we strolled into the airport and, with time to spare before the departure, El and I managed to stop deliberately vexing each other by busying ourselves with some duty-free shopping, last-minute annoying of the stony-faced soldiers lining the terminal and even a three-course lunch. Of course, fitting in the three-course lunch was not quite the feat it sounds like, as the lauded repast ("Bargain ten thousand dong for you, lady!") consisted of Coke, a small plate of noodles and a serviette. Still, it was good for roughage.

When we were finally called to board our Vietnam Airlines flight, we were gripped with a fervent nonchalance. From what we could see, our gleaming plane wouldn't even have pissed on the Lao Aviation junkheap we'd taken to Luang Prabang if it had been on fire, and it was far superior to the little twenty-seater that had gotten us to Saigon from Nha Trang. Its logo wasn't falling off, it had two, actually inflated wheels and its wings didn't look as if they were being held on with office staples. As we discovered when we took our surprisingly spacious seats, the hostesses wore uniforms and they even had safety equipment. It was all rather civilised.

*

Which was a hell of a lot more than I could say for Cambodia.

From the instant we shuffled into the feverish sprawl that was Pochentong Airport, we got the feeling of having miraculously travelled back in time to a place before rules, baths and prosthetics. Short, smooth-faced brown people were screaming, scamming, slithering and hopping around the stinking terminal in a frenzy of confusion. We had no idea what they were all doing there and, by the looks of it, nor did they. It was if they'd all decided to go hang out at the airport to cause as much unnecessary chaos as humanly possible, and they were doing a bloody good job. It was more anarchic than anarchy, and if I'd thought Saigon was crazy, then this place was throw-away-the-key fucking bonkers.

As we shoved and sorry-ed our way through the bedlam to pick up our visas and book El's ticket back to Bangkok, where she was to connect with her return flight to Japan, I was struck by two things. I'd known that a massive proportion of Cambodia's population was missing limbs of some description, thanks to a proliferation of landmines still lurking about in the countryside, but I hadn't been prepared for this. Nearly every person at the airport, staff included, was missing, if not a leg or an arm (sometimes both) then a finger or an eye. Unlike in Australia, where the handicapped are afforded special facilities and consideration, the disabled here semed to be such a majority that it was the able-bodied who were smiled upon with indulgence. Everyone else was booted and trodden on like common mongrels.

The other thing that caught my attention was the average age of the populace. Had the world known more about Cambodia than its tragic past, riddled with savage ethnic cleansing programs and fat old Pol Pot, the country could have been a real swingin' singles destination. Everyone we clapped eyes on looked to be under the age of thirty-five. From pilots, who were thankfully in command of all their body parts, down to passport-control guys, beggars and general idlers, everybody was in the flush of their youth. And nobody, but nobody, wore glasses. Between smoking out the back and stealing books from the library (old habits die hard), I'd studied Cambodia at school and the one thing I remembered was that the Khmer Rouge had taken it upon themselves to rid the country of old folks and intellectuals in their quest for the ultimate peasant-based utopian society. Apparently, these folks didn't go for geeks, and an "intellectual" meant anyone in specs—it was one way of getting rid of all those pesky large-print books in the library anyway.

El and I were too taken aback by the wretched scene at the airport to utter a single word until we'd picked up our visas and were standing, somewhat guiltily, outside. Yet again, our limbs were coveted objects, as was our dosh, and we couldn't offer the zillions of beggars swarming around us any of either. We hadn't managed yet to score ourselves any Cambodian riel—so-called to distinguish it from the fake money of its neighbours—and there was no way any of my appendages were coming off, no matter how hard they tugged. We'd already established that at Cu Chi. All we could do was shrug dolefully and count the seconds before we hopped a moto taxi outta there.

✳

Far from being a one-off jaunt into a mondo bizarro of poverty and woe, it turned out that the airport was little more than a diluted version of Phnom Penh itself. The city was absolutely, one hundred per cent fucked up. Thousands of wires and sparking cables, hung between termite-chewed poles, choked the smoggy sky above deliriously frantic streets clogged with what seemed to be every motorcycle on the planet. Disintegrating multi-storey buildings held up by exhausted shopfronts buckled beneath the weight of the billions of families who called each one home, their presences advertised by a rainbow of laundry hanging off the balconies. The lame, the insane and the starving loped past street vendors selling dried fish guts and bottled water, and naked children ran shrieking through the rubble.

Yet somehow, beneath the screaming poverty, the limbs-per-citizen ratio of four to twelve and the crumbling façade of its streetscape, Phnom Penh felt phenomenally alive. It was different to Saigon, which, despite its monkeys and itinerant barbers, was a city on the up, and it was centuries away from the neon lure of Bangkok, but Phnom Penh was nonetheless galvanic. Despite having nothing tangible going for it, unless you're looking for somewhere to start a discount prosthetic business, there was an air of optimism slicing through the place. I had a weird feeling I was going to like it here.

And half a minute later, I loved it.

Clutching our moto drivers with freshly-sprouted talons, El and I were zooming through the most ridiculous traffic we'd ever encountered on the way to the Capitol Hotel. But it wasn't until my driver turned to shout "Very close now!" in my already-buzzing ear that things went completely berserk.

"We're close!" I cried to El as her moto bashed into mine in an attempt to avoid running over a sleeping child in the road. "Nearly there!"

She nodded and looked over her shoulder, the usual paranoid response to being in the hands of someone who doesn't hold with rear-view mirrors or cautious glances at the road. So when she turned back to me with the most perplexed, bordering on horrified, look on her face, it didn't mean much to me. Probably just another family of fifteen crammed on to the one bike. I turned to get a look.

"Holy crap!"

It was an elephant. Not an elephant with a sign reading "Elephant rides, 50 riel," not an elephant leading a parade in a funny hat, not an elephant balancing on a ball in some kind of street circus; just an elephant with some sleeping guy on its back, ambling nonchalantly through the equally insouciant traffic. It moseyed along the jam of droning motos and rusty bicycles at the pace of a tortoise with nobody but us giving it a second thought. When I excitedly tapped my driver and pointed back to it, he didn't even bother to shrug, and simply veered slightly to let it go by. I leaned over to touch its leg as it groaned past and was filled with electric shivers. I'd ridden elephants as a child in safari parks, but to casually reach out and touch one in the middle of a traffic jam was something else.

This was definitely my kind of place.

*

Unfortunately, the Capitol was not.

Collapsing on the corner of two preposterously busy streets, the Capitol guesthouse and restaurant was swarming with farang of every description: young, old, stoners, drunkards, the annoyingly sober and the smug. Each and every one of them looked irritating, and it took only a brief glance to see that more than half of the honkies hanging out in the café beneath the hotel were wearing grubby Tin Tin shirts. It was also quite clear that many of them had been in Cambodia for a long time and were hellbent on letting everyone know it. Over copies of the xeroxed, English-language Cambodian Daily, thirtysomething guys who had cultivated the Pancho-cum-anthropologist look (scruffy beard, headband, thick glasses, faded destination T-shirt) strove to out-yell each other in discussions about Cambodian politics which served only to tell involuntary eavesdroppers that they were longtimers. I don't know what it is about a lot of independent travellers that makes them look down on people who haven't been in a place as long as them, even if they've only been there five minutes themselves, but there's a lot of misguided territorialism going down in that particular subculture. And the more unconventional the destination, the more hardcore is their protectiveness of "their" turf. It looked like Cambodia was pretty damned off-beat.

With riel in our pockets, thanks to the dodgy moneychanging service at the Capitol's front desk, and our gear ditched in our ill-ventilated cellblock upstairs, El and I ignored the superior glowers getting thrown at us by two girls with beaded hair and slumped at one of the café's plastic tables, unsure of what to do next. El, harbouring hopes of getting away from the sneering tourists, wanted me to ring Wazza immediately, while I just wanted to stuff my face. "I'll call after lunch, I swear," I said, drooling over a menu reading "Samwiches, $1." It had been a long time since I'd seen bread and I was stinging for something exotic like a cheese and tomato sanga.

You've gotta love the French. I never thought that I—who was once kicked out of a sharehouse by a stuck-up French couple because, as they said, "Zee Australian geerl eez zo dirty and coarze!"—would ever say that, but as soon as our "samwiches" arrived, I was filled with the glory of all things Gallic. Well, at least the glory of their gastronomic habits. Instead of getting two soggy flaps of white bread caked with processed cheese sheets and runny tomato chucked at us, our lunch arrived in the form of a crusty baguette placed delicately beside two foil-wrapped triangles of camembert and a whole, garden-fresh tomato. Booting the French out of your country was understandable, but keeping their cuisine pointed to evidence of genius among the Cambodians.

"Mon dieu!" El belched as she picked the remaining crumbs from her plate. "What a treat. Now," she passed me a cigarette, "how about we call that mate of yours?"

I inhaled luxuriously and settled back in my chair, watching with idle amusement as a dozen moto drivers clamoured over a hapless tourist who had straggled into the street. "Sure," I breathed, "any second now."

She looked at me in disbelief. "I wish Mama Hanh was here to see this, you lazy wench." I shrugged and put my feet up. It was hot, I was slack and besides I was still subconsciously trying to piss off El. I was really going to miss her.

"Okay then, fine. Give me his number and I'll go make the call." I nodded and began to slowly riffle through my bag for my address book. "And I'll leave you to your pals."

I looked up and within a millisecond, I was up. About a dozen

Yanks were thundering into the café, bellowing orders for beer while shoving aside the ragged beggars who were trailing them like gulls behind a trawler. It was a rankling scene which had been played out countless times during our fiasco in Southeast Asia but, for some reason, it felt intolerably worse this time. It didn't take me long to figure out why. Each and every one of them was wearing the despised correspondent's vest.

I realise there are other types of apparel which may be more richly deserving of reproof than the correspondent's vest, such as the rah-rah skirt, the pointy boot or anything worn by Mariah Carey. But, apart from Mariah Carey, the misguided souls who put these things on their bodies aren't actively pretending to be something they're not, whereas the jerks gadding about in correspondent's vests really think they can gain some sort of credibility by dressing up as Dan Rather on a night in Baghdad. And unlike rah-rah skirts, pointy boots and Mariah Carey, which are all in thankfully short supply in places like Phnom Penh and Long Hoa, correspondent's vests are legion in the third world. People like our imaginatively named Correspondent Vest in Vietnam and the screaming seppos in the Capitol have done such damage to the vest's reputation that real correspondents now refuse to wear them, opting instead for the ubiquitous blue chambray shirt and beige chinos. Unlike the correspondent's vest, neither of these have many pockets for storing important, newsworthy notes or rolls of film. So the next time you bemoan the demise of in-depth reporting, you'll know who to thank.

"Right," I said, gathering my things with a quite unfamiliar haste. "Outta here." The vests were clamouring dangerously close to our table, and unless I wanted to give real correspondents a riot story to file, it was time to haul arse.

*

Given our ineptitude in similarly workaday situations, I honestly don't know how either of us actually thought we'd be able to use a Cambodian payphone. It was hard enough for us to catch a bus, order a pizza or get along with our peers, let alone make a phone call. Yet we were still disappointed when, after ten minutes of kicking, bashing and throttling the receiver, all we could get was a dial tone that sounded like someone giving birth. It was as if the phone was some kind of techno-banshee, forewarning us of our imminent demise. Or at least the death of our egos.

Completely dejected, we gave up after giving the phone one last boot. Suddenly, everything sucked; El was leaving in the morning, I would be left Waz-less and mateless in the company of gibbering halfwits in sweat-stained headbands, and we'd just proven ourselves to be too feebleminded to make a basic phone call. Even if some smart-arse came along and gave me forty cents, I couldn't call someone who cared.

"Well, this is typical," El moaned, glaring at the useless phone. "My last day and we still can't do anything right. Christ." She stared across the road at the Capitol, her eyes turning red and watery.

I fidgeted around awkwardly, trying to think of something cheery to say, but I couldn't find a word. What could I say? "Chin up there, El. Let's go vest shopping to take your mind off it"? It was miserable and lousy and she was right. We couldn't do anything right.

Or maybe we could. Sure, we couldn't perform basic tasks to the standard of say, a trained ape, and we couldn't waltz into a new place without unleashing some degree of pandemonium, but we had one thing going for us: Dumb Luck.

With Dumb Luck on our side, we'd managed to bumble our way across four third world countries without getting lynched, pummelled by outraged locals or sucked into a farang contingent—which, while irritating us senseless, would probably have made for a much easier journey. Thanks to Dumb Luck, and an admittedly copious use of profanity, we'd wriggled our way out of countless tricky situations and had gone to places those too afraid to rely solely on Dumb Luck would never see. By allowing Dumb Luck to lead the way, we'd become independent, fearless (or at least slightly less terrified), kick-arse chicks who could handle anything. Well, a few things. So what if we weren't skilled in the arts of foreign telephony? Who really cared if we annoyed a few hippies along the way? And what did it matter that we were essentially gormless as fuck? We'd made it to where we'd wanted to go, and to most places in between, and we'd done it alone. I reckoned we rocked.

"Is that 'My Way' you're humming there?"

"Huh?" I looked up from my reverie and flashed her a cheesy, heartfelt smile. "You know, El, we've actually done alright."

She looked at the beeping, crazy streetscape thoughtfully, as if seeing it for the first time, and I guessed she was running through, as I just had, the trials and tribulations we'd overcome to get this far. "I guess we have," she said, turning back to me. "We're still freaks, but."

Suited me fine.

Chapter Twenty-three

The Most Godforsaken Place on Earth

Our egos reinflated and soppy affirmations of our travelling prowess over and done with, we decided to spend the rest of the afternoon kicking around the one place we were at least vicariously familiar with: the Killing Fields.

For two people who had only just departed from the Misery Zone, this could have been a dodgy choice of locales in which to boost our spirits, but we had nowhere else to go. Hanging out at the Capitol was definitely out of the question, its café by that stage teeming with people who needed to talk less and bathe more, and we didn't have any way of finding Waz now that we'd murdered the one payphone in the vicinity. Besides, I felt somehow duty-bound to make a pilgrimage to the mass grave-cum-tourist attraction, and I wanted to do it while El was still around. If I'd been freaked out in a cave full of lifeless statues and had nearly lost it crawling around in replica war tunnels, I didn't want to be alone in a place no doubt haunted by the souls of the forty thousand unfortunates murdered there by Pol Pot and his cronies.

Braving the lunatic traffic and the uppity looks from the café collective, El and I crossed the road and marched over to the rabble of moto drivers hanging out on the corner. As the drivers went through the hallmark ritual of brazenly ogling us and slapping each other on the back, I was filled with a sudden dread. How were we going to ask these guys to take us on an afternoon jaunt to a place that might well have been the end of the line for many of their friends and families less than two short decades ago? I felt like a sick weirdo, a voyeur taking advantage of the tragedy of a nation by traipsing out to a plot of unholy ground as if I were going on a picnic. I felt ill.

But if I was queasy, then the drivers were positively hearty. A lifetime steeped in misfortune and turmoil had strengthened rather than dampened their spirits and they'd obviously found a way of coming to terms with their past that didn't involve wailing and gnashing their teeth anytime anyone mentioned a trip to the countryside. Besides, they were probably used to taking hordes of tourists out there every day. There wasn't a great deal else to do in Phnom Penh.

The first man I'd laid eyes on in Southeast Asia who came anywhere near my towering height beckoned me to his motorbike, and I went more than willingly; with his distinctive Khmer latte-coloured skin, almond-shaped eyes and devastating smile, he was utterly divine. And with the plain gold ring on his left hand, he was also utterly married. But while that threw all of my erotic plans out the window, it had no effect on my sightseeing ones. I just wouldn't be seeing as much as I wanted to, that was all.

"Of course," he said in clear, intelligent English. "I will take you, and my friend," he gestured to another impressive-looking Khmer beside him, "will take your friend." I called out to El, who was busy getting mobbed by a throng of admirers, and turned back to the driver.

"Sareth is my name," he smiled, holding out his hand. I introduced myself and he patted his moto seat. "Before we go straight there, you should go first to the Security Prison."

I gawked at him in dumbstruck confusion. Why? Had I done something wrong? Was this standard procedure?

"The Security Prison is actually the Tuol Sleng Genocide Museum," Sareth explained. "It was once a high school before Pol Pot turned it into a torture centre during his regime. Many people, about twenty thousand, died there in horrible ways. Out of all the people to go through there, only seven people came out alive."

"Jesus," I whispered. "And it's now a museum?"

"Of a sort," Sareth said in his peculiarly well-spoken English. "They have left it almost exactly as it was in 1979. You can walk around the cells and everything."

"Jesus," I repeated. Coming hot on the heels of our expedition to the bombed wasteland of Cu Chi, I wasn't altogether sure I wanted to make a habit of loitering around this kind of scene. "I dunno."

He nodded to El's driver and turned back to me as he started up his bike. "Believe me, it is necessary. It will help you understand what happened to our country."

✳

By the time we pulled up outside Tuol Sleng, I already had a better idea of the horrors that had ravaged the small nation, as well as a supreme admiration for its people. As we'd puttered down muddy backstreets lined with shantytowns en route to the museum, Sareth had told me how the Khmer Rouge had killed or kidnapped nearly every member of his family—part of the despised intellectual class—when he'd been a young boy. He'd managed to escape execution solely through luck and good hiding places, but had been witness to dozens of terrifying murders.

"You must be extremely bitter," I'd said, mentally kicking myself for the understatement. Beer was bitter. Sareth must have been psychopathically rancorous.

Amazingly, he wasn't. "And neither are most of the Khmer people. You see, everyone in this country has lost someone, sometimes whole families like me. It was an awful nightmare but it's over. This country has grieved and suffered enough. Now, we believe, it's time to look to the future."

I was still awe-struck with wonder at the almost unnatural healthiness of Sareth's, and apparently his countryfolk's, attitude towards life when I hopped off the bike. When El pulled up, I could see she was experiencing the same whirl of emotions.

"How amazing are these people?" I asked her as we walked towards the entrance. "I still hold a grudge against people that pissed me off in Year 5."

"Mega," El replied. Her driver had endured a similar youth to Sareth's and was also of the opinion that things could—and would—only get better. "I can imagine being none too sane if I'd been through all that hell. Actually, I'm not feeling so hot just coming to this place." We stopped at the gate and took in our surroundings. Minus the barbed wire and barred windows, the complex could have been any high-school campus on earth, with its nondescript buildings and central courtyard. But there was no way anyone could mistake this plot as a haven for higher learning or sophomoric malarkey. There was a terrible feeling about the place and I found myself breathing through my hand, which was clamped across my mouth. It was the deathliest place in the world.

Half-clinging to each other, we shelled out the two-dollar entry fee to a lame woman at the door and were told to wander about as we chose. "You can go inside anywhere you want and take many pictures," she said. "We want the world to know of this evil."

I guessed that, considering Tuol Sleng had closed down in 1979 and had gotten a fair write-up in my guidebook, the world already had a fair idea about it. I just wished I'd known more about it. Maybe then I wouldn't have been bordering on nausea when I got there.

But probably not. No matter how many times you read the words "blood-smeared walls," the reality cannot truly hit home until you've accidentally leant against one. And all those bland historical statistics mean nothing until you've tripped over Genocide Victim No. 3651's spiked-iron foot shackle.

Due to either shoddy housekeeping or a desire to prove just how repellent humans can be to one another, the cells at Tuol Sleng had been left untouched since 1979. Dark stains clung like ghosts to the walls, the floors and, in one particularly frightening room, the ceiling. Metal beds which had been relieved of their mattresses, if indeed they'd ever had any, crouched angrily in the middle of the cells, some with torn shreds of prison rags still speared on the springs, while a miscellany of sinister-looking iron things hung all over the place. The original barbed wire still wove a menacing tapestry around many of the cell doorways where their captors had sought, as one of the many information boards noted, "to prevent the desperate victims from committing suicide." I was filled with indignation and rage, not to mention a wallop of guilt. Not that I could've done much about this particular situation, given that I was probably busy learning long division at the time.

"Oh, God," I wailed, reading the sign on a nearby building. "I can't take any more of this. Look, El." I pointed out "The Security Regulations": in spartan English they detailed the do's and don'ts that every prisoner was expected to know by heart, lest they receive "many shocks with the electric wire." And with everything from crying to being "a fool" listed as out of bounds, I could only thank God that I hadn't been hanging around in Cambodia circa 1979. I would've been toast.

"C'mon," El grabbed my hand and pulled me away from the disturbing sign. "I don't think we need to see any more."

Oh, but we did. To get out of the complex, we had to pass through another building that bore agonisingly human testament to the crimes of the Khmer Rouge. As much as we would've liked to, there was no ignoring the raw horror of the place: wallpapered with thousands of black-and-white photos of the victims of Tuol Sleng, many of them women and children, the hall was full of torture devices and the personal effects of those who had died there. A vandalised bust of Pol Pot glared defiantly from the dusty corner it was banished to, while an entire wall was taken up with a map of Cambodia created wholly from human skulls. I was trembling and El was growing paler by the minute. I wondered how people like Sareth, or the volunteers who calmly spent each day surrounded by this tragedy, could do it. Optimism was one thing, but a complete resistance to legitimate nervous breakdowns was another. These people were natural endorphin factories.

*

After immersing ourselves in the ghastly realism of Tuol Sleng, we weren't super keen on getting to the Killing Fields or, as the Khmers called them, Choeng Ek. But Sareth and Thy, El's driver, would have none of our protestations. They'd seen how affected we were by our brief gander at the cell blocks, and were deadset on getting us out to the Killing Fields to really drive the message home. While I understood that showing foreigners around these places might in some way contribute to the healing process, I also had the vague inkling that Sareth thought I—with my large camera, incessant pestering and noticeable dearth of correspondent's vests—was some kind of overseas journalist, out here to bring the plight of the Cambodian people to the world. What he probably didn't understand was that the world already knew. And didn't really give a stuff. Apart from featuring in the brief "Conflict in Southeast Asia" chapter in Year 11 history texts and getting a rare look-in on the late news when Princess Diana had strolled the minefields, pre-Parisian tunnel, to the Western world Cambodia didn't exist. If the Cambodians wanted any sort of international exposure, they were going to have to start playing cricket. And with up to ten million landmines still lurking in the countryside, that wasn't the best of ideas.

"Fine," we chorused. "Killing Fields are go."

✳

Maybe because it was teetering on twilight or maybe because we'd had a gutful of, well, guts, we didn't stay very long at the Killing Fields. The last stop down a long, unpaved path that skirted vast tracts of empty land posted with multilingual landmine warnings, Choeng Ek could almost have been mistaken for a picnic area from the outside. But the minute we strolled, carefully, across the grass towards it, we could see this was no place for a family outing. Not unless your kith and kin were all hardcore Marilyn Manson fans: the Killing Fields were a major skull-fest.

A memorial stupa containing a symbolic pile of skulls and ragged remains of clothing kept grim watch over the scrabbly patch of earth fenced with barbed wire. It was here, among the tired shrubs and thin earth, that the stormtroopers of the Khmer Rouge had killed and disposed of forty thousand of their own countrymen, women and children, under the orders of "Brother Number One." Like Tuol Sleng, the Killing Fields had a nasty, unmistakable aura of death. But just in case any obtuse farang failed to pick up on this, or indeed the grisly shrine at the entrance, they were brought up to date quick smart, thanks to grim signs pointing to things like the "MASS GRAVE OF 166 VICTIMS WITHOUTH [sic] HEADS."

Unwilling to linger too long around the skull skyscraper, El and I trod gingerly along obvious (read: mine-free) paths, which skirted the hills and ditches that indicated mass graves. Apart from us, the Killing Fields were deserted, Sareth and Thy wisely having waited with their bikes, and the impending sunset added an extra touch of melancholy to the place. Not that it needed any help; along with Tuol Sleng, the Killing Fields could easily lay claim to the title of Most Godforsaken Place on Earth.

Although we'd pulled up at Choeng Ek determined to give it the respectful attention it deserved, in the end all we could manage was a quick lap before traipsing back to the bikes. But I didn't feel we'd done it, or its multitude of victims, any injustice. I felt that Sareth could finally be proud of me; I did understand the brutal past of his country, and it was none too pretty. But more importantly I had grasped that, because of people like him, this brutal past would be trampled beneath a stampede towards a bright new future. That's what I hope for, anyway.

Chapter Twenty-four

Slum Runners

Our headlights were on by the time we got back into central Phnom Penh and, while Sareth and Thy warned us that wandering aimlessly through the city at night was, to say the least, highly inadvisable, we decided to hop off before reaching the Capitol. We were in no rush to get jiggy with the farang, most of whom would be drunk by now, no doubt spouting pseudo-Khmer poetry, and besides, it was fun walking around at night. By day, an Asian city could be a slap in the face—too much information. In the glare of the sun and choking under the weight of the heat and stifling crush of humanity, it was easy to feel overloaded. And while staggering around in the dark didn't offer much when it came to getting your bearings, it was sometimes pleasant allowing yourself to get lost in the mystery, bathed in the cool streetlights and enveloped in dinner smells.

Note the use of the word "sometimes" in the previous paragraph.

The instant our drivers reluctantly gave in to our cajoling and booted us off in the middle of some unlit urban wasteland, we realised that we were complete morons. Sure, it was lovely to wander the streets of some lazy, riverside haven like Nong Khai, saffron in the air and gentle families on their stoops. But trolling around the lawless slums of a city whose sector of less peacefully inclined denizens reportedly had no qualms about lynching the odd foreigner was another matter entirely. I'd read somewhere that the not quite defunct Khmer Rouge were still paying unscrupulous locals over a thousand dollars for every Westerner delivered to them alive. Well, as long as they weren't totally dead. Otherwise they only got eight hundred bucks. Considering the yearly wage in these parts averaged about sixty dollars per person, I gathered that this could be a rather tempting offer to anyone who came across a stray farang prancing around witlessly in a place they really shouldn't have been. Like, for instance, this place.

A rather feeble "oh" was about all I could manage as we stood in the middle of what I guessed was meant to be a street, watching Sareth's and Thy's tail-lamps disappear into the gloom. As their pinprick lights faded to nothing, I was struck by the realisation that I may well have jinxed us with my stupid "We're not so dumb after all" speech earlier that afternoon. By all accounts, we certainly were dumb, if not certifiably retarded. Who else would turn down an early-evening motorbike ride with two beautiful, if unavailable, exotic men who wanted nothing more than to safely deliver us to our lodgings?

"Well," El muttered. "Nice night for it. I guess we'd better ramble." Thankfully, this tour of Skid Row had been agreed upon by both of us as we'd careened through the twilight, giving neither party cause to rip the head off the other for being such a nitwit. With nobody to blame but ourselves, there was nothing we could do but accept our fate and start walking.

A few streetlights had overcome the standard Phnom Penh adversities of power-outages, flying rocks and electricity board incompetence, managing to cut occasional swaths of light through the heavy darkness. As we crept along, they would sometimes offer us rare glimpses into the lives of those who lived there. Wherever there was. It wasn't Park Avenue, that was for sure.

The rare buildings that hadn't been reduced to mounds of granite by bombs or overuse looked and smelled like decayed teeth. Unlike in the downtown area, there were no shopfronts or advertising signs attached to the gasping edifices, and similarly little evidence of human habitation. But little didn't necessarily mean none, and a couple of times we spotted figures sliding through the shadows, leading to almost complete loss of bowel control on our part. Or at least my part.

But it was when we heard what sounded like a shot followed by what sounded very much like a scream that we really, truly went bananas. Until then, we'd been content to exist in the temporary realm of the shit-scared, clinging to each other and riding the odd freak-out with soothing words and made-up prayers. But with that shot, or whatever it was, it was all over red rover. No more shuffling or whistling in the dark. We were so gone, I hadn't even realised I'd left yet.

For what seemed like a geological aeon, we pounded and puffed down black streets, alleyways and vacant lots. Having no idea where the hell we were going, where we'd been or even who or what had made that incredibly realistic impression of a pistol shot, this wasn't the best idea. We could've ended up straight back where we'd started, or worse. But when you're shitting yourself, there's nothing better you can do than run. At least you might make it to a toilet on time.

"Stop!" I gasped, collapsing against a half-standing building. Not counting our sprint through the Cu Chi forest, I hadn't used my body for anything but abuse in ages and I was sure I was dying. A shot in the head would've been preferable to the slow burning that was eating my lungs. Or maybe that was nicotine. Whatever, I was in agony.

"Get up," I heard El croak from somewhere. "There's an open shop around the corner. I think we're nearly in town."

Lungs afire and legs a-jelly, I hauled myself up and painfully trotted towards her voice. Miraculously, I could see the light. For a millisecond I wondered if it was the light, before smacking myself upside the head for being so melodramatic. No heavenly aura would waste its time glowing over a café decorated in sun-bleached Angkor Beer posters and tatty plastic furniture.

"Oh God, yes," El cried. "Look!"

I looked. All I could see was the same shitty café and the dark shapes of a few of its patrons.

"That guy sitting down," she yelped excitedly. "He's a farang!"

Never in my wildest dreams did I think either of us would hover so close to orgasm simply from encountering another deadbeat of similar persuasion, but there we were, practically flying across the road to revere what we'd reviled for so long.

El got there first, with me loping breathlessly behind. Two steps from the shadowy figure in the chair, I watched El as she tapped him on the shoulder.

"Excuse me," she said, as I pulled up behind her. The man took a sip from his beer and turned slowly around.

"Yes?"

"Waz!" I exclaimed.

＊

It was Wazza alright. While I had morphed into a gibbering fool, smothering him in relieved kisses, and El had forgone her usual mouthiness to gawk silently at us like a stunned mullet, Waz was the same token Bloke I'd met at the pub a lifetime ago.

"That'll do," he rasped, attempting to peel me off him. "What the bloody hell are you doing here?"

I backed away, mid-smooch, in horrified bewilderment. Had I crashed his country? "Waz, don't you remember I told you."

He cut me off. "Not in Cambodia, you dumb biddy." Wazza, our saviour, had obviously taken congeniality lessons from Mama Hanh at some stage. "I mean here. Don't you know where you are?"

El and I looked sheepishly at each other and shrugged. Waz just sighed and snapped at a nearby waiter for more beers. "You're in the most dangerous part of town," he explained. "This is where all the worst whores and their pimps live. There's about three murders a night." Our eyes widened as he went on. "No sane white person comes to this dump unless they're after a cheap fuck or a bullet." Not appearing overly suicidal, I could only guess as to what Waz was doing down here.

"Anyway," he said, pausing to light a filterless cigarette. "I'm glad we found each other. I need you."

As we gratefully sipped our beers, Wazza told us about a party he was throwing at his bungalow digs down south in a beach town called Sihanoukville. "It's gonna be huge, entertainment and everything, and I want you to come down and help me promote it. Whaddya say?"

I couldn't even find the words. It was all too perfect. Instead of winding up pimpmeat in some disease-riddled brothel, or worse, left without El in the pretentious swamp of the Capitol, I was saved. Our journey together was over, but I was going on. I was making a fresh start in a new place and it was going to rock. Whatever troubles had plagued me in the past were history. Like Cambodia itself, I was vaulting forward into a bright new future.

"Just one catch," Wazza said, breaking my reverie. "We're all booked out for once, so you'll have to share your bungalow with the entertainment guy. He's a musician, a traveller like you."

"Great!" I enthused. I really meant it this time too. Waz had broken the anti-farang spell for me and I was looking forward to meeting some new people all of a sudden. It was going to be fantastic.

"The poor bastard's broke and staying in one of these hellholes," Waz continued. "I'm meant to pick him up here." He squinted into the night. "And yep, here he comes now." He nodded and waved into the darkness.

A long shadow strolled towards us and broke into the light.

"Hey, groovers," Pancho said.

Epilogue

I'd never really had any interest in going to Outer Mongolia . . .